THE ITALIAN JOB
A CHELSEA THRILLER
STARRING
ANTONIO CONTE

MARK WORRALL

The Italian Job: A Chelsea Thriller Starring Antonio Conte
Copyright Mark Worrall 2017

THE MORAL RIGHT OF THE AUTHOR HAS BEEN ASSERTED
Apart from any fair dealing for the purposes of research or private study, or criticism or review, as permitted under the Copyright, Designs and Patents Act 1988, this publication may only be reproduced, stored or transmitted, in any means, with the prior permission in writing of GATE 17, or in the case of reprographic reproduction in accordance with the terms of licenses issued by the Copyright Licensing Agency. Enquiries concerning reproduction outside those terms should be sent to the publishers.

enquiries@gate17.co.uk
Twitter: @gate17marco
cover photograph: Disco Debs Coady @cfunofficial
cover design : GATE 17

CONTENTS

ACKNOWLEDGMENTS 1
PREFACE 7
ANTICIPATION 11
PRE-SEASON 15
THE BIG KICK OFF 26
SEPTEMBER 2016 35
OCTOBER 2016 47
NOVEMBER 2016 59
DECEMBER 2016 68
JANUARY 2017 82
FEBRUARY 2017 98
MARCH 2017 115
APRIL 2017 135
MAY 2017 167
REVIEW 193
STATISTICS 2016/2017 207
TRANSFERS AND LOANS 2016/2017 209
ALSO BY MARK WORRALL 211

ACKNOWLEDGMENTS

A massive thank you to Disco Debs Coady @cfcunofficial for the fantastic photo of Antonio Conte which graces the cover of this book. Taken 18 March 2017 at the bet365 stadium (Stoke City 1 Chelsea 2), Debs has captured the very essence of Conte. Check out her superb Blues photoblog www.cfcunofficial.com

Thank you also to Theresa Magee @bluebaby67 for regular supplies of life-saving hot chocolate brought pre-match to the cfcuk fanzine stall with a smile during the bleak and bitter winter months. At the same place, but not at the same time (yet) Mark Yates @WalterOtton, cheers for the JD & coke and occasional salmon. Jason Marco @chucklescabbie you can take a bow also for always being first with the breaking team news.

Matchday banter Blues in regular order of appearance at the cfcuk stall... I think: Bonesy, Peter Carroll, Steve Mabey, Steve (the brilliant but sadly now retired Gate17 steward) Seymour, David Johnstone, Peter Kemp, Neil Beard, Paul Canoville, Paul and Pearl Tungate, Tim Rolls, Roger Cumberbatch, Kerry Dixon, Terri Fisk, Julie Osbourne, Louise Osbourne, Raymondo Howden, Peter Trenter, Liz Nurse, Alexandra Churchill, David Chidgey, Alex the Mod, Justine Snell, Neil Wilcox, Enrico Castagnetti, Salvatore Orsini, Anna Lucia Orsini, Giuseppe Merola, Shaun McRonald, Carol Ann Wood, Alison Fradgley, Aggy Kyriakou, Dan Silver, Cliff Auger, Tom Broderick, Kalman Soos, Caroline Rice, Frances Clarke, Stuart Kinner, Ken Barkway, Patrick Niles, Kelvin Barker, Mark Meehan, Michelle Brand, Dane Greenfield, Andy Byrne, Garrison, Sid Celery, Rory Jennings, Chris Axon, Sam Simons, Clive O'Connell, Tony Davis, Nick Howe, Clayton Beerman, Julie Carr, Mark Wyeth, Neil Smith, Jeff Warren, Chris Vassallo, Charles Jackson, Tony Glover, Alan Bird, Bryan Marriott, Richard Schaller, Pater Sampson, Martin Wickham.

Overseas Blues who always stop by when they are in town for a game: Paul Ross, Carol Ross, Paul McEvoy, Oran Tully, Ollie Paillette, Julien Vauchel, Jerome Loubeau, Andy Wray, Beth Wild, Jan Hammarback, Tony Kullberg, Tomas Wilhelmsson, Harri Hemmi, Jake Cohen, Dan Dormer, Mike Neat, Steve Neat, Frank Visone.

My Gate 17 mates: Big Chris, Tantric Dave, Salisbury Rog, Alright Pav, Saucy Seb, Siciliano Sandro.

*Per la mia cara mamma Giovanna.
Ti dico solamente una sola parola: Grazie! XXX*

"It's not important where you win, it's important to win."
Antonio Conte

PREFACE

This preface to *The Italian Job* could quite easily have been entitled *The Winter of Discontent* or *You're Not Special Anymore*. Chelsea's brutally horrible and unexpected demise from being Premier League champions in May 2015 to a team in disarray less than six months later culminated with legendary Blues manager José Mourinho being sacked on 17 December 2015.

It was a divisive period among the London club's supporters.

Three days previously, a 2-1 defeat away at Leicester City, Chelsea's ninth loss in 16 top-flight games, had left the title holders marooned in 16th place in the table… Blues owner Roman Abramovich could take no more. Mourinho, no stranger to controversy, had had a very public falling out with club doctor Eva Carneiro towards the end of the opening match of the campaign, a 2-2 home draw with Swansea, and things had gone from bad to worse as tales of dressing room unrest bubbled to the surface… and rusted in the public eye. The team had lost its spirit, the players their mojo… something had to change… and in the Abramovich era at Chelsea typically that meant one thing. The manager had to go! The shock! The horror! Mourinho sacked! Incredible!

Social media sites erupted. Keyboard warriors duelled. Friendships were fractured. Mourinho's achievements in two stints as manager at Stamford Bridge had brought silverware aplenty. Three Premier League titles, the FA Cup, three League Cups and the Community Shield were won under the watch of the Portuguese and it was understandable, especially given the fact that six months previously Chelsea had recently won the league by a margin of eight points, if many fans thought Mourinho deserved more time to see if he could remedy matters. Whether they were in the majority or not will never be known. Certainly, there were plenty of chants and makeshift banners proclaiming support for the Special One, however there were also many stiff upper lips to be seen… people who had grown tired of Mourinho's fractiousness and the fact that Chelsea, just like the first time around, had become all about him.

The arguments rumbled on through Christmas and into the New Year, and fingers were still being pointed while ever-avuncular Guus Hiddink, parachuted in to do his interim manager thing, was trying his best to placate planet Chelsea. Approaching his 70th year, Hiddink was only ever going to be a short-term fix... the big question was, who would Abramovich appoint as Mourinho's long-term successor?

Having lost out on one enduring target, Bayern Munich boss Pep Guardiola, to Manchester City, and seen Atletico Madrid main-man Diego Simeone, perceived my many to be the obvious choice should Abramovich fail to lure Guardiola to SW6, distance himself from the job, it looked like Chelsea were struggling to find the right man to replace Mourinho. Outgoing City manager Manuel Pellegrini, former Chile national team boss Jorge Sampaoli and Juventus chief Massimiliano Allegri all jockeyed for position as bookmakers' favourite. By mid-February however, it was Allegri's countryman, Antonio Conte, manager of the Italy national team, whose odds to take on arguably the most difficult job in football suddenly shortened.

46 years of age at the time, Conte's CV was certainly impressive. Having won five Serie A titles plus the Champions League and UEFA Cup as a player with Juventus, the former Italy international midfielder had gone on to manage the Turin club to three consecutive Scudetto's before succeeding Cesare Prandelli as Azzurri boss in August 2014.

The more Conte's background and attributes were scrutinised, the more he looked like the right fit for Chelsea. Parallels were drawn with fellow Italian Carlo Ancelotti who had walked the walk as a player and manager in Serie A before arriving at Stamford Bridge in June 2009 and winning an historic Premier League and FA Cup Double in his first season. Of course, Ancelotti had fallen foul of Abramovich's as yet at the time unsated desire to win the Champions League, but among the Chelsea faithful he was widely respected... loved even. Personally, and not because of my Italian heritage, I thought media-friendly Ancelotti was the best manager we'd had in years... so yes you're right in deducing that I was in the camp that had grown tired of Mourinho's abrasiveness and self-absorbed one-upmanship.

Of all the choices available, I was convinced Conte was the best. With his appointment imminent, I found some photos showing his now fabulous thatch of hair looking curiously much thinner. A miracle had taken place at some point. I made a collage and took to Twitter @gate17marco ... *if Conte can restore Chelsea's fortunes as successfully as he has restored his hair, we will be champions again soon!*

4 April 2016

Antonio Conte's appointment on a three-year contract as 'First Team Head Coach' at Stamford Bridge was announced. "I am very excited about the prospect of working at Chelsea Football Club," said the Italian. "I am proud to be the coach of the national team of my country and only a role as attractive as manager of Chelsea could follow that. I am looking forward to meeting everyone at the club and the day-to-day challenge of competing in the Premier League."

Amen to that!

Conte had become the fifth Italian to manage Chelsea following on from Gianluca Vialli, Claudio Ranieri (who by now was on the spectacular verge of guiding Leicester to the Premier League title), Carlo Ancelotti of course… and totally remarkable Blues legend Roberto Di Matteo.

Now, the season couldn't end soon enough!

Out with the old, in with the new!

Forza Conte!

Vinci Per Noi!

ANTICIPATION

Following his appointment, among the first things Conte gave his seal of approval to was the retention of 35-year old veteran Chelsea captain, leader, legend John Terry who signed a new one year contract in May 2016. The new Blues boss clearly recognised not only the value of having revered club stalwart Terry around him at Stamford Bridge, but also the benefit of getting the club's supporters on his side from the get go.

So far so good, and the fact that Chelsea fans were about to see exactly what Conte was all about as a manager in granular detail as he took charge of Italy in France at EURO 2016 got the pot called anticipation bubbling away nicely.

The Azzurri's emphatic 2-0 victory over hotly fancied Belgium in their opening Group E game saw that pot boil over as social media sites lit up hailing Conte's tactical master-class. Alternating between 3-4-3 and 4-4-2, Italy's average-looking team made short work of a Belgium side packed with stars including Chelsea players Thibaut Courtois and Eden Hazard. It was a triumph of passionate substance over flattering-to-deceive style. Italy's goals coming from journeymen Emanuele Giaccherini (a recent Sunderland loanee) and Graziano Pelle, then of Southampton underlined this aspect of the game.

Defensively, Conte's system revolved around playing three centre-backs and one of these, Leonardo Bonucci of Juventus, had looked imperious when nullifying Belgium's attacking threat. A wonderful defence-splitting pass which assisted Giaccherini's goal showed Bonucci's all round ability and it seemed logical that Conte would be chatting to the 29-year old regularly about joining him in London. That was certainly the hope among Chelsea supporters purring at what they has just witnessed.

Italy followed up their victory over Belgium with a functional 1-0 win over Sweden. In a game of few chances, Conte's decision to replace Pelle with Simone Zaza on the hour proved pivotal late on when Zaza headed the ball into the path of Eder who sealed victory with a fabulous 88th minute strike. Once again, Italy never really looked like conceding with Bonucci putting in another robust display augmented by eye-catching distribution.

Surely Roman would have his chequebook out and sign Bonucci. Central defence had been a well-noted problem area for Chelsea during the previous disastrous season. Terry, although still a lion-heart, was ageing fast. 21-year old Kurt Zouma had proved himself in the position but was currently returning from injury, while Gary Cahill, 30, had struggled with consistency… then there was Branislav Ivanovic, 32… another lion-heart, but a player whose game had unfortunately gone to pieces. Academy graduate Jake Clarke-Salter, 18, was viewed as needing the benefit of a season on loan to further his experience, while 20-year old Andreas Christensen, who had shone brightly playing for Borussia Monchengladbach, was tied into a curious two-year loan deal with the Bundesliga outfit. Conte of course would have been well aware of all this… which made Bonucci's signing even more probable. Come on Roman, let's be having him.

Conte rotated his Italy side for their last Group E fixture which the Azzurri lost 1-0 to Ireland, but the result was of no consequence as qualification to the knock-out stage of the competition had already been assured. Spain were lying in wait. Interestingly enough, Abramovich had attended their Group D match with Croatia with reports suggesting suggested he was at the Stade de Bordeaux to take a close look at striker Alvaro Morata who duly obliged the Russian with a goal. The 23-year old had started his professional career with Real Madrid and just spent two seasons with Juventus netting 27 goals. Ah there was that intriguing Juve connection again.

Having sold Morata for £16 million in July 2014, a couple of weeks previously Real had exercised a £23.6 million buy-back clause to bring the player back to the Bernabeu… a deal which presented the Champions League winners with the opportunity to move him on at a substantial profit should they choose to do so.

Italy v Spain. Bonucci v Morata. Abramovich had a ringside seat while I sat in front of the big screen at Cheam Sports Club with a flagon of San Miguel. Chelsea supporters everywhere watched the match with as much interest as fans of the two countries involved.

Italy outclassed Spain waltzing to a comfortable 2-0 win thanks to goals from Giorgio Chiellini and Pelle. Conte deployed Mattia de Sciglio and

Alessandro Florenzi as wing-backs with dazzling and devastating effect, and had it not been for some stellar David De Gea goalkeeping the margin of Italy's victory would have been much wider.

Sharp-suited Conte cut a passionate, animated figure in the technical area. We were onto something with this man... with his methodology... everything really. Like entranced blue and white moths, Chelsea supporters fluttered to a hitherto unseen flame, their words of praise flickering across Twitter timelines.

Abramovich no doubt heaved a sign of relief. But what of Spain striker Alvaro Morata? He had gone into the game with three tournament goals, but was restricted to 28 touches of the ball by Italy. Subbed off after 70 minutes, and with Spain subsequently heading home, hyperbole about the striker dissipated.

As Italy prepared for a quarterfinal tie with World Champions Germany, news that Belgium international striker Michy Batshuayi had been given special dispensation by Red Devils' head coach Marc Wilmots to meet with Chelsea's team doctor to undergo a medical ahead of a proposed £33 million move to Stamford Bridge took Chelsea supporters by surprise.

39 goals in 97 appearances for Standard Liege in Belgium's Division A had brought Batshuayi to the attention of France Ligue 1 side Olympique de Marseille who'd paid £4.5 million for his services in August 2014. 26 goals in 62 games for Marseille and progression to represent his country raised his profile further... that being said, I wasn't alone among the Blues fraternity in saying Michy who? When the story broke.

At 22-years of age, given his achievements to date, Batshuayi definitely had an appeal... but if Chelsea were to add another Belgian to their ranks, it was his prolific countryman, former Blue Romelu Lukaku, discarded by Mourinho, and now making a name for himself with Everton, who was the more obvious choice. At 23-years of age, and with 60 Premier League goals to his name already, Lukaku was forever declaring he had 'unfinished business' at the Bridge, he'd probably cost double what Chelsea were prepared to pay for Batshuayi... but surely he'd be worth it. The question was asked, was Batshuayi signed at Conte's request... or was it the work of Chelsea technical director Michael Emenalo?

2 July

Conte's career as Italy manager came to an end in Bordeaux as the

Azzurri, having drawn 1-1 with Germany in 90 minutes and survived extra time, lost 6-5 on penalties and bowed out of the EUROs. There was no disgrace in defeat for the Italian's or their charismatic coach whose last roll of the dice in the tournament, replacing Giorgio Chiellini with Simone Zaza in the final moments of extra time, presumably because he rated Zaza's ability to convert penalties higher than Chiellini's, backfired miserably as the Juventus striker, having pirouetted in a ridiculous manner up to the ball, blasted his spot-kick wide of Manuel Neuer's goal.

PRE-SEASON

13 July

Antonio Conte arrived at Chelsea's training complex in Cobham and oversaw his first training session. Conte had visited the facility previously following his appointment to introduce himself to the squad… but this was the real thing now. Tracksuit on, it was time to start making assessments and planning ahead.

There was much to admire about the confident, relaxed manner in which Conte conducted himself during his first press conference the following day. Speaking in English, there was no drama, no one-upmanship and no Ranieri-esque Italian riddles… well apart from the observation that at Stamford Bridge "there is a small flame flickering that can become a towering inferno."

When asked about the squad he had inherited Conte said, "In the last two days, I saw the players with the right attitude, right behaviour and with a great will to fight for the shirt and to go back very soon to compete to win the title."

With the big kick off to the new season just a month away, and Conte's preparations for the campaign having commenced already… the widely held view among Chelsea supporters was that the sooner the new manager was able to work with the full complement of what would be his preferred starting XI the better… and that included international players returning from extended holidays and any new signings the club might make.

Conte hinted at the importance of this during his press conference. "In the coming days, we can buy one, two, three players. Players that can reinforce us for the season as it will be very, very tough."

Without the distraction of European competition, the Blues boss' key focus would be the Premier League… "to fight for the title, to be there at the end of the season"… was how the Italian succinctly put it.

Clearly, Conte had a plan that he presumably had been developing since his appointment at the start of April. A shortlist of transfer targets would have long since been drawn up and discussed with Roman Abramovich and his cabal of advisors and yet beyond Michy Batshuayi the Russian was yet to splash the cash on players who could make a difference.

Abramovich's hesitancy / reluctance / torpor… it never really transpired what the real reason was… to sign the players that Mourinho had identified at the end of the Blues title winning 2014/15 campaign as requirements to take Chelsea to the next level had contributed to the Portuguese's spectacular downfall. Hopefully a lesson had been learned… but had it?

The previous summer it had all been about signing Everton centre back John Stones and Juventus midfielder Paul Pogba… the deals failed to materialise (thankfully it would later seem in the case of Stones) yet it was clear to Mourinho then where he believed Chelsea needed to be stronger.

There had been on going speculation linking big money defenders Leonardo Bonucci of Juventus and Kalidou Koulibaly of Napoli with Chelsea, and rumours had recently intensified that Leicester City midfielder N'Golo Kante could be on his way to the Bridge for £32 million… but it was all just talk. Conte's management of Italy at the EUROs demonstrated a capability to get an average-looking team to punch above its weight, but despite Leicester's recent heroics, the Premier League, as Chelsea had recently found out, was an unforgiving environment for teams that failed to address problem areas.

15 July

Chelsea arrived in Austria for a week-long training camp.

16 July

N'Golo Kante signed a five-year contract to play for Chelsea. Hurrah! What a great signing. The 25-year old France international midfielder had played a pivotal role in Leicester's stunning Premier League title triumph and Blues supporters were already referring to him as the new Claude Makalele. If Kante could be anywhere near as good as 'Maka' was during his Chelsea heyday, then Conte's life as boss at the Bridge would be made much easier. One less thing to worry about. Onwards!

Later the same day, Chelsea played their first pre-season friendly fixture.

Rapid Vienna 2 Chelsea 0
Allianz Stadion
Attendance: 28,000
Referee: Harald Lechner

Chelsea (4-2-3-1): Asmir Begovic, Branislav Ivanovic, John Terry (c), Papy Djilobodji, Baba Rahman (Ola Aina h/t), John Obi Mikel (Nathaniel Chalobah 58), Nemanja Matic (Bertrand Traore 78), Willian (Kenedy 72), Ruben Loftus-Cheek (Oscar h/t), Victor Moses (Christian Atsu 80), Diego Costa (Loic Remy 72).

Rapid Vienna (4-5-1): Novota (Strebinger h/t), Schosswendter (Dibon), Schrammel (Auer 84), S.Hofmann (c) (Murg 55), Grahovac, Szanto (Nutz 81), M.Hofmann (Sonnleitner 81), Schobesberger (Entrup 84), Schaub (Schwab 77), Pavelic, Joelinton (Tomi).
Scorers: Joelinton 8, Tomi 82

Rapid Vienna hosted Chelsea at their all-new Allianz Stadion in the Austrian capital and christened their new home with a 2-0 victory. Diego Costa and Academy graduate Ola Aina had Chelsea's best chances to score, but it was a losing start for Conte who had named an experienced (albeit still shorn of international stars) maiden starting XI.

20 July

WAC RZ Pellets 0 Chelsea 3
Worthersee Stadion
Attendance: 7,800
Referee: Christian-Petru Chiochirca

Chelsea (4-2-4): Asmir Begovic, Branislav Ivanovic, John Terry (c) (Matt Miazga 89), Papy Djilobodji (Michael Hector 58), Ola Aina, Oscar (Nathaniel Chalobah 73), Nemanja Matic (John Obi Mikel 85), Willian (Christian Atsu), Bertrand Traore (Ruben Loftus-Cheek 58), Victor Moses (Kenedy 89), Diego Costa (Michy Batshuayi 58).
Scorers: Traore 41, Loftus-Cheek 84, Chalobah 90

WAC RZ Pellets (4-5-1): Kofler (Dobnik h/t), Klem (Rosenberger h/t), Standfest (Augustin 62), Zundel (Baldauf h/t), Rnic (Drescher h/t), Sollbauer (Berger h/t), Wernitznig (Tschernegg h/t), Offenbacher (Nutz h/t), Huttenbrenner (Rabitsch h/t), Prosenik (Trdina h/t), Topcagic (Hellquist h/t).

Conte registered his first win as Chelsea manager in the Blues next friendly in Klagenfurt against curiously-named Austrian Bundesliga outfit WAC RZ Pellets. Bertrand Traore, Ruben Loftus-Cheek and Nathaniel Chalobah found the net in a comfortable 3-0 victory. Victor Moses, playing high up the pitch, caught the eye as he had done in the first friendly against Rapid Vienna… little did we know what Conte had planned for the Nigeria international who since his £9 million signing from Wigan Athletic in August 2012 had been involved in more loans than a high street bank.

24 July

Chelsea touched down in Los Angeles as Antonio Conte's pre-season training preparations moved from Austria to California. A Blues party of 30 flew from London to the west coast of the USA and had a few days to acclimatize themselves before facing Premier League rivals Liverpool in a 'friendly' (I'd always struggle with that word where the Anfield club are concerned) at the Rose Bowl in Pasadena.

27 July

Liverpool 0 Chelsea 1
Rose Bowl
Attendance: 53,117
Referee: Baldomero Toledo

Chelsea (4-2-4): Asmir Begovic, Ola Aina, Gary Cahill, John Terry (c), Cesar Azpilicueta; Cesc Fabregas, Nemanja Matic, Willian (Pedro 67), Bertrand Traore (Michy Batshuayi 67), Ruben Loftus-Cheek (Nathaniel Chalobah 72), Victor Moses (Juan Cuadrado 67).
Scorer: Cahill 10
Sent off: Fabregas 70
Booked: Cahill 24

Liverpool (4-5-1): Karius, Randall (Markovic 63), Lovren (c) (Wisdom 63), Klavan, Moreno (Branagan 82), Stewart (Arnold-Alexander 82), Ejaria (Henderson 63), Grujic (Lallana h/t), Mane (Ojo 63), Coutinho (Wisdom 63), Firmino (Ings 63).
Booked: Moreno 6, Grujic 12, Erajia 39, Lovren 53, Stewart 72

An early headed goal from Gary Cahill settled a predictably feisty match against familiar foes. The assist was provided by assist-king Cesc Fabregas, though the midfielder would blot his copybook later on being shown a straight red card for a late tackle on Ragnar Klavan. Conte started the game

THE ITALIAN JOB

with Bertrand Traore and Ruben Loftus-Cheek playing up front with Willian and Victor Moses fielded out wide… and of the quartet, it was match-sharp Moses who appeared to have the greatest understanding of his manager's tactics.

"I like my team to play with great aggression and high intensity," said Conte grittily after the game. "We train to prepare for that, because I want that my team has an identity." The Chelsea manager's philosophy was a sound one, fools would not be suffered gladly and it was already clear that the dressing room dramas that beset the previous campaign would not be tolerated.

30 July

Real Madrid 3 Chelsea 2
Michigan Stadium
Attendance: 105,826
Referee: Younes Marrakchi

Chelsea (4-2-4): Asmir Begovic (Thibaut Courtois h/t), Ola Aina, Gary Cahill, John Terry (c), Cesar Azpilicueta, Oscar (Nathaniel Chalobah h/t), Nemanja Matic, Willian (Juan Cuadrado h/t), Bertrand Traore (Victor Moses 75), Ruben Loftus-Cheek (Michy Batshuayi h/t), Pedro (Eden Hazard 65).
Scorer: Hazard 80, 90+1
Booked: Traore 28, Pedro 33, Cahill, 42.

Real Madrid (4-4-2): Casilla (Yanez 64), Carvajal (Danilo h/t), Varane (Lienhart 64), Nacho, Marcelo (c) (Tejero 64), Vazquez (Odegaard 64), Kovacic (Llorente 64), Casemiro (E Zidane 64), Asenio (Febas 64), Mariano, Morata (S Diaz 64).
Scorers: Marcelo 19, 26, Mariano 37.
Booked: Casemiro 57, E Zidane 78.

Real Madrid defeated Chelsea 3-2 at the 'Big House' in Ann Arbor Michigan. A phenomenal crowd of 105,826, a record 'official' attendance for a Blues game, saw the La Liga side race into a 3-0 half-time lead before a late Eden Hazard brace made the score more respectable.

In truth, the game was a rude awakening for Antonio Conte who saw Marcelo run Chelsea ragged down the right flank, the Brazil left-back scoring twice in a breath-taking first-half for the Champions League winners. Marcelo was also involved in the build up to Real's third goal scored by Mariano, and if their manager Zinedine Zidane hadn't elected to make wholesale changes to his line-up in the second-half, the La Liga side's margin of victory could have been embarrassing.

Post-match, Conte underlined his understanding of Chelsea's soft underbelly. "It is important to keep concentration and to work together," said the Italian. "I know it is fatiguing to work without the ball but if we stay compact, like against Liverpool, we can win. If we lose this compact, if we think one, two or three players don't want to work without the ball, it is possible we see another bad season."

3 August

AC Milan 1 Chelsea 3
US Bank Stadium
Attendance: 63,101
Referee: Edvin Jurisevic

Chelsea (4-2-4): Thibaut Courtois, Ola Aina (Branislav Ivanovic 59), John Terry (c), Gary Cahill, Cesar Azpilicueta, Namanja Matic (Nathaniel Chalobah 29), Cesc Fabregas (Oscar 59); Willian (Juan Cuadrado 79), Bertrand Traore (Eden Hazard 52), Diego Costa (Michy Batshuayi 59), Victor Moses (N'Golo Kante 52).
Scorers: Traore 24, Oscar (pen) 70, 87

AC Milan (4-3-3): Donnarumma, Abate (Montolivo 60), Paletta, Romagnoli (Vergara 67), Calabria (Vido 81), Kucka, Poli, Bonaventura, Suso (Zanellato 81), Luiz Adriano (Honda 67), Niang (Matri 81).
Scorer: Bonaventura 38
Booked: Romagnoli 5, Calabria 64

Another big crowd saw Chelsea round off their Stateside tour with a welcome win against somewhat fallen Serie A giants AC Milan. Bertrand Traore opened the scoring with an early header at the US Bank Stadium in Minneapolis. Giacomo Bonaventura leveled with a peach of a free-kick just before the break, but it was Oscar, on as a second-half substitute for Cesc Fabregas, who grabbed the plaudits scoring twice late on. N'Golo Kante made his first appearance in a Chelsea shirt when replacing Victor Moses shortly after the lemon break.

*****

With five pre-season games under his belt and one still to go before Chelsea kicked off the new Premier League campaign at Stamford Bridge against

THE ITALIAN JOB

West Ham United, Antonio Conte had to be under no illusions about the enormity of the challenge he faced if he was to resurrect the club's fortunes.

Worryingly for Conte, addressing last season's critical problem area, defence, seemed to have stalled. Since the Italian's appointment in April, Chelsea had been linked with numerous players who could bolster / replace a backline that had capitulated all too often in the past year and although these rumours persisted still no transfer business had been done to alleviate concern.

John Stones of Everton, for so long on the Stamford Bridge radar, looked set to join Manchester City, while recent targets Leonardo Bonucci of Juventus and Napoli's Kalidou Koulibaly appeared to be going nowhere.

Curiously, while Conte had used pre-season to tinker with his options further forward, for the last three games against Liverpool, Real Madrid and AC Milan he had settled on a back four of familiar trio Cesar Azpilicueta, veteran skipper John Terry and Gary Cahill supplemented by promising Academy product Ola Aina.

With centre-back Kurt Zouma still rehabbing and unlikely to be available for selection until mid-September and Baba Rahman's stuttering form resulting in the £21.7 million left-back being shipped out on loan to Schalke, Conte had so far been forced to paper over last season's defensive cracks while he waited for the Chelsea board to sign credible reinforcements. Now, with just a final friendly against Werder Bremen to drill down his starting XI for the big kick off, the chances were that it was going to be a case of same-old-same-old defence-wise for the Blues opening fixtures.

It was reasoned by many supporters, me included, that West Ham (h), Watford (a), Burnley (h) would provide the old rear guard with a reasonable chance of putting in collectively competent displays… but Chelsea's next two opponents that followed, Liverpool (h) and Arsenal (a), could easily exploit any fragility. As it transpired, this foresight would prove to be uncannily accurate… and horrible. But then as the saying goes… it's always darkest before the dawn.

5 August

Papy Djilobodji was sold to Sunderland for a remarkable transfer fee of £8 million. Why remarkable? Papy had been signed a year previously from Ligue 1 said Nantes for £2.7 million and managed just one appearance for

Chelsea as an added time substitute for Radamel Falcao (I know, try not to laugh) in a League Cup tie away at Walsall (23 September 2015) which the Blues won 4-1. Papy was then sent out on loan to Werder Bremen in January 2016, a stint which included a two-batch ban following a sending off for making a throat-slitting gesture.

"Chelsea Football Club thanks Papy for his service and wishes him well for the future," said a somewhat bizarre statement on the Blues official website following his transfer to the Black Cats. It was a decent piece of business to be fair, and there would be more crazy-looking deals to follow.

7 August

Werder Bremen 2 Chelsea 4
Weserstadion
Attendance: 23,611
Referee: Sven Jablonski

Chelsea (4-1-4-1): Thibaut Courtois (Asmir Begovic 82), Branislav Ivanovic, Gary Cahill, John Terry (c) (Michael Hector 77), Cesar Azpilicueta (Ola Aina 75); N'Golo Kante (Nathaniel Chalobah 82); Willian (Moses 70), Oscar (Ruben Loftus-Cheek 75), Nemanja Matic (Cesc Fabregas h/t), Eden Hazard (Pedro 70); Diego Costa (Michy Batshuayi 70).
Scorers: Hazard 7, Oscar 9, Diego Costa 45, Pedro 90
Booked: Matic 32

Werder Bremen (4-4-2): Wiedwald, Sternberg, Moisander (Diagne 56), Caldirola, Guwara, Bartels, Junuzovic, Fritz (c), Yatabare (Kainz), Kruse (J.Eggestein 89), Pizarro (Thy h/t).
Scorers: Pizarro 33, Thy 65
Booked: Fritz 69

Chelsea's pre-season fixture programme was completed with an entertaining 4-2 win in Germany against Bundesliga side Werder Bremen. A tidy-sized crowd saw Eden Hazard and Oscar put Chelsea 2-0 up inside 10 minutes before veteran former Blue Claudio Pizarro (it seemed like decades ago he was at the Bridge... it was in fact 2007-2009) pulled a goal back for the home side. Diego Costa made it 3-1 just before half time and while Lennart Thy's 65th minute goal reduced the arrears Pedro slotted home late on to underline Chelsea's undeniable superiority.

Conte opted for a 4-1-4-1 formation, with Kante shielding the back four. Being the final game before the start of the season, the thought was that this would be what the Italian had in mind for the West Ham game.

With the exception of Fabregas, whose exclusion paved the way for the immediacy of Kante's expected inclusion, this was the Chelsea of old. Admittedly, Conte had a clear way of working that was different to what had gone before… but there were concerns the new manager was not being backed by the board as the Blues laboured to bring in fresh faces.

Chelsea's on going frustration as they tried to resolve central defensive concerns via the transfer market showed no sign of abating. The question was, were the Blues architects of their own apparent misfortune? Was a lack of managerial continuity the real reason behind the continued failure to replace once imperious central defensive duo of veteran skipper John Terry and long-departed partner Ricardo Carvalho?

One time Chelsea target John Stone's had recently become the world's second most expensive defender when the 22-year old centre-back joined Manchester City from Everton for £47.5 million. The costliest backline player on the planet remained David Luiz whom the Blues had sold to Paris Saint-Germain for £50 million in June 2014.

Luiz, originally viewed as Carvalho's successor, had signed for the London club in January 2011 from Benfica as a 23-year old for £21.3 million. The Brazil international soon established himself in then manager Carlo Ancelotti's side, and his swashbuckling style of play coupled with a knack of scoring important goals made him a firm favourite with the fans who spoke of him in glowing terms as future captain material.

A year after Luiz arrived at the Bridge, Chelsea signed Bolton Wanderers defender Gary Cahill for £7 million, and a month later 15-year old Denmark youth international centre-back Andreas Christensen joined from Brondby on a free transfer. Ancelotti had by now been sacked as Blues manager and replaced by Andre Villas-Boas… himself about to be sacked and replaced on an interim basis by assistant Roberto Di Matteo.

In May 2012, Di Matteo guided Chelsea to Champions League glory and Luiz played a prominent part in the triumph converting his spot-kick in the penalty shootout against Bayern Munich to help seal a stunning win. In the same match, squad player Cahill replaced suspended Terry and acquitted himself well.

Di Matteo, rewarded for his efforts by being appointed permanent Chelsea manager, was sacked later that year and replaced on a temporary basis by Rafa Benitez.

Under Benitez, in May 2013, the Blues won the Europa League. Luiz scored in both legs of the semi-final against Basel ensuring passage to the final against his former club Benfica which Chelsea won 2-1. With Terry missing out on another European final, this time through injury, Cahill partnered Luiz at the back and again stepped up to the mark. Christensen meanwhile, now an established member of Chelsea's youth team, played the same month in the side that lost to Norwich City in the FA Youth Cup Final.

The return of José Mourinho to manage Chelsea in June 2013 was trumpeted from the rooftops by exultant supporters. The self-anointed Special One set about remodelling the Blues favouring those players who played the José way and marginalising those who didn't even if it rankled with the fans.

Among the high-profile victims of Mourinho's cull were two-time Chelsea Player of the Year Juan Mata, sold to Manchester United in January 2014 and Luiz who departed six months later. Signing for the Blues for £12 million from Saint Etienne in the same transfer window that Mata departed was 19-year old centre-back Kurt Zouma. While Zouma stayed on in France with the Ligue 1 side for the rest of the season, Christensen continued to make a name for himself as part of Chelsea's academy team who defeated Fulham in the final of the FA Youth Cup.

Deputising for Cahill and/or Terry, Zouma enjoyed significant game-time in Chelsea's title-winning season that followed and earned rave reviews when deployed as a defensive midfielder by Mourinho in the League Cup Final win over Tottenham Hotspur.

Christensen, who featured for the first team against Shrewsbury Town in an earlier round of the competition, completed the season winning the UEFA Youth League and also made his Premier League debut as a substitute in the final game of the season against Sunderland.

With Zouma clearly earmarked by Mourinho as one half of his centre-back pairing for the future at the Bridge, the Portuguese identified Stones as his potential partner but Chelsea failed to reach an agreement with Everton over his transfer and the deal floundered as would the Blues… spectacularly so!

Christensen meanwhile was sent out on a two-year loan to Borussia

Monchengladbach and proved his worth being voted Player of the Year as the German side finished fourth in the Bundesliga. Already a fully-fledged Denmark international, Christensen has been the subject of a recent £14.5 million bid from Gladbach which Chelsea so far had resisted.

José Mourinho's sacking, his replacement by interim boss Guus Hiddink… and the subsequent hiring of Antonio Conte appeared to have further muddied central defensive waters already clouded by the injury sustained by Zouma in February 2016 and the terms of Christensen's loan deal. In any case, there was every chance that Conte had no idea who Christensen was when he'd signed on the dotted line at the Bridge hence the interest in the more familiar Serie A figures of Leonardo Bonucci who was clearly staying put with Juventus and Kalidou Koulibaly who was being held to ransom by Napoli whose hard-bargaining chairman Aurelio De Laurentiis was reported to be asking Chelsea to pay a ridiculous £60 million for the Senegal international.

The evidence was compelling. Chelsea's persistent chopping and changing of managers was continuing to hamper the club's chances of establishing a long-term centre-back partnership as each new boss brought with him his own ideas about which players were potentially right for the role.

THE BIG KICK OFF

15 August 2016

Premier League
Chelsea 2 West Ham United 1
Stamford Bridge
Attendance: 41,521
Referee: Anthony Taylor

Chelsea (4-1-4-1): Thibaut Courtois, Branislav Ivanovic, Gary Cahill, John Terry(c), Cesar Azpilicueta; N'Golo Kante; Willian (Pedro 80), Nemanja Matic, Oscar (Michy Batshuayi 85), Eden Hazard (Victor Moses 85), Diego Costa.
Scorers: Hazard (pen) 47, Costa 89
Booked: Kante 3, Diego Costa 20, Azpilicueta 75, Pedro 90+3

West Ham United (4-1-4-1): Adrian, Antonio (Byram 52), Reid, Collins, Masuaku, Nordtveit (Payet 66), Ayew (Tore 34), Noble (c), Kouyate, Valencia, Carroll.
Scorers: Collins 77
Booked: Collins 21, Antonio 46

Antonio Conte's reign as Chelsea manager got off to a nervy but winning start in an edgy London derby with West Ham at Stamford Bridge. The game was goalless at the end of tense first-half, but Eden Hazard broke the deadlock from the penalty spot shortly after the restart converting from 12 yards after Cesar Azpilicueta had been tripped in the box by Michail Antonio.

The Blues looked to be holding out for a 1-0 win until James Collins fired home for the Hammers following a poorly defended corner. Fortunately for Chelsea, with West Ham in the ascendancy, a determined-looking Diego Costa fired home an 89th minute winner ensuring Conte had three points at the first time of asking as Blues boss.

THE ITALIAN JOB

The Italian, who'd been greeted at the start of the game with a spectacular banner display draped from the upper tier of the Matthew Harding Stand, oozed charisma, style and passion from the technical area and his desire to win had clearly percolated into a Stamford Bridge dressing room desperately lacking in ambition last season.

Antonio Conte, does it better. Makes me happy. Makes me feel this way, sang Chelsea supporters to the tune of Chaka Khan's classic disco banger *Ain't Nobody*. Not everyone was up for this chant as the tune was already being well overused elsewhere... a simple masterpiece would eventually replace it.

Against a Hammers side compiled of many new faces, the Blues boss sent out a starting XI well versed in meshing together when the mood takes them. Remarkably, or not as a lot of us who were at the Monday night game discussed openly, N'Golo Kante was the only new face from the Chelsea side that kicked off last year's shocking campaign against Swansea City... at least the France international lived up to his billing as the best signing of the summer by putting in an imperious display and dragging up the calibre of performance of defensive midfield partner Nemanja Matic.

The duo shielded and gave confidence to the familiar, much-criticised backline of Cesar Azpilicueta, skipper John Terry, Gary Cahill and Branislav Ivanovic, so much so that keeper Thibaut Courtois had very little to do, and they also recycled the ball well for Eden Hazard, Willian and Oscar who tormented West Ham and were able to get striker Diego Costa involved in the game.

Ironically, it was the mercurial Hazard and combative Costa, two players whom last season appeared to have given up on Chelsea, and, in the process, tested to breaking point the patience of Blues supporters, who found the net.

Appointing Conte manager as early as April had to go down as a masterstroke on the part of the Chelsea board as he had clearly reconstructed the mind-sets of the duo who once more looked like the players whose goals went a long way to delivering the title in 2015.

Hazard fizzed with malevolent intent throughout the contest, and looking trim, fit and energetic, Costa was also back to his bristling best... hustling, harrying and making a general nuisance of himself. An early booking for dissent, a controversial late challenge on goalkeeper Adrian which might have got him sent off on another day, and an even later goal had the punters purring. On this type of pugnacious, predatory form, the

Brazil-born Spain international was right up there with the leading strikers in the game.

Conte had already spoken out, challenging Costa to prove how good he was and he certainly rose to the occasion against the Hammers yet the usual question marks remained. At least the persistent stories linking the striker with a move back to Atletico Madrid appeared to have dissipated, however there were new reports suggesting the he had been 'offered' to Napoli and Inter Milan as Chelsea cleared the decks for Romelu Lukaku's return to the Bridge for a colossal fee!

Having gambled by sending promising young forward Bertrand Traore out on loan to Ajax, Conte was currently reliant on Costa and summer signing Michy Batshuayi. The latest Lukaku talk could prove unsettling for both players... but perhaps more so Batshuayi, who'd come off the bench against West Ham and nodded down the ball for Costa to score the winner.

Conte was understandably happy after the game. "Every manager when they arrive at a new club tries to bring their philosophy and we have only been working with the players for one month, but I'm pleased," he said with a twinkle in his eyes. "I'm very happy with the attitude and behaviour of the players and to have a great team it's important to have the right spirit."

20 August

**Premier League
Watford 1 Chelsea 2
Vicarage Road
Attendance: 20,772
Referee: Jon Moss**

Chelsea (4-1-4-1): Thibaut Courtois, Branislav Ivanovic, Gary Cahill, John Terry (c), Cesar Azpilicueta, N'Golo Kante, Pedro (Victor Moses 71), Oscar (Michy Batshuayi 73), Nemanja Matic (Cesc Fabregas 78), Eden Hazard, Diego Costa.
Scorers: Batshuayi 80, Costa 87
Booked: Cahill 20, Costa 56, Hazard 90+2

Watford (3-5-2): Gomes, Cathcart, Prodl, Britos; Amrabat, Behrami, Capoue (Doucoure 84), Guedioura (Vydra 89), Holebas (Zuniga 90), Deeney (c), Ighalo.
Scorer: Capoue 55

THE ITALIAN JOB

Booked: Deeney 19, Britos 69, Holebas 70, Behrami 90+4

Chelsea came from behind to beat Watford 2-1 at Vicarage Road as late goals from substitute Michy Batshuayi and Diego Costa overturned a fine Etienne Capoue strike for the home side which had looked like being enough to give the Hornet's all three points.

The Blues enjoyed the lion's share of possession for much of the contest but created little in the way of chances up until the final phase of the game when Antonio Conte's tactical substitutions paid dividends. Batshuayi equalised with 10 minutes to go and then Cesc Fabregas, on for Nemanja Matic, teed up Costa with a wonderful defence-splitting through ball which the surly striker swept past Heurelho Gomes for the winner.

The feel good factor that came from snatching victory from the jaws of defeat could not be underestimated. As witnessed in Monday's season-opening victory over West Ham, Conte's passion and shrewd tactical acumen coupled with another late, late Costa goal delivered all three points and maintained Chelsea's 100% start to the campaign. A fabulous Fabregas cameo coming in a week when the Spain international had been rumoured to be departing Stamford Bridge was a timely reminder of his creative genius while Batshuayi showed enough quality to merit a start against Burnley next weekend.

Watford's goal was a defensive mishap redolent of last season. Capoue was allowed the freedom of Chelsea's penalty area when finding the net. The late unavailability of Willian through injury saw the Blues over-reliant on Eden Hazard with the Brazilian's replacement Pedro offering little in the way of creativity or ammunition for Costa who found himself yellow-carded for the second game in succession and indeed once again was somewhat fortunate to remain on the pitch this time following a theatrical dive.

The inclement conditions at Vicarage Road did not dampen Conte's ardour for the game as he lived and breathed every kick of the ball and barked orders from the technical area. It was a surprise given Chelsea's lack of incisiveness in the first-half, and the fact that Watford scored in the 55th minute, that it took the Italian until the 71st minute to make changes… but his substitutions had the desired effect and won the day.

"I'm happy for the commitment and attitude of the players. It shows a good family, a good team," said Conte after the game. The family. La famiglia. We liked that… Don Conte, Godfather of the Chelsea family.

23 August

EFL Cup Second Round
Chelsea 3 Bristol Rovers 2
Stamford Bridge
Attendance: 39,266
Referee: Keith Stroud

Chelsea (4-2-4): Asmir Begovic, Cesar Azpilicueta, Gary Cahill, Branislav Ivanovic (c), Ola Aina (John Terry 78), Cesc Fabregas, Nemanja Matic, Victor Moses, Michy Batshuayi, Ruben Loftus-Cheek (Oscar 82), Pedro (Eden Hazard 75).
Scorers: Batshuayi 29, 41, Moses 31
Booked: Pedro 47

Bristol Rovers (4-2-3-1): Mildenhall, Leadbitter, Lockyer (c), Hartley, Brown, Sinclair, O Clarke, Bodin (Easter h-t), Lines, James (Taylor h-t), Harrison (Gaffney 66).
Scorers: Hartley 34, Harrison 49.
Booked: Easter 71, Taylor 85

Chelsea progressed to the next round of the EFL Cup at the expense of Bristol Rovers but they were made to work harder than expected at Stamford Bridge by the League One outfit whose endeavours were fairly reflected by the final score-line of 3-2.

The Blues dominated the first-half, and two quick goals in succession around the half-hour mark from Michy Batshuayi and Victor Moses suggested the floodgates might open, but Rovers battled back and Peter Hartley reduced the arrears moments later. Batshuayi, making his full Chelsea debut, restored the home side's two-goal advantage before the break, but it was the visitors who took the initiative shortly after the interval when Ellis Harrison scored from the penalty spot and they might have levelled the tie but for an outstanding save from deputy keeper Asmir Begovic.

After two excellent cameo appearances from the substitutes bench, Batshuayi showed what he could do given a full 90 minutes. Two goals and a healthy, clean appetite for the game suggested that Chelsea might have unearthed a gem... even if he did cost £33 million! It was also good to see Victor Moses, who'd shone in pre-season given a start and repay Conte's faith with a goal. It wasn't all positive news though. The Blues continued inability to keep a clean sheet provided concerned food for thought.

THE ITALIAN JOB

Without the indefatigable N'Golo Kante, despite facing lowly opposition, Chelsea's midfield had flagged noticeably after the break when concentration levels in general seemed to wane.

"We must understand that when you have the opportunity to kill the game, you must kill the game," said Conte who'd clearly been unnerved by Rovers' fight back. "It's a pity because we were dominating the game but then we suffered. Tonight I knew the English cup, I knew the atmosphere, and I can tell these games are very tough for all."

27 August

Premier League
Chelsea 3 Burnley 0
Stamford Bridge
Attendance: 41,607
Referee: Mark Clattenburg

Chelsea (4-1-4-1): Thibaut Courtois, Branislav Ivanovic, Gary Cahill, John Terry (c), Cesar Azpilicueta, N'Golo Kante, Willian (Victor Moses 76), Nemanja Matic, Oscar, Eden Hazard (Pedro 80); Diego Costa (Michy Batshuayi 80)
Scorers: Hazard 9, Willian 41, Moses 89
Booked: Oscar 30, Ivanovic 43

Burnley (4-4-2): Heaton, Lowton, Keane, Mee, Ward, Arfield (Gudmondsson 56), Defour (O'Neill 55), Marney (Tarkowski 71), Boyd; Gray, Vokes
Booked: Keane 49

Chelsea cruised to a comfortable 3-0 victory over Burnley at Stamford Bridge making it three Premier League wins out of three for Antonio Conte. The Blues bossed the game from start to finish and the result was never in doubt from the 9th minute when Eden Hazard opening the scoring. Willian doubled the home side's advantage just before half time and Victor Moses who replaced the Brazil international in the 77th minute wrapped up proceedings with a late goal.

With the game effectively over as a contest by half-time, Conte could have used more of the second period to make better use if the substitutes available to him. Functional late changes meant academy graduates Ruben Loftus-Cheek and Ola Aina were left kicking their heals on the bench when further top-flight experience, particularly for Aina might have been beneficial.

It was noticeable that Stamford Bridge was bubbling with enthusiasm for Conte... the feel good factor associated with a 100% start to the campaign seemed to have all but banished the woeful memories of last season. Obviously Chelsea would face far sterner tests than Burnley were able to provide, but the Italian already had his players well-drilled and looking lean and hungry. We went home happy.

The Burnley result represented a first clean sheet of the season proper for Conte as Chelsea manager, and the Italian was clearly delighted by what he had seen. "I'm pleased to score the goals, it's always important to score one more goal than your opponent, but to keep a clean sheet is also important for the confidence of the whole team."

The Blues boss with what would appear to be foresight on his part also added, "It's important to keep the last season in our mind. When there is a difficult situation it is important to look behind to find new strength to go forward." Unfortunately, Conte's look-behind-you mantra to his players was about to fall on a few deaf ears. Maybe they were still getting used to his philosophy.

31 August

Transfer deadline day.

"I don't want to buy a player only to buy him, I want to buy the right player for Chelsea, for the present and for the future. A good prospect. It's important we make a good investment." Antonio Conte.

The eye-brow raising, headline-grabbing, last-minute deals which saw Marcos Alonso and David Luiz sign for Chelsea at the conclusion of the transfer window had an element of desperation about them that had plenty of supporters questioning the merit of the Blues manager's words.

It was clear that neither player was anywhere near the top of Conte's shopping list... if indeed they were on it at all when the Italian first drew up his plans to revitalise the London club's flagging squad following his appointment in April.

Having paid Fiorentina £23 million for 25-year old left-back Alonso, a player whose unspectacular career-to-date had included stints at Real Madrid, Bolton Wanderers and Sunderland and smacked of unfulfilled potential, Chelsea won the surprising-transfer-stakes by a country mile when re-signing 29-year old centre-back David Luiz from Paris Saint-Germain for £32 million.

What exactly was Conte planning to do with the duo?

To date, in his short career as Chelsea manager, the Italian had already displayed the type of ruthless streak needed to address the torpor that riddled the Stamford Bridge dressing room last season. Cesc Fabregas had found himself to be the first high-profile casualty. A regular place on the bench followed by a January transfer window exit seemed likely for the Spain international given Conte's clear preference to pair £30 summer signing N'Golo Kante with Nemanja Matic in Chelsea's midfield engine room.

Did the arrivals of Alonso and Luiz put at immediate risk the starting places of two of the Blues current backline that had started every Premier League game this season to date? Successive victories over West Ham, Watford and Burnley had given Conte the best possible start in the top-flight, but without the luxury of typically feeble Champions League group stage opposition to provide autumnal opportunities to tinker with his starting XI, the Italian was left with just EFL Cup matches in which to experiment. Having made a meal of beating lowly Bristol Rovers at home in the last round of the competition, Chelsea next opponents would be reigning top-flight champions Leicester City away at the King Power. Would Conte use the match against the Foxes to hand first starts to Alonso and Luiz… or might he have already done so in the Premier League?

The acquisition of Alonso suggested that Conte would like to field Cesar Azpilicueta at right full-back… his natural side. But there was a curious déjà vu aspect to this possibility that intimated things may not play out this way. In July 2014, Chelsea under the management of José Mourinho, had paid Atletico Madrid £15.8 million for the services of specialist left-back Filipe Luis who had just been nominated as the best defender in La Liga.

Luis however couldn't usurp Azpilicueta from the left-back berth and Mourinho was by now settled on playing Branislav Ivanovic at right-back. A year later, Luis returned to Atletico for an undisclosed fee and Chelsea signed Ghana international left-back Baba Rahman from Bundesliga side Augsburg for an initial £14 million and almost £10 million in contractual add-ons. In the torrid campaign which followed, Rahman failed to break through and the 22-year old also failed to impress Conte in pre-season and was now back in Germany on loan at Schalke 04.

Would Alonso be the first specialist left-back signed by the club since the legendary Ashley Cole to nail down an immediate and regular first-team place, or would Conte persist with the current Azpilicueta / Ivanovic arrangement and view the new man as a squad player? There was plenty debate to be had which included on-going concerns over 32-year old Ivanovic's problems dealing with pace. Looming league fixtures against Liverpool and Arsenal, teams bristling with attacking prowess, suggested Conte had a big call to make… and the Chelsea manager's life was now further complicated by the arrival of Luiz.

Luiz's theatrical and somewhat erratic defensive displays were as well-documented as Conte's love in Italy of playing three central defenders with two wing-backs buccaneering forward to provide ammunition for two strikers… a template he had yet to utilise in this country.

Did Conte plan to field Luiz as a ball-playing enabler alongside long-established centre-back duo Gary Cahill and veteran skipper John Terry in this way? With his 36th birthday looming, Terry was at risk from fatigue and injury. Given Luiz's issues with concentration, as a defensive combination, this trio had a jittery look about it that could buckle against top class opposition. Then there was Kurt Zouma to factor into the equation. The 21-year old France international broke through into Chelsea's first team under Mourinho, and would certainly have been ahead of one of Cahill or Terry at the time of Conte's appointment had injury not already cut short his season.

Ivanovic, Alonso, Azpilicueta, Cahill, Terry, Zouma, Luiz. What would Conte do when he reshaped his defence? The exclusion of Fabregas was evidence enough of the Italian's single-mindedness when it came to the pursuit of his version of excellence, but maybe that was an easier call to make given the abilities of Kante and Matic. Such astute stubbornness could and would bring with it more surprises, but at the time none of us supporters had any real clue what was about to happen.

SEPTEMBER 2016

6 September

In the midst of an international break, it was the England Under 21 side that provided food for thought rather than anything that transpired on the senior front as far as Chelsea's bevy of international stars was concerned.

Blues academy graduates Nathaniel Chalobah and Ruben Loftus-Cheek served up a timely reminder of their abilities when scoring in a 6-1 rout of Norway… a game in which one of Chelsea's on-loan army of players Lewis Baker, currently furthering his football apprenticeship in the Netherland's Eredvisie with Vitesse Arnhem, also found the net.

Interestingly enough, the match also saw Manchester United starlet Marcus Rashford score a hattrick. 18-year old Rashford broke through in to United's first team last season under Louis Van Gaal, but the arrival of José Mourinho… and Zlatan Ibrahimovic… at Old Trafford had clipped the high-flying youngster's first team wings. What a surprise!

As far as Chelsea were concerned, it looked like another huge case of déjà vu. Batshuayi's arrival at the Bridge and the retention of Diego Costa was without doubt the catalyst for Bertrand Traore being sent out on loan to Ajax. 21-year old Traore had impressed when given chances during what was a difficult season for Chelsea and his 'departure' had been met with a collective sigh by Blues supporters as frustrated as the young players themselves must be at the continuation of what was widely-viewed as a loan cycle of despair.

And so the pedals went round again. New boy Alonso being widely tipped to play at left-back enabling Conte to switch 27-year old Cesar Azpilicueta to right-back meant two things. The beginning of the end of 32-year old Branislav Ivanovic's Chelsea career and a lack of first team opportunities for promising academy starlet Ola Aina. Like, Chalobah, Loftus-Cheek, Baker and Traore, 19-year old Aina would no doubt find himself kicking his heels on the Blues bench before an almost inevitable loan move.

Conte had certainly had a good look at Chalobah, Loftus-Cheek and Aina and deemed that they are not quite ready to serve his demanding purposes. Why gamble on youth when Roman Abramovich was continually prepared to bankroll buying in players who could already hit the ground running?

Given Abramovich's unrelenting impatience with managers who could not deliver trophies season-in-season-out, unless Conte found a way to do this, the likelihood was he would go the way of his predecessors. He would anyway... eventually... they all do... and then another man comes in... and the sequence of intense pressure and scrutiny begins again... and academy hopefuls continue to fall by the wayside. If I'd had a boy instead of my blessed little daughter Misty Blue and he was showing promise at the glorious game, would I let him sign for Chelsea? Good question. Head v Heart... Money v Happiness... First team football... yes or no?

11 September

Premier League
Swansea City 2 Chelsea 2
Liberty Stadium
Attendance: 20,865
Referee: Andre Marriner

Chelsea (4-1-4-1): Thibaut Courtois, Branislav Ivanovic, Gary Cahill, John Terry (c), Cesar Azpilicueta, N'Golo Kante, Willian (Victor Moses 77), Oscar (Michy Batshuayi 88), Nemanja Matic (Cesc Fabregas 76), Eden Hazard, Diego Costa.
Scorer: Costa 18, 81
Booked: Costa 41, Courtois 59, Hazard 89, Terry 90+2

Swansea (3-5-1-1): Fabianski, Fernandez, Amat, Kingsley, Naughton, Fer, Cork (c) Ki, Taylor (Barrow 41), Sigurdsson (Rangel 88), Llorente.
Scorers: Sigurdsson (pen) 59, Fer 62
Booked: Fer 26, Fernandez 42, Amat 48

Chelsea failed to win for the first time under Antonio Conte in a feisty encounter with Swansea at the Liberty Stadium. Diego Costa opened the scoring as the Blues dominated the opening phase of the game, but the wheels came off early on in the second-half for the visitors.

THE ITALIAN JOB

In the 59th minute, Thibaut Courtois, left stranded by a back-pedaling defence that had been caught napping on the counter-attack, tripped Gylfi Sigurdsson in the box. The FA's new 'double-jeopardy' rule meant Courtois was booked rather than sent-off by referee Andre Marriner who awarded a penalty that Sigurdsson duly converted.

Three minutes later John Terry and Gary Cahill combined to have what could be politely termed as a bit of a shocker. 30 yards out from Chelsea's goal, Terry squared an innocuous-looking ball to Cahill who appeared not to be aware of the game around him. Leroy Fer raced in and clearly fouled the Blues centre-back when dispossessing him before beating Courtois.

Notwithstanding the hysteria that followed Marriner's obvious myopia, had Cahill been concentrating, he would have been more likely to retain possession and clear the ball. It could also be argued that Terry put his teammate under unnecessary pressure when it might have made more sense to sweep the ball up field. Twitter trolls went mental, masturbating themselves over their keyboards in a knuckle-dragging frenzy of barbed vitriol directed principally at Cahill.

By the time Costa salvaged a point for Chelsea with an acrobatic goal, the Blues striker was fortunate to still be on the pitch. Having been booked earlier in the game, he was infinitely lucky not to receive another yellow card for a blatant dive that was as theatrical as the bicycle kick he later pulled off to score.

In his post-match summary, Conte concluded that in respect of Swansea's first goal Chelsea must "improve in some situations" and that the second was a "great mistake of the referee's". Cahill was so incensed with Marriner's failure to penalise Fer that he took to Twitter to share his frustration posting a video clip of the incident and the word "Incredible" followed by nine angry-face emojis. (The tweet was subsequently deleted.)

Significantly as it would transpire, Chelsea skipper John Terry strained the ligaments in his left ankle following a late Fer challenge and although he completed the game, he left the Liberty Stadium on crutches. Although Terry would go onto to make a full recovery, the window of opportunity was beckoning for David Luiz. Would the former Blues cult hero be able to take advantage of the situation? Not just yet!!

16 September

Premier League
Chelsea 1 Liverpool 2
Stamford Bridge
Attendance: 41,514
Referee: Martin Atkinson

Chelsea (4-1-4-1): Thibaut Courtois, Branislav Ivanovic (c), Gary Cahill, David Luiz, Cesar Azpilicueta, N'Golo Kante, Willian (Victor Moses 83), Nemanja Matic (Cesc Fabregas 83), Oscar (Pedro 83), Eden Hazard, Diego Costa.
Scorer: Costa 60
Booked: Willian 45+1

Liverpool (4-3-3): Mignolet, Clyne, Lovren, Matip, Milner, Lallana, Henderson (c), Wijnaldum (Stewart 89), Mane, Sturridge (Origi 57), Coutinho (Lucas 81).
Scorers: Lovren 17, Henderson 35
Booked: Lucas 88

Liverpool ended Antonio Conte's unbeaten start as Chelsea manager winning 2-1 at Stamford Bridge in a game which endorsed the belief widely held by many Blues supporters that previous early season results had represented something of a false dawn.

Captain for the night in the absence of the injured John Terry, Branislav Ivanovic conceded a needless free-kick in the 17th minute which was worked via Philippe Coutinho to Dejan Lovren who took advantage of a dormant Chelsea defence and placed the ball beyond Thibaut Courtois.

Liverpool were well in control of the game when Jordan Henderson doubled their advantage in the 36th minute with a 30 yard screamer... 10 minutes later when referee Martin Atkinson blew for half-time, boos could be heard from sections of the home support. Each to their own and all that, and I guess if people pay £45/£50 and more for a ticket they are entitled to boo... but I hate(d) hearing it.

Caught up in the midst of this rude awakening was David Luiz making his second debut for Chelsea. Blues supporters, and there were plenty, who'd questioned the wisdom and dare I say sanity of re-signing the curly-haired 'Geezer' continued their grumbles and given what had just been witnessed... to be fair they appeared well-founded.

THE ITALIAN JOB

Chelsea made a fist of the game in the second-half, playing with what Conte later described as "good intensity"… and while another Diego Costa goal tightened up the contest, begrudgingly I'd had to admit Liverpool were good value for their win. The sight of an animated and clearly vexed Conte raging in the technical area was some consolation… the Blues boss would be having words with his players at the end of the game.

Friday night football was the first horrible aspect of this defeat… a weekend ruined before it had got properly started. And the second? Nasally-whining sounds of self-entitlement bubbling up from the corner of The Shed where corralled Liverpool supporters spent the evening reminding us "rent boys" that they'd "won it five times". That didn't go down too well either.

Reflecting on the defeat Conte humbly stated, "I'm guilty because I'm the coach and it means I have to work more." It was refreshing to hear. Would a certain Special One have ever admitted fallibility, or would he have just blamed his players? Answers on a postcard please.

With his finger on the pulse of the problem the Blues boss concluded, "We must feel the danger in every single moment of the game if we want to win and think like a great team. We must pay attention and be focused."

Imagine if he'd told his players to write that out 100 times… like a school master taking detention making pupils do lines.

Pay attention and be focused
Pay attention and be focused
Pay attention and be focused

20 September

EFL Cup Third Round
Leicester City 2 Chelsea 4
King Power Stadium
Attendance: 29,899
Referee: Robert Madley

Chelsea (4-2-4): Asmir Begovic, Cesar Azpilicueta, Gary Cahill (c), David Luiz, Marco Alonso, Cesc Fabregas, Nemanja Matic, Victor Moses, Ruben Loftus-Cheek (Diego Costa 67), Michy Batshuayi (Nathaniel Chalobah 80), Pedro (Eden Hazard 90).
Scorers: Cahill 45+1, Azpilicueta 49, Fabregas 92, 94
Booked: Matic 83, David Luiz 109

Leicester (4-4-2): Zieler, Simpson, Wasilewski, Morgan (c), Chilwell, Gray (Amartey 90+1), Drinkwater, King, Schlupp, Musa (Vardy 76), Okazaki (Ulloa 75)
Scorer: Okazaki 17, 34
Sent off: Wasilewski 89
Booked: Drinkwater 87, Wasilewski 52, Chilwell 103

Chelsea came back from 2-0 down to beat Leicester 4-2 in what in the end proved to be an emphatic EFL Cup 3rd Round victory at the King Power Stadium.

A combination of lackadaisical goalkeeping and error-strewn defending gifted Shinji Okazaki a brace of goals inside 35 minutes at which point the visitors looked to be heading out of the competition. Once again, Chelsea's backline looked rudderless... lacking cohesion and genuine leadership. There was a horrible groundhog day aspect to this and opposing teams, with full sight of the Blues Achilles heel, were continuing to savage it.

Fortunately, Gary Cahill pulled a goal back before the break to give Antonio Conte's side breathing space and after Cesar Azpilicueta levelled the tie shortly after the restart there was only going to be one winner.

The late introduction of Diego Costa for the disappointingly ineffective Ruben Loftus-Cheek and Eden Hazard for Pedro proved to be telling factors. Marcin Wasilewski's irresponsible forearm smash on Costa resulted in a second yellow for the Leicester defender, and Chelsea made the most of the man advantage in extra time when Fabregas found the net twice in quick succession on the back of scintillating play by Hazard to kill the tie

THE ITALIAN JOB

off.

Going 2-0 down once again, and on the back of last Friday's disappointing home defeat to Liverpool, the pressure was on Chelsea. Defeat would have been undoubtedly problematic for Conte as he tried to manage a club with the most impatient owner in world football... however what eventually turned out to be a stirring victory provided a much needed morale-boosting fillip for the Italian and his players, especially match winner Fabregas who had been frozen out of Premier League action.

Making his debut, £23 million specialist left-back Alonso initially failed to instill confidence that he might succeed where expensive recent predecessors Baba Rahman and Filipe Luis flopped but he improved in the second period providing hope for the future though it was evident he needed more time to settle into the English game.

Travelling Blues supporters had been in fine voice throughout the game even at 2-0. Conte described the fans as "incredible" which was thoroughly decent of him. Should I have a dig at Mourinho here? No, leave it Marco... let it go.

The Blues boss also advised there was work still to be done. "We know that we can improve, I repeat this. The only way I know is to continue to work very hard and to improve on different aspects. I am sure we can improve and I will try with all my strength to do this."

*****

Beating the reigning Premier League champions in the EFL Cup was a decent way to bounce back after the Liverpool loss, but thoughts soon turned to Chelsea's next opponents, Arsenal.

In recent years, trips to the Emirates had been fruitful with memories still fresh in the mind of Didier Drogba scoring when he wants and the various home-seat emptying 'fire drills' that had been set off by Chelsea asserting their authority over the Gunners. Even last season, the Blues had made a mockery of their troubles by beating Arsenal home and away thereby putting a significant dent in the title hopes Arsene Wenger had for his team... but given on going defensive dramas I felt less confident about the forthcoming encounter. In fact I wasn't confident at all.

Pay attention and be focused
Pay attention and be focused
Pay attention and be focused

24 September

**Premier League
Arsenal 3 Chelsea 0
Emirates Stadium
Attendance: 60,028
Referee: Michael Oliver**

Chelsea (4-1-4-1): Thibaut Courtois, Branislav Ivanovic (c), Gary Cahill, David Luiz, Cesar Azpilicueta, N'Golo Kante, Willian (Pedro 70), Cesc Fabregas (Marcos Alonso 55), Nemanja Matic, Eden Hazard (Michy Batshuayi 70), Diego Costa.
Booked: Ivanovic 28, Diego Costa 83
Arsenal (4-2-3-1): Cech, Bellerin, Mustafi, Koscielny (c), Monreal, Coquelin (Xhaka 32), Cazorla, Walcott, Ozil, Iwobi (Gibbs 69), Sanchez (Giroud 79).
Scorers: Sanchez 11, Walcott 14, Ozil 40

Arsenal took Chelsea's defence to the Finsbury Park branch of Sketchley's in a traumatic first-half for captain Brana and company. Gary Cahill was at fault not for the first time in recent weeks when allowing Alexis Sanchez to leave him for dead and score after 11 minutes, and Theo Walcott doubled the Gunners advantage three minutes later following a move which flummoxed the Blues static backline. Five minutes before half-time Mesut Ozil left N'Golo Kante trailing in his wake to put Arsenal's three up and kill the game off.

Pay attention and be focused
Pay attention and be focused
Pay attention and be focused

See what happens if you don't? Antonio Conte must have flown into an apoplectic rage at half time.

It made for horrific watching. To add to Chelsea's calamitous defensive display, Cesc Fabregas, handed a first Premier League start against his former employers by Conte following his two-goal heroics in midweek against Leicester failed to get going. At the interval, thoughts returned to that blissful day at the Bridge in 2014 when Chelsea thrashed Arsenal 6-0… was this going to be the day the Gunners properly avenged that defeat? The portents didn't look good.

There were no changes at half-time, but on 55 minutes Conte sent on

THE ITALIAN JOB

Marcos Alonso for Fabregas and switched to three at the back, with the Spaniard and his countryman Cesar Azpilicueta deployed either side of Ivanovic, David Luiz and Cahill…damage limitation for sure… and a glimpse into the future as Chelsea stood firm and enjoyed more possession.

The darkest moment comes before the dawn… right… well it was pitch black that night… and Twitter predictably went into a full meltdown with the usual predictably anonymous keyboard warriors (giving the impression that they had personally played football at the highest level) demonizing Conte and calling for Brana and Cahill to be hung drawn and quartered.

Once again, the Chelsea manager's philosophy served to pour oil on troubled waters. "I was a footballer and it happens that in one game you don't have a good performance for many reasons, but I hope to improve this situation." I could imagine him reasoning with his players and them listening. The "I was a footballer" bit was powerful, it resonated… it suggested that Conte knew how to resolve matters. "We've had defeat in two big games. For this reason we must be humble and understand the moment and that we need to work a lot to improve and change our story."

*****

I was still frustrated. Of course I was, but on the pitch, if the truth be told there was nothing new to tell. A desperate defence playing in front of a goalkeeper who at every international break intimated he would rather live in Madrid than west London. A player (Branislav Ivanovic) piping up to say the team didn't stick to the manager's game plan. Conte had to find a way to sort out this dogs breakfast before things got too messy again and Chelsea's owner started barking… and then biting. God help us!

At least Costa and Hazard had been able to cover for the deficiencies behind them in the Blues opening matches against West Ham, Watford, Burnley and Swansea… but against serious opponents in Liverpool and Arsenal it was a case of mission impossible.

I figured a fit again John Terry should provide the organization and leadership lacking in the games he missed and Kurt Zouma would return to provide further options at the back… but it wasn't an ideal situation. Having assessed the squad following his appointment in April, it was evident that Conte had requested at least one world-class central defender be brought in during the summer transfer window… he was given Marcos Alonso and David Luiz.

Granted, N'Golo Kante was a decent signing… but one swallow didn't make a summer and Conte had admitted he was losing sleep trying to figure out a solution with the resources he had available.

It all sounded horribly familiar... and it was. It was well over a year since the penny dropped that the root of the London club's problems may be in the boardroom rather than the dressing room.

José Mourinho hadn't been able to improve the squad that had cantered to the 2015 Premier League title. Mourinho wanted Paul Pogba and John Stones, but the Chelsea board failed to deliver and provided him instead with Pedro, Baba Rahman... and future Sunderland legend Papy Djilobodji. Legendary goalkeeper Petr Cech was sold to Arsenal... and then there was the curious case of striker Radamel Falcao brought in on loan despite having flopped spectacularly at Manchester United. Stars of the team, in particular Hazard and Costa, looked unfit and uncaring... and Mourinho's opening day touchline spat with Eva Carneiro had set a ball rolling that would eventually knock the Portuguese over.

A catalogue of defensive disasters and associated defeats led to the inevitable. Abramovich sacked Mourinho. Abramovich's right hand man, technical director Michael Emenalo put his head above the parapet and advised the world that there had been "palpable discord" between the manager and the team.

Exasperated Blues supporters raged about the glaring deficiencies of Emenalo's CV and many pointed their fingers of blame for Mourinho's cataclysmic demise at the Nigerian who was brought into the club as a scout in 2007 by former manager Avram Grant... another Abramovich hire with a questionable football pedigree. At the time of joining Chelsea, Emenalo remarked that the chance of working for Grant was "a wonderful soccer education... like studying for your PhD at Harvard".

Emenalo's comment bordered on the ridiculous even then... now it reads like a laughable example of the 'it's not what you know, it's who you know' culture that had pervaded Chelsea since Abramovich bought the club in 2003. Currently pulling the boardroom strings at the Bridge... Marina Granovskaia who previously worked for the Russian at his oil company Sibneft where the head of corporate finance was Eugene Tenenbaum another trusted consultant at SW6 alongside Chelsea chairman Bruce Buck, a corporate lawyer who worked on the deal to sell 72% of Sibneft to Gazprom in 2005. Beyond Buck being a Blues fan and Emenalo's underwhelming career with the likes of Notts County, San José Clash and Maccabi Tel Aviv... Abramovich's current cabal of advisers were hardly steeped in the wisdom of football.

Poaching Peter Kenyon from Manchester United to be Chelsea chief executive in 2003 had been a masterstroke on the part of Abramovich. Kenyon's role in replicating United's giddy success at the Bridge could not be underestimated. Often maligned by Blues supporters during his time at Stamford Bridge because he is a lifelong Red Devils fan, Kenyon was a football man who knew how to spend the Russian's money. Kenyon left his role in 2009 and was replaced by protégé Ron Gourlay… another former United employee who also lacked popularity with Blues fans but seemingly got the job done. Gourlay resigned his position in October 2014 having overseen the Double triumph of 2010 and Champion's League glory in 2012.

From that point on, Abramovich's Chelsea world had become increasingly insular though the ambition to be a stellar football club clearly remained.

A billion pounds spent and yes, trophies aplenty have been won… but right now nothing appeared joined up. The glittering academy had evolved into an embarrassing white elephant that churned out loan fodder and continued to frustrate its graduates as much as the fans clamouring to see promising youths progress to the first team. Then there were the plans for a state-of-the-art new stadium where Chelsea's galacticos would play in front of 60,000… currently, the project seemed like a rich man's folly because the club couldn't get the basics right.

It was no wonder Conte was having sleepless nights.

Pay attention and be focused
Pay attention and be focused
Pay attention and be focused

26 September

Roman Abramovich paying his latest manager Antonio Conte a visit at the London club's state-of-the-art coaching facility at Cobham fuelled intense speculation about the nature of the meeting.

Coming on the back of successive Premier League defeats to Liverpool and Arsenal, games in which the woeful shortcomings of the Blues porous defence had been exposed yet again, it was little surprise that Abramovich felt the need to speak directly with Conte and view the players in training.

Following Saturday's 3-0 loss at the Emirates, stand in skipper Branislav Ivanovic had commented that the team "didn't believe" in what they were doing... words which no doubt alarmed Abramovich as much as the emphatic nature of Chelsea's loss.

Assessing the mood in the camp then seemed a fairly obvious thing to do. Conte was clearly feeling the intense pressure to succeed that comes with the manager's job at Stamford Bridge and words of reassurance from his boss, if that's indeed what he received, would go some way to remedying the problem of insomnia the affable Italian had spoken of recently. That's what I hoped for. Breathing space for the gaffer, and with an international break due following the coming weekend's away fixture with Hull City... a time to rethink tactics.

OCTOBER 2016

1 October

Premier League
Hull City 0 Chelsea 2
KCOM Stadium
Attendance: 21,257
Referee: Anthony Taylor

Chelsea (3-4-3): Thibaut Courtois, Cesar Azpilicueta, David Luiz, Gary Cahill, Victor Moses (Pedro 85), N'Golo Kante, Nemanja Matic, Marcos Alonso, Willian (Nathaniel Chalobah 89), Diego Costa, Eden Hazard (Oscar 81).
Scorers: Willian 61, Diego Costa 67
Booked: Moses 35, Matic 41.

Hull City (4-1-4-1): Marshall, Meyler, Livermore, Davies (c), Robertson, Clucas (Huddlestone 81), Snodgrass, Henriksen (Hernandez 71), Mason, Diomande (Maloney 63), Mbokani.
Booked: Livermore 42, Robertson 79

Chelsea returned to winning ways brushing aside Hull City 2-0 at the KCOM Stadium. Excellent second-half goals from Willian and Diego Costa were enough to seal a comfortable victory and Blues boss Antonio Conte delighted in the fact that his new-look Juventus and Italy-esque 3-4-3 formation worked out positively bringing with it a much needed clean sheet as well as three very welcome points.

Conte dropped Branislav Ivanovic to the bench opting to play Cesar Azpilicueta, Gary Cahill and David Luiz across the back with Victor Moses and Marcos Alonso deployed as wing-backs. Against Hull, the new template looked reasonably robust with Moses and Alonso giving Chelsea added impetus going forward which in turn energized Willian and Costa in particular who looked every inch a player at the top of his game leading the line with aplomb and focusing on his football rather than getting involved in the tempestuous spats that saw his card regularly marked yellow by referees.

Speaking about the new system after the victory Conte appeared relaxed and in control. 3-4-3 was his baby and he was going to nurture it. "It can be a big change in the tactical aspect. More than the system, what's important is the principles, then you can change. This week we've worked a lot, we must find the right way to be more compact. A clean sheet is important for the confidence. We are working very hard and we must continue in this way."

The Twitter trolls were nowhere to be seen that night. Maybe they were sleeping with the fishes. The Godfather had a great script and Don Conte in his role as Chelsea's Godfather also had a great script.

"Chelsea is a great team and I try to choose the best team because I want to win, the club and fans want to win. We have different options, that's normal. Together we win, together we lose."

Fantastic! I wondered if Conte liked the odd Limoncello... my favourite Italian tipple. He seemed like a really decent fella to have a few drinks with. Proper Chels as we say down at the cfcuk stall on matchday.

*****

Of course the international break provided thinking time... too much to be honest... but at least things appeared to be making more sense on planet Chelsea. It felt as if those horrible disasters against Liverpool and Arsenal had to happen so that Conte could move the Blues on from the past... and move them on he had. Even so, the harsh reality that had become apparent over the opening seven games of the season made it feel right now that Chelsea were still in the Premier League equivalent of no mans land. Always capable of despatching those teams that perennially occupied the middle / lower ground or yo-yoed too and from the Championship... the Blues had fallen behind in the race to occupy those precious places which guaranteed European... and in particular Champions League football.

With irascible owner Roman Abramovich not known for tolerating excuses or failure, Conte knew he must find a way to make up the initial ground already lost on the current top four... leaders and title favourites Manchester City, Tottenham Hotspur, Arsenal and Liverpool.

Chelsea currently sat in 7th place, three points off 4th place and so the gap was not insurmountable. Next up for the Blues were a brace of intriguing home games against stuttering reigning champions Leicester City... and José Mourinho's Manchester United.

Having set his revised stall out against Hull, there was no reason to suggest that Conte wouldn't employ the same tactics against a Leicester side who appeared to be saving their best for the Champions League this season. The return from injury of John Terry and long-term absentee Kurt Zouma would provide the Chelsea manager with more options at the back, and he might well need them when Mourinho's stuttering Man U arrived in SW6.

11 October

Bookmakers odds on Conte getting sacked shortened dramatically... without apparent reason... thankfully! Twitter went into overdrive (I was told)... I'd stayed away from it with purpose. Why wind yourself up with such nonsense?

15 October

Premier League
Chelsea 3 Leicester City 0
Stamford Bridge
Attendance: 41,547
Referee: Andre Marriner

Chelsea (3-4-3): Thibaut Courtois, Cesar Azpilicueta, David Luiz, Cahill (c), Victor Moses (Ola Aina 80), N'Golo Kante, Nemanja Matic, Marcos Alonso, Pedro (Nathaniel Chalobah 67), Diego Costa, Eden Hazard (Ruben Loftus-Cheek 80).
Scorers: Diego Costa 7, Hazard 33, Moses 79
Booked: Azpilicueta 51

Leicester (4-4-2): Schmeichel, Hernandez, Huth, Morgan (c), Fuchs, Albrighton (King 73), Drinkwater, Amartey, Schlupp (Mahrez 66), Vardy, Musa (Slimani 66).
Booked: Huth 26

Chelsea cruised to a comfortable 3-0 victory over a lacklustre Leicester City side at Stamford Bridge. Antonio Conte's side dominated the match from start to finish, and the result was never in doubt from the moment Diego Costa opened the scoring in the 7th minute with his 7th goal of the season. Eden Hazard doubled the Blues advantage just after the half-hour mark and Victor Moses rounded off a resounding win against the reigning Premier League champions 10 minutes from time.

Three well-crafted goals and a clean sheet on the back of some wonderful free-flowing football provided plenty of reasons to be cheerful for Chelsea supporters. Admirable passing play from wing-backs Marcos Alonso and Moses who joyfully celebrated his goal with a somersault gave the Blues an added dimension, while Hazard's renewed appetite for the game and eye for goal helped make short work of Leicester.

Nathaniel Chalobah, who'd replaced Pedro in the 68th minute, was given a rousing reception by Chelsea supporters keen to see the promising academy graduate do well. Chalobah didn't disappoint either providing the assist for Moses' goal with a deft piece of trickery.

Conte swept away the somewhat ridiculous rumours that he was about to be sacked by masterminding an emphatic win that came with another very welcome clean sheet. It was very much in evidence that the Blues had competently adapted to the Italian's three at the back / wing back system and, to his credit, with the exception of Willian, sadly absent on compassionate leave following the death of his mother, he'd deployed the same starting XI that faced Hull… and they didn't let him… or us down.

In Moses we'd found a new cult hero… *deh deh deh deh, Victor Moses* chanted the Matthew Harding Stand hijacking the fabulous early '80s Pigbag tune *Papa's Got a Brand New Pigbag*.

If there was a slight negative to the day it was Diego Costa's curious antics towards the end of the game which served as a reminder of the tempestuous side of the striker's nature that when unleashed usually spelt trouble of some sort.

Being one booking from an immediate suspension, and mindful of Chelsea's next opponents being Manchester United, many Blues supporters thought that with his side two up before the break and coasting to an easy win, Conte would have withdrawn Costa thereby avoiding any possible scenario which could have resulted in a yellow card and a ban for the United game. Evidently, Conte had other ideas and clearly wasn't fazed by such a possibility as Costa remained on the pitch for the full 90 minutes.

67 minutes into the match, Leicester manager Claudio Ranieri made a double substitution replacing Ahmed Musa and Jeffrey Schulpp with Riyad Mahrez and Islam Slimani. Conte countered this by replacing Pedro with

THE ITALIAN JOB

Nathaniel Chalobah and switching from 3-4-3 to the 3-5-2 with Eden Hazard going up front alongside Costa.

Conte, his usual animated self, barked instructions from the technical area to ensure his players were aware of the tactical revision and a couple of minutes later Costa was seen signalling to the bench with a rolled hands gesture indicating he wanted to come off.

My first thought was, 'bollocks!' Costa was injured… my second that he was concerned about picking up a yellow card… my third that he was unhappy with whatever Conte was communicating. This latter assumption was subsequently reported widely as being the reason for Costa's request to come off though there was a subjective element to this as the player remained tight-lipped about the incident.

Conte wouldn't be drawn on Costa's reasoning for requesting to be withdrawn, but he made it prescriptively clear after the game that substitutions were 100% his call. "I decide (about substitutions). Me, every single substitution. I take the responsibility in every situation, in positive or negative situations. It's always my decision," said the Italian who also revealed that the striker's importance on the pitch was such that it outweighed the risk factor involved in him getting booked.

All things considered, there was a theatrical box-office element to the Costa / Conte spat… if that's really what it was… which was certain to be revisited time and again in the build up to the United game and the return of The Special One to the Bridge.

José Mourinho and Costa had had a much-publicised disagreement during the course of a run-of-the-mill Champions League game against Maccabi Tel Aviv the previous November. Despite being en-route to a 4-0 victory in Israel, Costa was lambasted from the touchline by Mourinho and dropped for Chelsea's next game away to deadly rivals Tottenham Hotpsur. With the Blues already underperforming, and stories of dressing room unrest bubbling away, José 's decision, coupled with the fact he had Costa warm up at White Hart Lane during the match with Spurs which ended 0-0 but didn't send him on didn't benefit Chelsea's cause in the slightest. Less than a month later Mourinho was sacked… and Costa was one of the players held accountable for his demise by fans sympathetic to The Special One's cause.

23 October

Premier League
Chelsea 4 Manchester United 0
Stamford Bridge
Attendance: 41,424
Referee: Martin Atkinson

Chelsea (3-4-3): Thibaut Courtois, Cesar Azpilicueta, David Luiz, Gary Cahill (c); Victor Moses, N'Golo Kante, Nemanja Matic, Marcos Alonso, Pedro (Nathaniel Chalobah 71), Diego Costa (Michy Batshuayi 77), Eden Hazard (Willian 77).
Scorers: Pedro 1, Cahill 20, Hazard 61, Kante 70
Booked: Pedro 1, David Luiz 40, Alonso 65

Manchester United (4-2-3-1): De Gea, Valencia, Smalling (c), Bailly, Blind, Herrera, Fellaini (Mata h/t), Rashford, Pogba, Lingard (Martial 65), Ibrahimovic.
Booked: Bailly 29, Pogba 74

A remarkable game for many reasons... the main three for me being...
1) The score. Chelsea didn't just beat Man U they destroyed them.
2) José Mourinho... humiliated... no hiding place.
3) Antonio Conte... the new hero... a man of the people.

We'd scarcely sat down when Pedro had us out of our seats opening the scoring inside the first minute. United simply couldn't live with Chelsea's pace and inventiveness and it was only a matter of time before another goal came. 21 minutes, Gary Cahill lashed in a poorly defended Eden Hazard corner ball. Shortly after the hour mark, Hazard drilled home a third for the Blues and N'Golo Kante completed the rout ten minutes later scoring his first goal for the club.

The victory moved Chelsea up to fourth place and, more significantly, to within one point of early Premier League pacesetters Manchester City... and in the managerial love affair stakes... for those who still lingered after Mourinho... it moved them on massively. The early Pedro goal and the way the Blues bludgeoned the Red Devils into submission removed any temptation for nostalgic, deferential *José Mourinho* chanting from the home crowd. Now it was all about new Chelsea. Remodelled Chelsea. Chelsea under Antonio Conte... and a better song for the man was essential.

Antonio, Antonio. Antonio, Antonio, Antonio.

THE ITALIAN JOB

The chant sung to the remarkably obscure melody of *Pop Goes The World* by Canadian band Men Without Hats (originally purloined by River Plate and later Crystal Palace for their repetitive *CPFC* chant which in October 2014 during a Blues / Eagles game at Selhurst Park Chelsea transformed to *Shit Football Team* and later *We're Top of the League*) reverberated around Stamford Bridge hailing Conte.

"I asked my players to start very strong and show quickly our desire to win this game, not only our fans but above all our opponent," enthused the Chelsea manager after the game. "It happened because we scored after 30 seconds. The most important thing was that we continued to play, and to try to score the second goal. It happened and I'm very happy."

Conte was happy. The players were happy. We were happy.

The old king was most definitely dead… long live the new king!

*****

Chelsea supporters were becoming more convinced by the game that Antonio Conte, if given sufficient latitude by Roman Abramovich, had the managerial ability and tactical nous to bring the glory days back to Stamford Bridge.

A notable absentee from SW6, had he been present to witness first-hand the demolition of Man U, Abramovich would have been all smiles at the way Conte and his players emphatically laid the ghost of Mourinho to rest. The manner of victory buried the lingering notion that the Portuguese might have remedied Chelsea's ills last season had he been given time to do so and the 'words' he had with Conte at the final whistle were a reminder of the unwanted controversies Mourinho is able to generate.

"You don't celebrate like that at 4-0, you can do it at 1-0, otherwise it's humiliating for us," the former Blues boss was reported to have said to Conte in Italian. Wow! How trite!

Despite all this and the ironic chant of *you're not special anymore* as his United team capitulated, there was no shadow of doubt that José would always remain a bona fide Blues legend for his many outstanding achievements as Chelsea manager… but the Mourinho of today, with all his marvels and machinations, was for Manchester United's supporters to contemplate and debate. He may bring them joy, he may bring them pain, but that wasn't our problem any more.

26 October

EFL Cup Fourth Round
West Ham United 2 Chelsea 1
London Stadium
Attendance: 45,957
Referee: Craig Pawson

Chelsea (3-4-3): Asmir Begovic, David Luiz, John Terry (c), Gary Cahill, Cesar Azpilicueta, N'Golo Kante, Nathaniel Chalobah (Eden Hazard 64), Ola Aina (Pedro 67); Willian, Michy Batshuayi (Diego Costa 55), Oscar.
Scorers: Cahill 90+3

West Ham United (4-2-3-1): Randolph; Kouyate, Reid, Ogbonna; Fernandes (Feghouli 67), Obiang, Noble (c), Cresswell; Lanzini (Ayew 78), Antonio (Zaza 82), Payet.
Scorers: Kouyate 11, Fernandes 48
Booked: Noble 65, Reid 76, Kouyate 90+3

A heavily-rotated Chelsea side were knocked out of the EFL Cup by West Ham United at a febrile London Stadium. An inspired Cheikhou Kouyate header gave the Hammers an early first-half lead and when Edimilson Fernandes rifled the ball home shortly after the break to double the home side's advantage the graffiti was on the wall for the visitors. Gary Cahill pulled one back for the Blues with the game deep into injury time, but it wasn't enough to change the course of events and there could be no complaints about the result.

As unfortunate as it was predictable, the game was marred by ugly crowd disturbances. Trouble at West Ham's opening set of fixtures at the former Olympic stadium had highlighted issues with seating, stewarding and policing in general… and with Chelsea having been allocated over 5,000 tickets for the cup tie with no apparent solution in place for a match with plenty of serious previous, the inevitable was bound to happen. The flagrant atmosphere kindled outside the stadium by police unfairly kettling Blues fans became increasingly volatile inside and culminated in riot police being deployed towards the end of the game. Plastic seats, bottles and coins were thrown and there were violent clashes redolent of the 1970s and '80s.

"Tearing up their own seats to chuck them at as. Nice one West Ham," tweeted @cfc_jb

Commander BJ Harrington, who led the police operation,

THE ITALIAN JOB

said: "Although the vast majority of people left the stadium peacefully and were well behaved, there were a minority of people who attended the match that were clearly intent on being involved in confrontation and violence."

No shit Sherlock!

"We welcome the condemnation from partners and have already started a post match investigation," continued Harrington. "We have already made seven arrests and will work tirelessly to identify people involved and bring them to justice."

When asked about the crowd trouble Conte offered a neutral response, essentially because he was unaware of what was going on. "I must be honest because I didn't see it, we were playing. I don't like this type of situation because it's important to always see the right atmosphere. In England we are used to seeing that and it's right to maintain that. I'm sorry about this situation."

Speaking about the defeat, Conte was typically philosophical. "I'm optimistic because I saw the right spirit and that's very important. You can lose or win but you must have the right spirit. If I see that, I see a clear future."

*****

While crowd disorder grabbed the headlines, on the football front the loss highlighted the fact that Conte's subtle changes to his preferred starting XI for Premier League games were flawed.

It would have been easy to cane the Blues boss for his decision to restore fit-again club legend John Terry to the heart of his new-look three-at-the-back defence, but perhaps the Italian needed this game to realise that time and tide wait for no man. Unfortunately, Terry had a fair degree of culpability for both West Ham's goals.

Credit was duly given to Conte for affording academy graduates Ola Aina and Nathaniel Chalobah starts… but was an intense London derby a sensible platform to do this?

Up front, Michy Batshuayi failed to seize the opportunity to make a name for himself. Handed a rare start, and despite showing promise and finding the net earlier in the season, Batshuayi appeared overawed by the atmosphere and looked nervous when fluffing a wonderful opportunity to equalise just before the break. An early substitution shortly after the interval wouldn't have done too much to improve confidence. Shame really... and unfortunately matters wouldn't improve for the young Belgian.

30 October

Premier League
Southampton 0 Chelsea 2
St Mary's Stadium
Attendance: 31,827
Referee: Mike Jones

Chelsea (3-4-3): Thibaut Courtois, Cesar Azpilicueta, David Luiz, Gary Cahill (c); Victor Moses (Branislav Ivanovic 87) N'Golo Kante, Nemanja Matic, Marcos Alonso, Pedro (Willian 78), Diego Costa (Michy Batshuayi 88), Eden Hazard.
Scorers: Hazard 6, Diego Costa 55

Southampton (4-3-3): Forster; Martina, Fonte (c), Van Dijk, Bertrand (McQueen 78); Clasie (Boufal 61) Romeu, Davis; Redmond, Tadic (Hojbjerg 78), Austin.

Chelsea blotted out the memory of the midweek horrors at West Ham with another smooth Premier League victory beating Southampton 2-0 at St Mary's. The Blues were a goal to the good inside 10 minutes when Eden Hazard nutmegged Saints keeper Fraser Forster and shortly after the break Diego Costa sealed a fourth top-flight win in a row for Antonio Conte with a wicked 22-yard curler that sailed joyfully into the net.

Chelsea's sparkling renaissance in the league owed as much to Conte's much-trumpeted switch to 3-4-3 as it did to the players fashioned in his own spirited image that he'd selected to embrace it.

Having made a promising and unbeaten start, the Italian's managerial capabilities were suddenly and dramatically put under the microscope as both Liverpool and Arsenal ruthlessly exposed and punished a Blues defence that had long since failed to recover the discipline and shape lost at the start of last season.

With the transfer window shut, Conte had had no option other than to work with the current members of Chelsea's squad. Given the depth of talent available, excuses being punted about the Blues failing to secure the signature(s) of one or more world-class defenders had fallen on deaf, unsympathetic ears.

THE ITALIAN JOB

The pressure was on Conte, but to his credit he displayed both fortitude and tactical nous by remedying Chelsea's ills in emphatic fashion. Smiles replaced the scowls of star players Eden Hazard and Diego Costa, both of whom had been heavily linked with moves away from the Bridge in the wake of the cataclysmic crumbling of Mourinho's Chelsea empire. Hazard and Costa were scoring goals for fun and they weren't the only men reenergised by Conte. Midfielder Nemanja Matic had rediscovered his mojo while defender Gary Cahill was playing with renewed confidence and flourishing as skipper.

Conte's remarkable reinvention of the ever-sparkling Victor Moses as a right-wing-back continued to garner the greatest attention but on the opposite flank, Marcos Alonso, an eyebrow-raising acquisition for sure was also silencing the doubters. Finger on lips... shhhhh. And then there was David Luiz! Given his endearing personality and eye for an opportunistic goal, Luiz had previously enjoyed legend-style status at the Bridge, but the Brazil international also had a careless streak that proved costly on more than one occasion. In truth, he was still in many fans eyes a disaster waiting to happen... but Conte appeared to have re-chipped him or maybe, at age of 29, the central defender had finally matured. Certainly, his robust and focussed displays thus far suggested so.

With indefatigable midfield dynamo N'Golo Kante shackling Chelsea together, suddenly the Blues had the look of a side that could mount a serious challenge for the league title. The thought was as nervy as it was exciting. As everyone knows, it pays not to get too ahead of yourself if you support Chelsea.

Perhaps the most intriguing aspect of Conte's revolution at Stamford Bridge was that whereas in the past there had been pressure brought to bear on previous managers regarding the futures of the old order of players who brought glory to the club... the likes of Petr Cech, Ashley Cole, Frank Lampard, Didier Drogba and John Terry, the current Blues boss had no such concerns.

Yes, there was only a place on the bench for a fit-again Terry, but at 35-years of age the veteran warhorse appeared to have accepted the fact that the world at SW6 was changing and he looked happy enough when applauding Chelsea's recent successes. JT could have no real complaints. He been given a chance by Conte in last weeks EFL cup tie with West Ham, but he'd toiled at the London Stadium as the Blues slipped to defeat.

Branislav Ivanovic and Cesc Fabregas were the other big names locked out of Conte's new system. Ivanovic like Terry had maybe had his day as a star player while Fabregas' propensity to blow hot and cold clearly didn't cut the mustard with the gaffer.

Despite recent triumphs, it was unlikely that Conte would view his current Chelsea team as the finished article, but barring injuries, they did look well-positioned to secure a precious Champions League berth which would have been a failure-is-not-an-option demand made of his new manager by Roman Abramovich.

NOVEMBER 2016

5 November

**Premier League
Chelsea 5 Everton 0
Stamford Bridge
Attendance: 41,429
Referee: Robert Madley**

Chelsea (3-4-3): Thibaut Courtois, Cesar Azpilicueta, David Luiz, Gary Cahill (c) (John Terry 84), Victor Moses, N'Golo Kante, Nemanja Matic, Marcos Alonso; Pedro (Oscar 71) Diego Costa, Eden Hazard (Michy Batshuayi 80).
Scorers: Hazard 19, 56, Alonso 20, Diego Costa 42, Pedro 65

Everton (3-4-3): Stekelenburg, Williams, Jagielka (c), Funes, Coleman, Barry (Davies 66), Cleverley, Oviedo (Mirallas 36), Barkley, Bolasie (Lennon 60), Lukaku.
Booked: Bolasie 15, Jagielka 30, Barry 64

Chelsea's obliteration of Everton brought with it the type of gushing praise that might have been construed as hyperbole by anyone who didn't see the game either live or in highlights format. The plain and simple fact was that Antonio Conte's side were every bit as good as the 5-0 score-line suggested. This was a fifth straight Premier League victory for the Blues, a run which thus far had featured 16 goals scored and zero conceded... and this latest result catapulted Conte and co. to the top of the table, albeit for a little under 24 hours when they were replaced by Liverpool following the Reds 6-1 hammering of Watford at Anfield.

Eden Hazard, on song again, put Chelsea ahead in the 20th minute with an angled shot, and Marcos Alonso doubled the lead moments later when he nutmegged Everton keeper Maarten Stekelenburg. Diego Costa made it 3-0 just before half-time, and Hazard scored his second of the evening shortly after the break. Pedro rounded off an emphatic win tapping into an empty net in the 65th minute at which point many of us started wondering what the final score might end up as... but that was it. Job done. 5-0

Antonio, Antonio. Antonio, Antonio, Antonio.

"The players deserve this because they show me great commitment and I can tell they are working very hard," said Conte after the game. "The team has more balance defensively, but we don't lose our offensive situation. We are creating more chances to score goals."

The Blues boss must however have ended the weekend feeling as frustrated as we supporters were... it was time now for another dreaded international break. Would momentum gained be lost? Worse still, would any of Chelsea 3-4-3 heroes succumb to injury?

9 November

Seven passengers including Chelsea season ticket holder Robert (Bob) Huxley were killed and 58 more injured when a tram derailed near Croydon.

14 November

Frank Lampard announced his intention to leave MLS side New York City.

Distraction from concerns about Chelsea's present run of form being halted came in the shape of club legend *Super Frankie Lampard* calling time on his two-year transatlantic flirtation with New York City FC.

Blues supporters took to social media in their droves to voice what appeared to be an almost uniform opinion that Chelsea should offer him a position at Stamford Bridge.

The word 'legend' has long been over-applied in football, however Lampard's unparalleled achievements in a stellar 13-year career at the Bridge elevated him way beyond the ever-increasing glut of players categorised this way.

648 appearances, a club record 211 goals, three Premier League titles, four FA Cups, two League Cups, one Europa League... oh and that never to be forgotten night in Munich when he skippered the Blues to Champions League glory made a compelling pro case in any argument that Lampard was Chelsea's best ever player.

THE ITALIAN JOB

Legend? No... Lampard deserved better than that... a footballing God maybe, a true icon whose place at the very front of the pantheon of Stamford Bridge greats was already assured for time immemorial.

Following his departure from SW6, Lampard's saintly halo had wobbled briefly in the eyes of some members of the Stamford Bridge faithful... particularly when he turned out for NYCFC parent club Manchester City. In an episode that appeared scripted in Hollywood, Super Frank subsequently scored against Chelsea... but the faint and dissonant anonymous Twitter cries of 'Judas' and 'mercenary' soon dissipated.

Not only was Lampard a gifted footballer... his friendly demeanour, good looks and charm made him virtually impossible to dislike. Even those fans of opposing clubs who regularly chided him with taunts of 'Fat Frank' and worse would begrudgingly admit that they would love to have had Lampard, who also racked up 29 goals when winning an impressive 106 England caps, playing for their team when he was at the peak of his powers.

So what was going to happen then? Was Frank about to make a superhero's return to Stamford Bridge? And if so in what capacity? Chelsea were yet to declare their hand regarding making an offer of employment to Lampard, and the 38-year old was remaining tight-lipped about his future, though he did declare via Instagram that he would be 'making an announcement very soon'.

Continuing with the filmic theme, Lampard's Chelsea story might be completed with a return to the club in a coaching capacity with a progression to assistant manager and then the top job... an accession that could coincide with the Blues returning to the Bridge when the proposed stadium redevelopment at Stamford Bridge was complete. 'Lamps' would then go on to win an historic quadruple in his first season as boss and eventually become Chelsea's most successful manager. An offer of the England job would inevitably follow and Lampard would finally retire from football altogether after guiding the Three Lions to World Cup glory on home soil of course.

It was a fanciful notion, but football has a remarkable habit of turning wild almost impossible dreams into reality... Chelsea's journey to Champions League glory being a pristine example.

The flip-side to this idea of nirvana for many Blues fans was that Lampard made it through the Blues coaching ranks but then things went horribly and spectacularly wrong... and as far as managers tales at Chelsea go, there's a nasty reversal of expectation that seems to be written into every chapter of the club's story. (Take note Antonio)

Lampard witnessed first hand the brutal demise of the man who signed him for Chelsea, Claudio Ranieri... then there was José Mourinho, Avram Grant, Luiz Felipe Scolari, Carlo Ancelotti, Andre Villas-Boas, Roberto Di Matteo... and he would have been well aware of the disastrous conclusion to Mourinho's second stint as Blues boss.

It would be horrible to see Lampard dragged into such a scenario, and the truth is he may well have been thinking to himself, 'you know what Frankie my son, I just don't need or want the grief'. Having already made well-received forays into TV punditry and quiz shows and being signed to the same talent agency as his television personality wife Christine Bleakley, the star midfielder had probably already considered that following in fellow football superstar Gary Lineker's managerial-avoidance footsteps to media stardom might be a far more sensible option than staying in the game.

Ultimately, it would be Lampard's personal and presently private ambitions that plotted the course of his future destiny. Whatever he chose to do, it would meet with the blessing of most Chelsea supporters who would always remain eternally grateful for the glory he helped bring to the club.

16 November

Antonio Conte was named Barclays Manager of the Month for October. Eden Hazard made it a Chelsea double, picking up the EA Sports Player of the Month award.

20 November

Premier League
Middlesbrough 0 Chelsea 1
Riverside Stadium
Attendance: 32,704
Referee: Jon Moss

Chelsea (3-4-3): Thibaut Courtois, Cesar Azpilicueta, David Luiz, Gary Cahill (c), Victor Moses (Branislav Ivanovic 89), N'Golo Kante, Nemanja Matic, Marcos Alonso, Pedro (Nathaniel Chalobah 80), Diego Costa, Eden Hazard Hazard (Oscar 90+2).
Scorer: Diego Costa 41

THE ITALIAN JOB

Booked: Azpilicueta 51, David Luiz 65, Kante 73

Middlesbrough (4-5-1): Valdes; Barragan, Chambers, Gibson (c), Fabio (Downing 71); Traore, Forshaw (Leadbitter 89), Clayton (Fischer 73), De Roon, Ramirez; Negredo.
Booked: Clayton 8, Chambers 74

Chelsea moved to the top of the Premier League as their compelling sequence of clean sheet victories continued with a 1-0 win against Middlesbrough at the Riverside Stadium. A scrappy Diego Costa goal just before half-time separated the sides, but it was good enough to make it six wins in a row for Antonio Conte's side whose on-going resilience and ability to get results was beginning to make them look like serious title contenders... though Blues supporters were keeping calm.

Conte fielded the same starting XI for a fifth game in succession, a Premier League record. The understanding Chelsea players clearly had with each other and their manager was formidable with Costa perhaps the brightest, shiniest example of the transformation. It was another game, another goal for the top flight's leading marksman who was perfectly placed to take advantage of a loose ball following an Eden Hazard corner just before the break. Equally pleasing as the winner, it was another match for Costa without a yellow card... probably another record if someone dared to look.

Chelsea's irresistible surge to the top of the Premier League brought with it compliments and analysis by the shedload. It was now 590 minutes since Thibaut Courtois had had to pick the ball out of the net... meanwhile the players in front of him had plundered 17 goals between them.

Courtois had finally stopped squawking about returning to his precious La Liga and what initially was considered to be a makeshift back three... Cesar Azpilicueta, David Luiz and Gary Cahill... had the resolute look of a trio that have been playing together for a decade.

Wing-backs Victor Moses and Marcos Alonso were continuing to defy the critics who questioned the validity of their inclusion by Conte while pulling the strings in Chelsea's midfield, unfaltering N'Golo Kante had already gone a long way already to proving himself to be the Premier League signing of the summer. There was never any doubt about the France international's pedigree and with Nemanja Matic another player revitalised by the manager, the Blues engine room was a hub of bristling energy.

Further forward, like Matic, Pedro, Hazard and Costa of course appeared reborn. Last season, Pedro didn't flatter to deceive he just deceived while Hazard became haphazard and Costa had developed the desperate disposition of a cornered street-fighter. Conte had got inside their heads and reprogrammed them.

"I'm pleased because we won a game in a different way if you compare it to our past five games," Conte advised after the gritty victory. "We won only 1-0 against a strong team with good organisation. At the moment we had to suffer, we suffered, but we never lost our compactness. It's very good."

This Chelsea team, Conte's Chelsea team, had developed a unique identity that not only made them a force to be reckoned with, but also a joy to watch. Again I had that thought. You know. And yeah, maybe it was too early to talk of winning the title in that ridiculous way they seem to do on the red half of Merseyside at some point every season... but victories over forthcoming opponents Tottenham Hotspur and Manchester City who had grand ambitions of their own could (and would) change that.

Whatever happened, Conte, with his passion, zest for the game, tactical nous, understanding of what makes players tick and team ethos had raised the Premier League bar this season and few would begrudge Chelsea their success should they become champions. Among the few would be Spurs... how that rivalry had blossomed over the past few years!

Pay attention and be focused
Pay attention and be focused
Pay attention and be focused

"Antonio, we do not lose at home to Spurs... Capisce?" I said, looking at Conte's face which adorned the latest issue of cfcuk.

26 November

Premier League
Chelsea 2 Tottenham Hotspur 1
Stamford Bridge
Attendance: 41,513
Referee: Michael Oliver

Chelsea (3-4-3): Thibaut Courtois, Cesar Azpilicueta, David Luiz, Gary Cahill (c), Victor Moses (Branislav Ivanovic 80), N'Golo Kante, Nemanja

THE ITALIAN JOB

Matic, Marcos Alonso, Pedro (Oscar 83), Diego Costa, Eden Hazard (Willian 76).
Scorers: Pedro 44, Moses 51
Booked: David Luiz 18, Willian 85

Tottenham (4-2-3-1): Lloris; Walker, Dier, Vertonghen, Wimmer; Wanyama, Dembele; Son (Winks 65), Alli (N'Koudou 73), Eriksen, Kane.
Scorer: Eriksen 11
Booked: Dembele 26

"Capisce?" Antonio understood all right.

Chelsea remained top of the Premier League after defeating Tottenham Hotspur 2-1 in a thrilling London derby at Stamford Bridge. Christian Eriksen's blistering long-range strike gave Spurs a deserved early lead, but the Blues fought back and Pedro levelled just before half time with a wonder goal of similar quality to Eriksen's.

Chelsea upped the ante after the break, and man-of-the-moment Victor Moses won the game with a show-stopping goal of his own. In doing so, Moses consigned Spurs to their first top-flight loss of the season while extending the Blues winning sequence to seven.

Having gone six Premier League games without conceding a goal, going behind early on against a visibly motivated Spurs side was a test of Chelsea's resolve but the Blues battled back, tenaciously turned the game around… and closed it out. Given Antonio Conte's understandable persistence with the same personnel and system that had served him so well for the previous six league games, there was always the danger that an opposing team might suss Chelsea out. Spurs did that for 20 minutes and Conte's animated rages on the touchline were evidence enough of the concerns he had about the way the Blues lost their shape early on.

The build up to the game had been as frenzied as you would expect for a high-profile London derby. Supporters of both sides had taken to social media talking up the chances of their respective sides.

There was an element of tongue-in-cheek jocularity about the 'invincibles' tag Spurs fans had labelled Mauricio Pochettino's team with. True, prior to the Stamford Bridge showdown, Tottenham were the only side yet to taste defeat this season in the Premier League, but their form in other competitions, principally the Champions League, had been woeful. Nevertheless there were grounds for optimism on their part and a hope that this time, finally, for the first time since 1990, Spurs would win at the Bridge.

Despite having lost his place in Conte's starting XI, John Terry would have impressed on his manager the fact that Chelsea don't do home defeats to Tottenham. Six months previously, they came close to ending that run. Coming to the Bridge and watching their team snatch a draw from the jaws of victory and seeing their title hopes crumble must have been painful for Spurs fans... pride swallowed once more... and yet the false bravado was in evidence again as they emerged from Fulham Broadway station singing *Chelsea rent boys we're coming for you.*

In the end there was the usual healthy dose of glorious unpredictability involved. It wasn't easy. Coming from behind never is, but Conte's tactics prevailed once again. Tottenham's high-line game caused the Blues no end of problems early on, and Eriksen's blistering opening goal for the visitors was due reward for sustained effort. But Spurs ran out of steam.

Was that really Pedro? Or had the Chelsea wide man metamorphosed into his former Barcelona teammate Lionel Messi? The Spaniard's wonder goal knocked the stuffing out of Spurs who moments later as the half-time whistle went were probably thinking 'oh no, here we go again' as they trudged off the pitch.

Psychology plays a big part in football. Belief cannot be underestimated. And if Pedro had been told by Conte that he was better than Messi, it was safe to assume that the affable Italian had told Victor Moses that he was better than Pele!

Having previously parted the red sea that was Manchester United, 'Holy' Moses currency was on the rise again. Causing problems for Spurs every time he took the ball forward, the wing-back was equally determined in the tackle and when he rifled home Costa's cut back following a scintillating run to be in the right place at the right time... it was a cue for rapturous Chelsea delirium. *One nil and you fucked it up* never sounded sweeter... trust me.

Amidst all the joy, I felt sad for one Chelsea player... Willian. On as a sub for Hazard late on in the game against Spurs and welcomed with a rousing rendition of *he hate's Tottenham, he hates Tottenham,* cruel fate had recently dealt the Brazil international a terrible blow when his mother had lost her battle with cancer. Previously, one of the first names on many Chelsea team sheets, compassionate leave had seen Willian lose his place to

Pedro and with the Blues blazing a trail to the top of the league in his absence there was no immediate way back.

There was some inevitable fan banter about winning the title. That's the feel-good factor that comes with beating Spurs… but Antonio talked us down from our giddy euphoria. "In this period to talk about this is not right, we have to improve a lot, we have a long way in front of us," said the Blues boss. "Above all, after this type of game we have to wait. It's important to stay humble and continue to work, trust in our work. Today we won against a really strong team."

As an eternally positive footnote to the evening's dramatic events, it's more than worth recalling that the 63rd minute of the game saw supporter rivalries put to one side as both sets of fans joined together in a spirited round of applause to commemorate 63-year old Chelsea season ticket holder Bob Huxley who had lost his life in the Croydon tram disaster two weeks previously.

28 November

A plane carrying players and staff of Brazil's Chapecoense football club crashed near Medellin in Colombia killing 71 of the 77 people on board. The football world was unified in mourning. Right around the globe, in matches that followed, a minute's silence was held as a mark of respect to those who lost their lives.

DECEMBER 2016

The momentum and belief Chelsea had gained from winning seven Premier League games in a row would be catapulted into the stratosphere should they defeat second place Manchester City at the Etihad in their next game.

Heading into the frenetic festive fixture period, victory for Antonio Conte's team would represent a giant stride forward in the title race… but it was a tall order, especially given the likelihood that City boss Pep Guardiola would have spent significant time reviewing Chelsea's previous game against Tottenham Hotspur.

Having taken the lead when Christian Eriksen breached the Blues defence for the first time in 601 top-flight minutes, Spurs, dominant for much of the first-half, paid the price for not pressing home their superiority and taking additional goal-scoring chances that came their way.

Prolific City striker Sergio Aguero and creative duo Kevin De Bruyne and David Silva were a cut above the Tottenham attack, and Guardiola would surely demand his players take the game to Chelsea from the first minute.
The Spurs 'scare' would certainly have given Conte plenty tactical food for thought ahead of the City game… probably not a bad thing given the daunting nature of the task ahead at the Etihad. The funny thing was though… why would Conte change anything? Would you really tinker with a team that can't stop winning?

Mauricio Pochettino had figured out all by himself that the way to beat Conte's system was to overpower Chelsea's midfield, play high up the pitch pegging the Blues back and thereby nullifying the threat of wing-backs Victor Moses and Marcos Alonso and isolating Eden Hazard and Diego Costa. Pochettino's problem was his team couldn't keep up the tempo, and a flash of goal-scoring genius from Pedro was all it took for Spurs to lose their initiative and shape.

Reversing a losing situation from a goal down wasn't an insurmountable task, two goals even... particularly against Tottenham whose luck was cursed at the Bridge... but away at City, Conte would have concerns about the likes of Aguero, De Bruyne and Silva getting in behind Chelsea's defence and it could come to pass that he might make a minor adjustment early on by playing four at the back to quash the expected early threat.

The flipside of course was that Conte may have looked at City's porous defence which had one clean sheet to its name in 14 previous games in all competitions and decide that attack was the best form of defence. Far from having a stable starting XI Guardiola didn't appear to know what his best team was and hadn't fielded the same backline in consecutive league fixtures since the opening weeks of the season. This lack of familiarity, and the erratic form of City goalkeeper Claudio Bravo could pay dividends for Chelsea.

Given Chelsea's next five opponents after the City game, West Brom (h), Sunderland (a), Crystal Palace (a), Bournemouth (h) and Stoke (h) represented a highly conceivable opportunity to pick up another five wins by the end of the year, a favourable result at the Etihad would embolden the Blues position as the bookies new favourites to win the title.

3 December

Premier League
Manchester City 1 Chelsea 3
Etihad Stadium
Attendance: 54,457
Referee: Anthony Taylor

Chelsea (3-4-3): Thibaut Courtois, Cesar Azpilicueta, David Luiz, Gary Cahill (c), Victor Moses, N'Golo Kante, Cesc Fabregas, Marcos Alonso, Pedro (Willian 49), Diego Costa (Nathaniel Chalobah 80), Eden Hazard.
  Scorers: Costa 60, Willian 69, Hazard 90
  Booked: Kante 49, Chalobah 90+7, Fabregas 90+7

Manchester City (3-4-3): Bravo; Otamendi, Stones (Iheanacho 78), Kolarov; Navas, Fernandinho, Gundogan (Toure 76), Sane (Clichy 69); Silva (c), Aguero, De Bruyne.
  Scorers: Cahill (own-goal) 45
  Sent off: Aguero 90+6, Fernandinho 90+7
  Booked: Otamendi 17, Navas 81

For the second game in a row, this time against fellow title challengers

Manchester City, Chelsea came from behind to register a stirring victory. Gary Cahill's own goal just before half-time gave City the advantage at the break, but once again Antonio Conte's side refused to lie down.

Kevin De Bruyne squandered an exceptional opportunity to double the home side's advantage but maybe the pressure of trying to prove his old employers were foolish to sell him got to the Belgium international as he fluffed his lines.

Thereafter, it went horribly and chaotically wrong for City.

On the hour mark, Cesc Fabregas, starting in place of Nemanja Matic who was side-lined by a stomach muscle injury, picked out Diego Costa with a trademark well-sighted pass and the prolific Chelsea striker hammered the ball past Claudio Bravo. 10 minutes later, Costa turned provider on a Chelsea counter attack finding substitute Willian running into space. The Brazilian had work to do, but wasn't going to be denied by Bravo beating the keeper with a drive into the bottom corner. Chelsea's vociferous travelling contingent gathered behind the goal celebrated wildly.

Eden Hazard's 90th minute goal wrapped up the points for Conte's side, but the excitement wasn't over yet. In injury time, City lost the plot. Sergio Aguero, criminally lunged at David Luiz with a 'tackle' that was both high and late. Another Chelsea substitute Nathaniel Chalobah joined in the resulting fracas and as Taylor gave Aguero his marching orders he was lucky to not see red as well. A fantastic photograph of Chalobah standing over a falling Aguero captioned 'everyone's a gangster until a gangster walks in the room' did the rounds of social media that evening. Fair play to the Chelsea kid.

Taylor's red card wouldn't remain in his pocket long as Fernandinho, who had thuggishly been kicking lumps out of Hazard throughout the game, was sent off for grabbing Cesc Fabregas by the throat. Fabregas turned the other cheek, but the sight of Diego Costa, who had earlier been replaced by Chalobah, tearing over from the bench made for a few nervy moments. Was the once pugnacious striker about to revert to his old self? Fortunately, Costa deployed himself in the unlikely role of peacemaker. Moments later, Taylor blew the final whistle! Phew! That was some game to win.

Eight wins in a row and counting… and the good news didn't stop there. As Chelsea marched on, the weekend would see Liverpool surprisingly lose at Bournemouth… a result left the Blues three points clear at the top of the Premier League.

Speaking after the match, Conte was clearly delighted with his side's performance and with Costa's exemplary behaviour. "I saw lots of character from my team and that's very important," said the Blues boss. "Diego is showing he is using his passion in the right way and I'm very happy about that."

Subsequently, there was an inevitable investigation into the outbreak of lawlessness, and both clubs were charged for failing to ensure their players conducted themselves in an orderly fashion and/or refrained from provocative behaviour. Following an Independent Regulatory Commission hearing, City and Chelsea admitted a breach of FA Rule E20(a) and received respective fines of £35,000 and £100,000. The fact that the Londoners had been previously charged and fined for breaching this rule on five separate occasions no doubt determined the comparative harshness of the punishment received.

*****

Antonio Conte's selection of Cesc Fabregas for the Man City game was fairly obvious given the injury to Nemanja Matic... but it still sparked plenty of debate. Chelsea's assist king duly teeing up Costa for the Blues equalizer was a timely reminder of his capabilities, but had Fabregas done enough against City to retain his place in Conte's starting XI should Matic be fit to return for the forthcoming game against West Brom, or would the 29-year old midfielder find himself sitting on the bench again?

It was an interesting question? Prior to the City match, Fabregas had started just three games under Conte. Decent performances in EFL Cup ties against Bristol Rovers and Leicester City, the latter bringing with it a brace of goals, earned the Spain international a call up for the Premier League game which followed the defeat of Leicester. Fabregas lined up against his former club Arsenal... and what followed has already been documented.

Having had the pre-season to assess Fabregas, a lack of game-time even before the much-trumpeted switch to 3-4-3 suggested that what Conte was seeing during coaching sessions and on the pitch didn't match his exacting requirements.

Given Fabregas' pedigree, it was only natural that rumours would start linking the player with a move away from Stamford Bridge with West Ham

United and AC Milan being talked about as possible destinations in the January transfer window. Surely Chelsea would resist any temptation to sell.

A lack of European football this season and an early exit from the EFL Cup saw Chelsea's fixture list a lot less cluttered than usual meaning opportunities for first team football were reduced. Fabregas wasn't the only player kicking his heels in frustration at the lack of game time coming his way, regularly on the bench alongside him were Brazilian duo Willian and Oscar... what would the future hold for the trio if their agents started agitating the marketplace?

9 December

Antonio Conte was named Barclays Manager of the Month for November with Diego Costa picking up the EA Sports Player of the Month. Pedro won the EA Sports Goal of the Month trophy for his wonder-strike against Spurs. Amen to that!

11 December

Premier League
Chelsea 1 West Bromwich Albion 0
Stamford Bridge
Attendance: 41,622
Referee: Mike Dean

Chelsea (3-4-3): Thibaut Courtois, Cesar Azpilicueta, David Luiz, Gary Cahill (c), Victor Moses (Cesc Fabregas 74), N'Golo Kante, Nemanja Matic, Marcos Alonso, Pedro (Willian 63) Diego Costa, Eden Hazard (Branislav Ivanovic 79)
Scorer: Diego Costa 76
Booked: Kante 48, Matic 88

West Brom (4-2-3-1): Foster; Dawson, McAuley, Evans, Nyom; Fletcher (c), Yacob; Brunt (Robson-Kanu 84), Morrison (Chadli 79) Phillips (McClean 79) Rondon.
Booked: Brunt 20, McAuley 29, Dawson 51, Yacob 56.

Chelsea secured yet another three points with a hard fought 1-0 victory over West Brom at Stamford Bridge. In a game of few clear-cut chances for the home side, Diego Costa capitalized on an error by West Brom defender Gareth McAuley and beat Baggies keeper Ben Foster with a clinical strike. This was Costa's 12th Premier League goal of the campaign, his fifth strike in six games… and a fitting match-winner.

If the Blues were to be crowned champions, it would be as a direct consequence of beating the type of dogged opposition that West Brom represented. Faced with time-wasting tactics and a succession of cynical fouls, Chelsea of old had been known on more than one occasion to lose their patience, discipline and shape, but Antonio Conte's well-drilled outfit remained calm and stuck to the manager's game-plan.

Despite the Etihad heroics of Cesc Fabregas, Conte restored fit again Nemanja Matic to his starting XI however the Serbia international was unable to exert his customary authority and was caught in possession too often for comfort. He looked to be the obvious candidate to be replaced by Fabregas but the manager stuck by him for the full 90 minutes.

"I know this league and it's very tough to win every game," said the Blues boss after the game. "To have nine wins in a row is fantastic. I hope to continue this. I'm pleased because I think our work is paying off a lot and for this I give thanks to my players every day."

With the fixture schedule looking busy heading into the festive period, Chelsea supporters were wondering if Conte might rotate his line-up slightly for the midweek trip to bottom of the table Sunderland.

Against West Brom, thigh-strapped David Luiz appeared to be suffering the after-effects of Sergio Aguero's felonious tackle perpetrated a week previously in Chelsea's win at Manchester City. Matic also looked out of sorts against the Baggies… was he fully fit? With just two days separating the West Brom and Sunderland games and then another two before a London derby with Crystal Palace was Conte running the risk of fatiguing key players and aggravating any underlying injury problems they may have?

Eden Hazard's welfare also needed monitoring. The Belgium international was kicked from pillar to post by West Brom and would probably still be counting his bruises in the Stadium of Light dressing room… perhaps Conte should consider resting him to the bench with a view to deploying him as an impact substitute as and when required.

The Blues boss also needed to consider the impact possible suspensions might have in the near term. Costa, Luiz and the midfield engine room duo of Nemanja Matic and N'Golo Kante were all one yellow card away a mandatory one game suspension. With four games remaining before the January amnesty came into play, Conte faced the real prospect of losing one or more of the quartet… was he bothered… and if so would he plan accordingly?

Commenting after Liverpool's recent 2-0 win over Sunderland, Reds manager Jurgen Klopp described David Moyes' side as the most defensive he'd ever seen. Klopp lost arguably his best player, Philippe Coutinho, to injury in that game, and Liverpool subsequently took one point from six in their next two league games against Bournemouth and West Ham… matches they were expected to win.

Already locked in a battle to avoid relegation, Sunderland's desperation for points could manifest itself in a similar way against Chelsea as it did against Liverpool. Klopp's side may have won the battle against Moyes' men, but they now seem to be losing the war… oh dear. All joking aside, Conte would only have himself to blame if he failed to heed the warning signs that were in front of him and the Blues lost their way as a result.

13 December

Chelsea were reported to have sanctioned the transfer of Oscar to Chinese Super League club Shanghai SIPG, managed by former Blues boss Andre Villas-Boas, for a staggering fee in excess of £50 million. Awash with money, would more denizens of the Stamford Bridge dressing room be tempted by Chinese riches in January?

The Blues youth team commenced their defence of the FA Youth Cup by steamrollering Cardiff City 5-0 in a Third Round tie at Aldershot's EBB Stadium. With former midfielder Jody Morris, himself a product of the Stamford Bridge academy, now at the helm, Chelsea's youngsters were bidding for a fourth straight competition triumph. A brace from Ike Ugbo plus goals from Mason Mount, Tariq Uwakwe and Jacob Maddox sent the kids one step of the way there.

14 December

Premier League
Sunderland 0 Chelsea 1
Stadium of Light
Attendance: 41,008
Referee: Neil Swarbrick

Chelsea (3-4-3) Thibaut Courtois, Cesar Azpilicueta, David Luiz, Gary Cahill (c), Victor Moses (Branislav Ivanovic 90+3), N'Golo Kante, Cesc

Fabregas, Marcos Alonso, Willian (Nathaniel Chalobah 89), Diego Costa, Pedro (Nemanja Matic 75).
Scorer: Fabregas 40
Booked: Pedro 56, Moses 90+2

Sunderland (3-4-3) Pickford, Kone, O'Shea (c), Djilobodji, Jones (Love 59), Denayer, Kirchhoff (Larsson 57), Van Aanholt, Januzaj, Defoe (c), Borini (Khazri 82).
Booked: Defoe 43, O'Shea 45+2, Borini 71

Chelsea opened up a six-point gap at the top of the Premier League with another gritty 1-0 victory this time against rock bottom Sunderland. Cesc Fabregas settled the match with a sweeping drive five minutes from half-time, but the Blues had keeper Thibaut Courtois to thank for securing all three points with the Belgium international making two world-class saves, the second in stoppage time, to deny the Black Cats at least a point.

After the match, Antonio Conte was swift to praise the Chelsea keeper. "For Thibaut it's more difficult because for the whole game you wait and you could lose concentration but he is a fantastic goalkeeper," said the Blues boss. He's "One of the best in the world, if not the best, and I'm pleased to have him in my team." I couldn't argue with that or the performance of Courtois, though I still had a nagging doubt about the Belgian's commitment to the cause.

The selection of Fabregas ahead of Nemanja Matic and Willian in place of Eden Hazard (reported to have a minor knee problem) answered the question about whether or not Antonio Conte might make better use of his squad for this game… and clearly, given the positive result the Italian might opt to continue to do so.

The importance of such matters had rightly been put into perspective before kick-off when five-year old Sunderland supporter Bradley Lowery, stricken with cancer, took to the field and beat Chelsea reserve keeper Asmir Begovic from the penalty spot. There was also a round of applause on five minutes for the brave youngster.

17 December

**Premier League
Crystal Palace 0 Chelsea 1
Selhurst Park
Attendance: 25,259
Referee: Jon Moss**

Chelsea (3-4-3): Thibaut Courtois, Cesar Azpilicueta, David Luiz, Gary Cahill (c), Victor Moses (Branislav Ivanovic 79), N'Golo Kante, Nemanja Matic, Marcos Alonso, Willian (Cesc Fabregas 64), Diego Costa (Michy Batshuayi 89), Eden Hazard.
Scorer: Diego Costa 44
Booked: Diego Costa 22, Kante 60, Fabregas 90+2.

Palace (4-2-3-1): Hennessey; Kelly, Dann (c), Delaney, Ward; McArthur, Ledley; Zaha, Cabaye (Campbell 79), Puncheon (Townsend 77); Benteke.
Booked: Ward 17, Cabaye 65.

Chelsea's impressive winning sequence stretched to a club record-equalling 11 at Selhurst Park with yet another 1-0 victory on this occasion over Crystal Palace. Blues striker Diego Costa settled matters with a fine headed goal shortly before halftime, but the top-flight's leading scorer also picked up a yellow card meaning he would be suspended for the Boxing Day match with Bournemouth at Stamford Bridge. Midfield dynamo N'Golo Kante would also miss the Cherries game courtesy of referee Jon Moss handing him a fifth booking for the campaign.

One of the more entertaining aspects of the game was Marcos Alonso's duel with in-form Palace winger Wilfried Zaha on the left flank. The Chelsea wing-back came out on top and also did well getting forward... so-much-so he might have scored twice. On the first occasion, Wayne Hennessey denied Alonso with a brilliant save from open play, on the second, with the Palace keeper rooted to the spot, the woodwork prevented a 25-yard free-kick from finding the net. Maybe a few quid on Alonso to find the net might be a smart move for punters trying to find some value betting on Chelsea... the winning streak had seen the bookies markedly shorten odds in just about every Blues-related betting market.

Also noteworthy was Antonio Conte's decision to afford Pedro a rest and use Cesc Fabregas intelligently from the bench. It showed the depth of the Italian's tactical planning. Right now the Chelsea manager appeared to have an answer for everything. A true football mastermind, Conte had taken the Blues to a level above every other team in the Premier League.

A couple of days after the Palace victory Conte shed some fascinating light on his reasoning behind the remarkable transformation to 3-4-3 he had engineered following the losses to Liverpool and Arsenal. "I had in my mind before the game against Liverpool, there was the will to change, but I waited for the right moment," he said cryptically. "After the defeats we changed something in me, in my players, in the club as well," he continued, opening up more. "We understood the way to go and have a different season compared to last season." It was engrossing stuff and it spoke volumes. "We found the right solution with the formation, but also improved the quality of our work in all aspects… the tactical aspect, the physical aspect and I am pleased for this because after these two bad games, we changed a lot."

Antonio, Antonio. Antonio, Antonio, Antonio.

An intriguing by-product of the 11 successive victories, 33 points, 25 goals scored, 2 conceded that comprised the current Chelsea hot streak that Antonio Conte had presided over was the nullifying effect on one of the perennial debates to be had by Blues supporters… namely the club's continued failure to find a player from within its academy ranks of sufficient calibre to make a lasting breakthrough to the first team.

Conte's current level of success was such that in respect of team selection the Blues boss had become virtually immune to criticism, and supporters social media rants about 'playing the youth' had long since evaporated. The kids would have to make do with a run out in the FA Cup in January. In Conte, Chelsea fans trusted… make no mistake about it!

25 December

I had a very Merry Christmas!!!

26 December

Premier League
Chelsea 3 Bournemouth
Stamford Bridge
Attendance: 41,384
Referee: Mike Jones

Chelsea (3-4-3): Thibaut Courtois, Cesar Azpilicueta, David Luiz, Gary Cahill (c), Victor Moses (Ola Aina 89), Cesc Fabregas, Nemanja Matic, Marcos Alonso, Willian (Nathaniel Chalobah 83), Eden Hazard, Pedro (Michy Batshuayi 90+4).
Scorers: Pedro 24, Hazard 49 pen, Cook (OG) 90+4
Booked: Pedro 63

Bournemouth (3-5-1-1): Boruc, Francis (c), Cook, Daniels, A Smith, Arter, Surman (Stanislas 66), Gosling, B Smith (Ibe 77), Wilshere, King (Afobe 66).
Booked: Wilshere 14

There was no evidence of any Christmas hangovers among Chelsea's players as they outclassed Bournemouth 3-0 at Stamford Bridge on Boxing Day setting a club record 12 straight Premier League wins in the process. A Pedro brace split by an Eden Hazard penalty and a late own goal by Steve Cook, sealed another three points for Antonio Conte's side who were unhindered by the absence through suspension of N'Golo Kante and Diego Costa.

The result underlined the Blues credentials as title favourites and the enforced changes of key personnel made no difference… right now there didn't appear to be a weak link in the armour of Conte or his first team squad.

The key talking point was Conte's decision to omit striker Michy Batshuayi from his starting XI… the Italian opted to field Hazard as a 'false 9' to cater for the absence of Costa and to be fair to the Chelsea manager, his decision was vindicated.

Allowed a licence to roam up front by Conte, Hazard was a constant thorn in the side for Bournemouth's backline who struggled throughout the game with his pace and creativity. There was an air of inevitability that such sublime skills might eventually draw a penalty, and it was Cherries defender Simon Francis who obliged, dumping the Belgium international on the floor in the box. A 50th Premier League goal followed for Hazard who was Chelsea's star turn on the day just shading out Pedro who blotted his two-goal copybook by picking up a fifth yellow card of the campaign for a needless foul on Harry Arter… an automatic suspension would follow for the Spaniard.

Bizarrely, Conte sent on Batshuayi for Pedro five seconds before referee Mike Jones blew for full time… you couldn't help but feel sorry for the 23-year old who might be entitled to wonder why Chelsea made him their second most expensive signing ever.

Speaking about his tactical decision to go with a 'false 9', Conte offered a crumb of comfort to Batshuayi. "We tried this in training and I think for us at the moment this situation is the best," said the Italian. "But I don't forget Michy because he is a young player with great talent. He is adapting to this league and its football. In the future, I trust in him."

*****

Victor Moses may have been the obvious choice in terms of picking a Chelsea player who had stepped up since Antonio Conte's arrival at the Bridge, but Pedro wasn't too far behind him in many supporters' eyes.

It's easy when you know how, and there was no doubting Pedro had the know how when Chelsea, at the behest of then manager José Mourinho, paid Barcelona £21 million for his services in August 2015. A product of the Catalan club's youth academy, Pedro scored 99 goals in 321 appearances for Barca winning La Liga five times and picking up three Champions League winners medals. On the international stage, he'd also won the 2010 World Cup and 2012 Euros with Spain before arriving at Stamford Bridge.

A very fine pedigree indeed… unfortunately for Pedro, despite scoring on his debut against West Brom, unbeknown to him (and everyone else) he'd joined Chelsea at the wrong time.

Given the subsequent upheaval that culminated with Conte's appointment, it would have come as little surprise if Pedro, destabilised by the goings on, had left in the summer, indeed the player had spoken openly about returning to the Camp Nou. Had he left, the 29-year olds departure would scarcely have registered with supporters already used to Chelsea rapidly churning through attacking midfielders.

Juan Mata, Andre Schurrle, Mo Salah, Kevin De Bruyne, Juan Cuadrado, are names that regularly cropped up in related conversations... and Pedro could easily have joined the list especially given that at the outset of this season he started just one of the first seven league games under Conte. Going 3-0 down to Arsenal certainly proved to be the catalyst for change in the Italian's game-plan, but a switch to 3-4-3 still saw no place for Pedro in Chelsea's starting XI. The Spaniard was given six minutes off the bench in the Blues 2-0 away win at Hull City and it would take a sad circumstance, namely Willian being granted compassionate leave to attend the funeral of his mother, which meant Conte had to make a change for Chelsea's next game against Leicester City.

Pedro was given the nod and played well, contributing an assist in a 3-0 win. Then followed the breath-taking 4-0 rout of Manchester United in which Pedro scored and assisted... it is in such games that reputations are made, and the value of the Spaniard's currency with Blues fans was on the rise... and it was enhanced markedly when he scored a stunning goal a few weeks later against Tottenham Hotspur.

It doesn't take much these days for the word legend to be trotted out by football fans... where Chelsea supporters are concerned, any player who enhances the Blues cause against Spurs might find his status elevated in such a way... for a few hours anyway.

31 December

Premier League
Chelsea 4 Stoke City 2
Stamford Bridge
Attendance: 41,601
Referee: Robert Madley

Chelsea (3-4-3): Thibaut Courtois, Cesar Azpilicueta, David Luiz, Gary Cahill (c), Victor Moses (Branislav Ivanovic 82), N'Golo Kante, Cesc Fabregas (Nemanja Matic 73), Marcos Alonso, Willian (Nathaniel Chalobah 84), Diego Costa, Eden Hazard.
Scorers: Cahill 34, Willian 57, 65, Costa 84
Booked: Moses 24, Fabregas 59, Alonso 70

Stoke City (3-4-3): Grant; Johnson, Shawcross (c), Martins Indi; Diouf, Adam, Allen, Pieters; Shaqiri (Bojan 61), Affelay (Imbula 61); Crouch.
Scorers: Martins Indi 46, Crouch 64
Booked: Diouf 70, Adam 86

THE ITALIAN JOB

Chelsea extended their club-record winning streak to 13 matches with a dramatic 4-2 New Years Eve victory over Stoke City at Stamford Bridge. When skipper Gary Cahill headed Chelsea into a half-time lead, it seemed the Blues would be on course for another routine victory, but Stoke refused to lie down and were back in the game immediately after the break when Bruno Martins Indi scored from close range.

Peter Crouch, a lanky nuisance for the Chelsea defence at every forward set-piece Stoke, mustered provided the nod down assist for Martins Indi's goal and he would score himself shortly after Willian, starting in place of the suspended Pedro, had restored the Blues lead.

Stoke's players were still congratulating each other moments after Crouch's equalizer when Cesc Fabregas picked out Willian with a sharp pass and the Brazil international fired home his second of the game... a timely reminder to Conte, if it were needed, of his value to the team.

Diego Costa, who'd worked feverishly hard up-front leading Chelsea's line, sealed all three points for Conte when rewarded for his endeavours with a late goal, his 14th of the season. The result meant the Blues had now equalled the English top-flight record for the number of consecutive wins in a single season set by Arsenal in the run in to their title-winning 2001-2002 campaign.

"Congratulations go to my players. To win 13 games in a row in this league is very difficult," said an ebullient Antonio Conte after the game. "My players showed they can adapt to the different kinds of game we face. They showed great commitment, work-rate and will to win. I'm delighted for them," he continued before delving into some more of his football philosophy. "Numbers are not important if you do not win the title. Now, they are fantastic and we are proud, but we must concentrate on the second part of the season."

Conte was right and Conte's final message before my thoughts turned to partying the night away got me wondering…

"Now, it's important to celebrate the arrival of the New Year, then to think of the next game against Tottenham."

What could possibly go wrong?

JANUARY 2017

1 January

I had a very happy New Year!!!

4 January

Premier League
Tottenham Hotspur 2 Chelsea 0
White Hart Lane
Attendance: 31,491
Referee: Martin Atkinson

Chelsea (3-4-3): Thibaut Courtois, Cesar Azpilicueta, David Luiz, Gary Cahill (c), Victor Moses (Michy Batshuayi 85), N'Golo Kante (Cesc Fabregas 79), Nemanja Matic, Marcos Alonso (Willian 65), Pedro, Diego Costa, Eden Hazard.
Booked: Pedro 18, Cahill 38

Tottenham (3-5-2): Lloris (c), Dier, Alderweireld, Vertonghen, Walker, Dembele (Winks 74), Wanyama, Eriksen, Rose, Alli (Sissoko 86), Kane (Son 90+3).
Scorer: Alli 45+1, 54
Booked: Wanyama 40, Alli 45+2, Rose 87

Chelsea's New Year celebrations (and mine) were soon forgotten on a perishing, cold night at White Hart Lane as Tottenham avenged the ignominy they had suffered in their last two games with the Blues by halting the runaway Premier League leaders in their tracks via a comfortable 2-0 win.

A pair of almost identical goals either side of the lemon break from Dele Alli... headers both assisted by Christian Eriksen, settled the match in Spurs favour, and the result ended Chelsea's hopes of a record-beating 14th straight top-flight victory.

THE ITALIAN JOB

The game was a rude awakening for Blues supporters and no doubt manager Antonio Conte and his players who had grown accustomed to teams not being able to live with the tempo associated with Chelsea's new system.

Spurs boss Mauricio Pochettino set up his team perfectly in a 3-4-2-1 formation to snuff out Conte's 3-4-3, and the Blues laboured as a consequence with Blues wing-backs Marcos Alonso and Victor Moses and midfielder N'Golo Kante all struggling to cope with the intensity of respective positional opponents Kyle Walker, Danny Rose and Victor Wanyama.

The Blues trio's struggles did not go unnoticed by Conte with each player eventually substituted… but by then the damage had been done. Truthfully, Tottenham bossed the match from the outset and deserved all three points. Despite this, Chelsea's away support remained vocal throughout the evening ensuring that the home crowd were regularly reminded that John Terry had won the *Double, Double, Double… and the shit from the Lane had won fuck all again…*

Understandably, Conte was disappointed after the loss… as we all were. But as usual the Italian's words of wisdom hit the nervy nail squarely on the head. "Now we have to restart, to continue to work and this defeat is totally different if you compare with our defeats in September, because at that moment we were not a team. Tonight we showed we are a strong team and this is important."

Too right Antonio. While the defeat was hard to bear, the sight of Chelsea five points clear of second-placed Liverpool at the top of the Premier League made took the edge off the situation, and the forthcoming FA Cup tie with League One side Peterborough United would provide Conte with the time he needed to rotate and rest key players and build them up psychologically to come again.

6 January

Loyal club servant John Obi Mikel announced he would be leaving Chelsea after 10 years to join Chinese Super League side Tianjin TEDA. Maligned and misunderstood by a narrow-minded section of Blues support who never failed to give him stick at the earliest opportunity, Mikel was in fact a serial winner who racked up 11 trophies in his time at Stamford Bridge.

Personally, I loved the fella... and will argue long and hard with any of his detractors that if they watch a replay of the 2012 Champions League final, they will see that the epic shift Mikel put in against Bayern Munich was the primary reason Chelsea stayed in contention to the final whistle.

Deaf perhaps to the harsh words from the stands... and humble to the last, Mikel's parting comments hopefully embarrassed those who'd chided him. "My biggest thanks must go to the Blues fans. You brought me into the Chelsea family, you sung my name, and were there with us every step of the way. Thanks to your support, on nights like in Munich, you made the impossible possible."

John Obi Mikel... Proper Chels... and that's legend status isn't it if you know what I mean.

8 January

FA Cup Third Round
Chelsea 4 Peterborough United 1
Stamford Bridge
Attendance: 41,003
Referee: Kevin Friend

Chelsea (3-4-3): Asmir Begovic, Kurt Zouma, John Terry (c), Gary Cahill (Ola Aina 57), Branislav Ivanovic, Cesc Fabregas, Nathaniel Chalobah, Pedro, Ruben Loftus-Cheek (Cesar Azpilicueta 69), Michy Batshuayi, Willian (N'Golo Kante 73).
Scorers: Pedro 18, 75, Batshuayi 44, Willian 52
Sent off: Terry 67
Booked: Fabregas 24

Peterborough (4-4-2): McGee, Smith, Bostwick, Tafazolli, Hughes (Binnom-Williams 83), Maddison (Taylor 57), Lopes, Forrester (c), Edwards (Samuelsen 57), Nichols, Angol.
Scorer: Nicholls 70
Booked: Forrester 23, Tafazolli 33

Antonio Conte made nine changes to the starting XI which lost to Tottenham, but this 'second-string' Chelsea side were still way too good for Peterborough. Livewire Pedro, deployed very effectively at left wing-back by Conte, opened the scoring in the 18th minute with a sweetly struck shot and the under-employed Michy Batshuayi doubled the Blues advantage just before half-time.

THE ITALIAN JOB

Willian increased Chelsea's lead shortly after the break with the goal of the game, firing home from 20 yards but it wasn't all one-way traffic. In the 67th minute, John Terry, making his first start since October, was caught out by advancing Peterborough striker Lee Angol and inadvertently floored the Posh player when going to ground himself on a pitch made slippy by the rain. With referee Kevin Friend determining that Angol was the last man, Terry was shown a straight red card and cut a dispirited figure as he trudged disconsolately to the dressing room.

Tom Nicholls gave the 6,000 travelling Peterborough fans something more to cheer about when pulling a goal back minutes after Terry's dismissal, but despite being down to 10 men for the final phase of the game Chelsea were still too good for the League One side and Pedro completed the rout with a decent strike on 75 minutes.

"I am pleased, when you change nine players it is never easy to play a good game and to be a team," said Conte after the match. "Today we showed we were a team. I'm pleased for those who have played less as they have showed me good form."

Among those who had played less who showed good form was defender Kurt Zouma returning to first team action for the first time since sustaining a knee injury in a league game with Manchester United almost a year ago.

22-year old Zouma had already established himself in Chelsea's first team prior to being side-lined and Blues supporters were as keen as Conte to see if the kid still had it in him. It was all good news. Against Peterborough, the France international displayed the spirit, mobility and physicality that had swiftly made him a fan favourite. Yes he looked rusty at the outset and had slipped when trying to intercept the through-ball which led to Terry getting red-carded, but criticism would have been harsh and the centre-back looked a steadfast deputy for any of Conte's current preferred back three of Gary Cahill, David Luiz and Cesar Azpilicueta.

Nathaniel Chalobah and Ruben Loftus-Cheek also excelled. The duo, both 20-years old, played with vibrant energy and unselfish enthusiasm and had chances to score. Chalobah in particular caught the eye and had a central role in Chelsea's opening two goals. Under Conte, Loftus-Cheek had clearly been developing into a more forward-thinking, progressive player and his link-up play was excellent.

Given the limited opportunities that had come his way since his big-money arrival at the Bridge, and the pressure of trying to impress Conte, it was understandable perhaps if Michy Batshuayi might try too hard... and certainly the 23-year old did early on in the contest. Following a well-taken goal just before the break, the Belgium international settled down and led the line well putting in type of shift that suggested to Chelsea supporters he would be more than capable of deputising for Costa if required. That said, the fans belief was that Conte simply didn't fancy him for the job. With the transfer window now open, would the Blues boss make a move for the type of deputy that he believed to be more capable?

11 January

Hammersmith and Fulham Borough Council planners unanimously approved Chelsea's proposals to build a new stadium on the site of Stamford Bridge. "We are happy to help usher in this exciting new phase in Chelsea FC's history", announced H&F Council Leader, Cllr Stephen Cowan.

As the virtual reality, social media cheers of Blues supporters who had been following the evening's procedures on Twitter (big thank you to journalist @danlevene for his minute-by-minute updates) reverberated 'loudly' around the world, the sense of relief among the Chelsea brethren was palpable.

Although there was clearly much work to be done before the works could commence, the fact that the new stadium would be sited where Chelsea had played football since their foundation in 1905 removed a shroud of uncertainty that had blanketed the Bridge since the 1970s when property developers first circled one of the most valuable pieces of real estate in the country.

During the Second World War, making reference to the on-going valiant efforts of the Royal Air Force pilots who were at the time fighting the Battle of Britain, Prime Minister Winston Churchill declared the immortal words, "Never in the field of human conflict was so much owed by so many to so few". It may be a strange analogy to use, but I recalled former Chelsea Chief Executive Ron Gourlay, a name otherwise easily forgotten to be honest, making a bold somewhat self-aggrandising claim in a 2014 interview with the *Evening Standard* that since he had replaced Peter Kenyon in 2009, the Blues fan-base had grown from 26 million to 400 million. That was a lot of Chelsea supporters... including me... presumably all happy with the news... who owed a huge debt of gratitude to the dedicated small band of fellow followers, among them the Chelsea Pitch Owners, whose slavish hard work and long-term campaigning had helped ensure that future

THE ITALIAN JOB

generations of Blues could see their team play at Stamford Bridge. Well done!

There were still issues and concerns associated with the as yet undecided venue where Chelsea will have to play their 'home' games while the existing stadium was razed to the ground and rebuilt... but they could be dealt with in due course.

Clearly, the long-term gain far outweighed the short-term (building works forecasted to take three years) pain, but the thought occurred to me that a lot could happen in football in three years, and while the hard core Blues support will always endure change and hiatus just as it has always done throughout the lean years in the pre-Roman Abramovich era, it would be vitally important that during the period of stadium redevelopment, Chelsea remained a competitive force... not only domestically, but on the European stage as well.

Right now, with Antonio Conte at the managerial helm, Chelsea were surfing on the crest of a wave of positivity. It may still have been too early to talk of winning the title or indeed the league and cup double, but Conte was clearly fashioning a team of winners... and in a grand inclusive manner. Could any other manager do a better job? No! Not for me anyway. Hopefully Abramovich would have the patience to give Conte the latitude he needed to lead Chelsea through the next pivotal phase in its history.

13 January

And in this respect, if Roman Abramovich needed a nudge regarding Antonio Conte's capabilities, the Italian becoming the first manager in Premier League history to scoop three successive Manager of the Month awards would have done just that.

Conte's latest award may have been performance-related, but later in the day his full repertoire of managerial attributes came to the fore when a story broke that Diego Costa had rowed earlier in the week with Paulo Bertelli one of Chelsea's fitness coaches. Costa had told Bertelli that he had a back problem and couldn't train... the coach disagreed and made his thoughts known to Conte. The drama played out amid tales of Costa having had his head turned by a reported £30 million a year salary offer from Chinese Super League club Tianjin Quanjian who were reported to also be dangling a £5 million signing on fee... and the outcome? Costa did not travel with the rest of the Blues team when they departed London for the forthcoming game with Leicester. "Go to China," Conte was alleged to have told his tempestuous striker. If Don Conte was cast in the role of Godfather, Costa might find himself sleeping with those infamous fishes if he wasn't careful. Unlike previous seasons, there was only one guvnor in the Chelsea dressing room. Conte. Enough said!

14 January

Premier League
Leicester City 0 Chelsea 3
King Power Stadium
Attendance: 32,066
Referee: Andre Marriner

Chelsea (3-4-3): Thibaut Courtois, Cesar Azpilicueta, David Luiz, Gary Cahill (c), Victor Moses, N'Golo Kante, Nemanja Matic, Marcos Alonso, Willian (Michy Batshuayi 83), Eden Hazard (Cesc Fabregas 78), Pedro (Ruben Loftus-Cheek 83).
Scorers: Alonso 6, 51, Pedro 71

Leicester (3-5-2): Schmeichel, Morgan (c), Huth (Okazaki 59), Fuchs, Chilwell, Mendy, Drinkwater, Ndidi, Albrighton (Simpson 76), Musa (Gray 71), Vardy.
Booked: Fuchs 51

Pre-match the media got their collective knickers in a twist over Costa and started trumpeting the player's 'fall out' with Conte as a potential disaster for Chelsea and the beginning of the end of their title bid. Reigning champions Leicester's form was patchy, but a 4-2 hammering of Manchester City the previous month had been a timely reminder of their capabilities. Would the Foxes turn the apparent disharmony in the league leader's camp to their advantage? Blues supporters had a feeling that the hacks and TV pundits were hoping this would be the case... and took great pleasure at the huge reversal of expectation.

Two well-struck goals from Marcos Alonso that Costa would have been proud of saw the drama surrounding the absent striker begin to evaporate. By the time Pedro headed home the Blues third Costa's absence was all but forgotten.

Antonio, Antonio. Antonio, Antonio, Antonio.

Coming on the back of the disappointing defeat to Tottenham Hotspur, and Conte's consternation with Costa, there was a huge amount of pressure on Chelsea to prove their title credentials, and, to their credit, that's exactly what they did... emphatically.

Once again the Blues boss was a ball of energy on the touchline. He lived and breathed the match as if he were playing in it. Maybe that was it... the secret to Chelsea's success. Conte was their 12th man. What an advantage!

Speaking on Soccer AM at Christmas, John Terry had provided an enlightening glimpse into his manager's somewhat unorthodox behaviour during games and how it affected him afterwards. "He's a really nice guy. He is absolutely sweating after the games. His shirt and suit comes off," said the Blues legend. "He has a towel around him in the dressing room to cool down. The animation!"

This probably explained why Conte was last on parade for post-match press conferences. Can you imagine Big Sam at Palace needing to calm down, have a shower and put on a change of clobber before speaking to the media? No. Me neither. Conte probably covered the same eight miles or so that midfielder N'Golo Kante did. Easy to see why the players took to him in the way they did. He was one of them... better than them even... world class... and he also had the stripes.

16 January

Antonio Conte spoke about his bond with the supporters. Sometimes when managers do such things it seems contrived, but Conte came across as genuine and honest. "The fans with me are always special, from the first day," said the Blues boss. "I remember for my first game they prepared a flag, an Italian flag," he continued enthusiastically. "It is fantastic to have this kind of relationship with great passion. I think I show this in every game and I think they are appreciating this." (We certainly were) "I hope to continue this way because it's important to always stay together... with the team, the players, the fan, the club, me, my staff. It's important to continue to work together."

17 January

Having spent Monday training on his own at Chelsea's Cobham facility while the rest of the first team had a day off, Tuesday saw a clearly fit Costa assimilated back into the fold by Conte. Now the question was would the Blues boss restore the 28-year old to his starting XI for the forthcoming game with Hull City?

Despite myriad rumours linking Costa with a move to China, Conte always maintained that the forward had a lower back problem stating this was the reason for the player being dropped. However, given the stellar sums of money washing around the Chinese Super League clubs, and the recent departure from London to Shanghai of Costa's native countryman and former teammate Oscar as well as Chelsea midfielder John Obi Mikel it would be understandable if the Brazil-born Spain international has been distracted recently… particularly given the disruptive influence of his money-chasing super agent Jorge Mendes who had been travelling around China the previous week.

Even though Chelsea ran out comfortable 3-0 winners against Leicester, they lacked Costa's presence and classic centre-forward's ability to lead the line. The creative triumvirate of Pedro, Willian and Eden Hazard, aided and abetted by wing-backs Victor Moses and two-goal Marcos Alonso proved more than a match for Leicester, and there was no reason to suppose that the quintet could not combine again to see off relegation-threatened Hull.

With Conte likely to rotate his team for the following weekend's FA Cup 4th Round tie with Brentford, a game that Costa, irrespective of fitness or personal stability would be unlikely to start, the Italian might decide to keep the striker fresh for Chelsea's next two Premier League games which had a season-defining look about them.

Tuesday 31 January Chelsea were due at Anfield to face Liverpool and four days later, the Blues would host Arsenal at Stamford Bridge. If Conte could mastermind victories in both games it could prove to be a huge psychological blow… not only to these opponents, but to Tottenham Hotspur, Manchester City and Manchester United as well.

Interesting times lay ahead.

18 January

Chelsea agreed to sell Patrick Bamford to Middlesbrough for £6 million plus a series of add-ons which could take the fee to £10 million. The deal represented a significant profit on the 23-year old striker who was signed from Nottingham Forest in January 2012 for £1.5 million but failed to make a first team appearance for the Blues. Having enjoyed successful loan spells at Milton Keynes, Derby County and at Boro where in 2014-2015 when he was voted Championship Player of the Year, Bamford had latterly failed to make an impact with Crystal Palace, Norwich and Burnley.

THE ITALIAN JOB

The benefit of such a whirlwind of moves on a young footballer's development was a regular topic of debate given the number of players Chelsea had on loan... but from a mercenary financial point of view... it was starting to prove tricky arguing a case against the Blues board for employing such a strategy. Bugger! Was Michael Emenalo actually a genius after all?

The spotlight remained on Chelsea's academy later in the day as the Under-18s continued their defence of the FA Youth Cup by thrashing Birmingham City 5-0 at Solihull Moors. Mason Mount bagged a hattrick and Cole Dasilva and Reece James completed the rout. Manager Jody Morris had by now opted to follow senior gaffer Antonio Conte's 3-4-3 set-up... the result proved that if you had the right calibre players it could be devastating at any level.

22 January

**Premier League
Chelsea 2 Hull City 0
Stamford Bridge
Attendance: 41,605
Referee: Neil Swarbrick**

Chelsea (3-4-3): Thibaut Courtois, Cesar Azpilicueta, David Luiz, Gary Cahill (c), Victor Moses, N'Golo Kante, Nemanja Matic, Marcos Alonso, Pedro (Willian 69), Diego Costa (Michy Batshuayi 85), Eden Hazard (Cesc Fabregas 69).
Scorers: Diego Costa 45+7, Cahill 80
Booked: Kante 42
Hull City (3-4-2-1): Jakupovic, Maguire, Dawson (c), Davies (Niasse 59), Elabdellaoui, Mason (Meyler 20), Huddlestone, Robertson; Evandro, Clucas; Hernandez (Diomande 74).
Booked: Dawson 6, Davies 25, Robertson 51

Well, well... in the end it came as no surprise that Antonio Conte reinstated Diego Costa to his starting XI... and it was even less of surprise when the striker, making his 100th appearance for Chelsea, opened the scoring driving home a Victor Moses cross in the 7th minute of first-half stoppage time. Gary Cahill made certain of the points near the end of the game heading home a Cesc Fabregas free-kick.

"You must tell me if I did well to put Diego in the starting XI," mused Conte after the game. "I have to make the best decision for the team, and if he wasn't ready to play, or my choice was bad, it's my fault, not the player's fault."

When asked about the speculation surrounding Costa's future at Chelsea, Conte was both deliberate and cagey. "Diego has two years left on his contract. He's very happy to stay with us and play for Chelsea. Now we must concentrate on the present and not look too far ahead. If we do that we risk losing the present, and that's more important than the future." I made a mental note to see if my bookie would take a bet on Costa not being a Blues player come August.

Football aside, the match was notable for two occurrences that highlighted how fragile precious life can be.

In the 13th minute, Hull midfielder Ryan Mason and Cahill accidentally clashed heads as the visitors defended a corner. Mason stayed down, and after a lengthy period of treatment was stretchered from the field wearing an oxygen mask. It was later announced that the player had suffered a fractured skull and had undergone surgery… the football world prayed. Fortunately, there would be a positive outcome for Mason who spent a week in hospital before being allowed home. No timeframe would be placed on his return to action.

In the 55th minute, the life of Chelsea supporter Carl O'Brien, a former groundsman at Stamford Bridge, was commemorated with a round of applause. Carl, 55, known as Wurzel to fellow fans, had been a home and away regular on the Blues scene for over 40 years… a shocking and unprovoked attack in a communal stairwell near his flat in Wallington, South London on 3 December led to his death from a brain haemorrhage 20 days later.

Carl's photo was displayed on the large monitors at half-time when stadium announcer Neil Barnett delivered a short eulogy and a banner was unfurled during the minute's applause which read R.I.P Carl 'Wurzel' O'Brien.

A police investigation into the attack which occurred on the same day as the first birthday of Carl's only grandchild Lily would subsequently lead to a 26-year old man being arrested and charged with murder. At the time of writing, the trial had been scheduled for July 2017.

*****

Chelsea's victory over Hull, coupled with title rivals Liverpool, Tottenham

THE ITALIAN JOB

Hotspur, Manchester City and Manchester United all dropping points left Antonio Conte's team eight points clear of Arsenal, the only other top six side to manage a win at the weekend. The Blues losing to Spurs at the beginning of the month had been a well-timed reminder that in football there is no room for complacency. Irrespective of form and position, every team in the Premier League was capable of 'working out' and surprising opponents... high-flying Liverpool being beaten 3-2 at 'fortress Anfield' by lowly Swansea the day before Conte and Co. beat Hull being the latest prime example.

Every player needed to remain focussed, and that started with the goalkeeper. While much had been made of Chelsea's robust three man defence of Cesar Azpilicueta, David Luiz and Gary Cahill, buccaneering wing-backs Marcos Alonso and Victor Moses and prolific if somewhat highly-strung striker Diego Costa, Thibaut Courtois' contribution (Sunderland away excepted) to the Blues renaissance had been somewhat overlooked.

Predictably, given the recent 'back injury' / 'China transfer' drama which saw Costa dropped by Conte, restoration to Chelsea's starting XI, and scoring the opening goal against Hull, was always going to see the striker grab the headlines and secure man-of-the-match plaudits.

At the other end of the pitch, the performance of Courtois who pulled off a series of fine saves, commanded his penalty area with authority, and was perfectly positioned for every Hull set piece, deserved equal if not more credit to that which Costa received.

Chelsea's goal difference at the time of +32 and 13 clean sheets was superior to that of any other Premier League side, and Courtois' diligence and fine goalkeeping form was right there at the heart of it. Consistency was the key.

By comparison, the weekend had seen Tottenham keeper Hugo Lloris calamitously gift Manchester City two goals in a game which finished 2-2. Similarly, City, after a blistering start to the campaign, had been bedevilled with problems in this area following manager Pep Gaurdiola's single-minded decision to dispense with the services of England international Joe Hart in favour of erratic former Barcelona 'sweeper-keeper' Claudio Bravo. Meanwhile at Anfield against Swansea, Liverpool goalkeeper Simon Mignolet had conceded the only three shots on target he faced... and he would have a large say in the outcome of Chelsea's game with the Reds at the end of the month.

Arguably the Premier League's best keeper, Courtois was essential to Chelsea's chances of winning silverware. Annoyingly, there were transfer window stories bubbling away again that the 24-year old, whose partner and child still lived in Madrid where he spent a successful three-year loan spell with Atletico, was looking to move back to the Spanish capital where Real were reported to be readying a sizable summer bid.

What the future would hold at Chelsea for Courtois, and what Conte had in mind for the position was unknown. Given the fact that Bournemouth had recently bid £10 million for back-up keeper Asmir Begovic, and might improve on that figure to try and push the deal through before the end of the month, with third choice 34-year old Eduardo an unknown quantity in English football, the Blues boss clearly had some thinking to do about the position. With the threat of injury always present, Conte had to retain the services of Begovic... he also needed to ensure that Courtois did not become distracted by thoughts of a return to La Liga.

28 January

FA Cup Fourth Round
Chelsea 4 Brentford 0
Stamford Bridge
Attendance: 41,042
Referee: Michael Oliver

Chelsea (3-4-3): Asmir Begovic, Kurt Zouma, John Terry (c), Cesar Azpilicueta (Kenedy 70) Pedro (Diego Costa 76), Cesc Fabregas, Nathaniel Chalobah, Nathan Ake, Willian (Branislav Ivanovic 64), Michy Batshuayi, Ruben Loftus-Cheek.
Scorers: Willian 14, Pedro 20, Ivanovic 70, Batshuayi 81 pen.
Booked: Chalobah 89

Brentford (3-5-2): Bentley; Egan, Dean (c), Bjelland; Colin, Yennaris, McEachran (Kerschbaumer 78), Woods, Barbet; Vibe (Jota 64), Sawyers (Hogan 64).
Booked: Colin 55

Chelsea coasted into the 5th Round of the FA Cup with an easy 4-0 victory over west London neighbours Brentford. Antonio Conte made nine changes to his starting XI, but this was no ordinary second string, the Blues simply had too much strength in depth... many Premier League managers would have been glad to have this line-up as their first team.

THE ITALIAN JOB

Willian opened the scoring with a trade-mark free-kick in the 14th minute and the contest was effectively over just six minutes later when Pedro made it 2-0. The biggest cheer of the day was reserved for Branislav Ivanovic who came on for Willian in the 64th minute, slotted into a wing-back role on the right flank, and promptly scored a few minutes later firing home a great goal. Michy Batshuayi completed the rout from the penalty spot after Ivanovic was fouled in the box.

Going into the game, there had been rumours circulating that Ivanovic was set to leave Chelsea in the transfer window, and as it transpired these stories proved to be correct though Conte was coy on the matter after the game. "Ivan knows well the situation and I'm pleased if he remains here, if he stays with us. But in this situation, for sure, the player must make the best decision for him, for his family,' said the Blues boss. "Ivan deserves great respect for his career at Chelsea. He played a lot of games, he won a lot with this team."

Conte was right in his summary. Ivanovic had played 377 times for Chelsea scoring 34 goals and winning eight major trophies. The respect aspect was a sore point for many match-going supporters angered by the social media trolling the player had suffered in the past 18 months when his form had dipped.

Soon to be 33, the time was right for Brana to move on. Like the recently departed John Obi Mikel, Ivanovic in my eyes was a Chelsea legend beyond question. That euphoric moment in extra-time at Stamford Bridge (14 March 2012) when he almost burst the Napoli net to settle a stirring Champions League tie 5-4 in Chelsea's favour and set the Blues on a remarkable path to glory will live forever in my memory.

As the Brentford game presented an opportunity to reflect on Brana's outstanding nine-year sojourn at the Bridge, so did it also provide a chance to reflect on what might have been for another player who was on Chelsea's books for a much longer period of time than Ivanovic… Josh McEachran, now plying his trade for the Bees.

Having signed for the Blues as a kid, highly-rated McEachran then progressed through the academy sides winning the FA Youth Cup in 2010. So prodigious were his skills that at 16-years of age Real Madrid tried to lure him to the Bernabeu. A Chelsea supporter, the youngster opted to stay at Stamford Bridge where he enjoyed a breakthrough season in 2010/11 making 17 first-team appearances. *He does what he wants,* we'd chanted in deference to the kid, but unfortunately for McEachran, then manager Carlo

Ancelotti was sacked at the end of the campaign... and as the managerial door span off it's hinges with comings and goings, opportunities fell by the wayside. A series of loan spells followed before he was eventually sold to Brentford for £750,000 in July 2015.

Against Chelsea, playing at the base of the Bees midfield, McEachran, now 23 years of age, showed some nice touches, but nothing to suggest that the Blues had made an error of judgement selling him on. Football can be a cruel game. If Ancelotti hadn't been sacked, things might have turned out differently... but then you could say that about many footballers careers. Imagine if Claudio Ranieri had not taken a chance on a very young John Terry... or signed Frank Lampard... enough said I guess.

28 January

Premier League
Liverpool 1 Chelsea 1
Anfield
Attendance: 53,157
Referee: Mark Clattenburg

Chelsea (3-4-3): Thibaut Courtois, Cesar Azpilicueta, David Luiz, Gary Cahill (c), Victor Moses, N'Golo Kante, Nemanja Matic, Marcos Alonso, Willian (Cesc Fabregas 83), Diego Costa (Michy Batshuayi 90+4), Eden Hazard (Pedro 72).
Scorer: David Luiz 24
Booked: Willian 79

Liverpool (4-3-3): Mignolet, Clyne, Matip, Lovren, Milner; Wijnaldum, Henderson (c), Can, Lallana (Origi 90), Firmino, Coutinho (Mane 75).
Scorer: Wijnaldum 57
Booked: Henderson 45, Milner 57

Chelsea were held to a 1-1 draw by Liverpool in a blink-and-you-missed-it, full-throttle encounter at rain-swept Anfield. David Luiz, taking full advantage of Reds keeper Simon Mignolet's unpreparedness, blasted home a free-kick midway through the first-half to give the visitors the lead against the run of play. Liverpool's equalizer came via a poorly-defended, close-range Georginio Wijnaldum header on 57 minutes. When Joel Matip brought down Diego Costa to concede a penalty with just 15 minutes left, the game looked set to go Chelsea's way... but Costa's spot-kick was soft and easily saved by Mignolet who was clearly motivated to atone for his earlier error.

THE ITALIAN JOB

It was a night of mixed fortunes for Chelsea who despite seeing Costa spurn the perfect chance to win the game still managed to conclude the night increasing their advantage at the top of the table to nine points as second-placed Arsenal contrived to lose at home to Watford. The Blues certainly appeared to be blessed with good luck this season, and such a positive could not be underestimated… a little fortune can go a long way in football.

Luiz, scoring his first goal for Chelsea since returning to the club, was outstanding. Not just for the perception and precision he displayed when seizing the initiative from Willian to hammer that free-kick past Mignolet, but also for the outstanding defensive qualities and valorous desire to play through the pain barrier after he sustained a knee injury 10 minutes before half-time.

Once again, Antonio Conte cut a dynamic, passionate figure on the touchline. Winning so clearly meant everything to the Italian. If he could have taken the penalty Costa squandered, he would have done… and he would have scored, you know that!

"When there are these type of games with high intensity it's very difficult to see the mistakes and to try to make the correction, but I think we played a really good game," said the Chelsea manager post-match.

It was a good match. A great match even. With hindsight, Conte's management of the in-form Pedro's game-time, namely fielding him against Brentford in the FA Cup and benching him for the Liverpool match was perhaps the wrong strategy, but maybe that was just nit-picking in the same way criticising Costa for his penalty miss was.

In summary, if anyone had said to me after that 3-0 loss to Arsenal back in September (a result that left Chelsea in eighth place in the league, eight points behind then leaders Manchester City) that come the end of the following January the Blues would head the chasing pack by nine points I would have asked them what hallucinogenic drugs they had been taking… and bought some for myself!

Glorious unpredictability, that's the wonder of Chelsea… and next up was the opportunity to exact revenge on Arsenal for that 3-0 defeat. Gunners manager Arsene Wenger had curiously declared after their 'shock' defeat by Watford that his side weren't mentally prepared for the game. Hopefully this curious state of mind would persist for a few days longer.

FEBRUARY 2017

1 February

Chelsea confirmed the sale for an undisclosed fee of Branislav Ivanovic to Russian Premier League side Zenit St Petersburg.

The Blues Under-18s romped to a 4-0 FA Youth Cup Fourth Round victory over Sheffield Wednesday at Aldershot's EBB Stadium. Trevor Chalobah, younger brother of occasional first-teamer Nathaniel, opened the scoring with further goals coming from Ike Ugbo, Mason Mount and Callum Hudson-Odoi. Interestingly, manager Jody Morris went with 4-3-3 as opposed to 3-4-3, but such was Chelsea's superiority the formation to be honest could have been 2-6-2 and the Blues would have still won at a canter.

2 February

Chelsea legend 'Sir' Frank Lampard announced his retirement as a player. Despite the fact that Super Frank, now 38 years of age, had left Stamford Bridge in June 2014 the news was still a big deal for Blues supporters who celebrated his achievements on social media.

The £11million Chelsea paid to West Ham United for 22-year old Lampard's services in June 2001 seemed expensive at the time... however to put the value of that fee in perspective, Fulham paid Lyon £13.5 million for Steve Marlet a few weeks later... Steve who? Exactly!

'Sir' Frank went on to become the Blues all time record scorer with 211 goals from 649 appearances in all competitions. In a glittering 13-year career at Stamford Bridge he won 11 major trophies and captained the Champions League Final winning side in 2012. Oh and he also won 106 England caps scoring 29 goals... 30 if you include the wonder-strike that crossed Germany's line in the 2010 World Cup but was never given.

If ever there was a footballer in the modern era deserving of a

THE ITALIAN JOB

knighthood, Frank Lampard was the worthiest of candidates…

Thank you for the memories 'Sir' Frank, maybe one day you will return to Stamford Bridge in a capacity that will thrill and inspire players and supporters once more.

4 February

**Premier League
Chelsea 3 Arsenal 1
Stamford Bridge
Attendance: 41,490
Referee: Martin Atkinson**

Chelsea (3-4-3): Thibaut Courtois, Cesar Azpilicueta, David Luiz, Gary Cahill (c), Victor Moses (Kurt Zouma 86), N'Golo Kante, Nemanja Matic, Marcos Alonso, Pedro (Willian 82), Diego Costa, Eden Hazard (Cesc Fabregas 82).
Scorers: Alonso 12, Hazard 52, Fabregas 85
Booked: Matic 69

Arsenal (4-2-3-1): Cech; Bellerin (Gabriel 16), Mustafi, Koscielny (c), Monreal, Coquelin (Giroud 64), Oxlade-Chamberlain; Walcott, Ozil, Iwobi, Sanchez.
Scorer: Giroud 90
Booked: Mustafi 22

PMT = Pre Match Tension. There was plenty of it around the cfcuk stall at Fulham Broadway before the 12.30pm kick-off with Arsenal. A stupid 'o' clock start to the day had left little time to gather thoughts let alone get the stall ship shape with fanzines, books and t-shirts and the accompanying rain didn't buoy the mood either.

There was a serious amount of banter had between the stall's regular habitués who tarried to discuss the matters at hand. If you do the Chelsea Twitter thing, you'll recognize some of them variously as @GrocerJackUK @tim_rolls @chucklescabbie @TrueblueTerri @ChelseatheLab @churchill_alex @stamfordchidge @Martin_Wickham @camberleycfc @zizzytheblue @goalie59 @chelsearog1966 and @kenbarkway… and the general feeling among them was one of nervously cautious optimism. In Conte we trust and all that. Without a doubt, the consensus was that a victory of any sort would hammer the final nail in Arsenal's faltering title bid while furthering our own hopes of Chelsea winning club football's greatest prize.

Curiously, for the first time this season... as far as I could recall, there was no sign of the Chelsea band playing *Blue is the Colour* that normally march past the fanzine stall once the police have closed Fulham Road to traffic an hour or so before kick off. I hoped it wasn't a bad omen... not that I'm superstitious.

In the stadium, it took just 13 minutes for the boys in Blue to settle the nerves of home supporters. Marcos Alonso leapt salmon-like to meet a crossbar rebound from a Diego Costa header nodding home past former Chelsea keeper Petr Cech.

The game ebbed and flowed in typical London-derby fashion for the balance of the first-half. N'Golo Kante's tigerish attitude to the game limited Arsenal's effective possession though Thibaut Courtois needed to be focused and on point towards the end of the opening 45 minutes particularly when he was tested by Gabriel.

So far so good. Chelsea needed another goal to kill the game off... a moment of brilliance perhaps... and then it happened... 53 minutes...

Eden Hazard picked up a recycled ball just inside the centre circle D of his own half. As he edged towards the half-way line and contemplated what to do next... with Arsenal trio Laurent Koscielny, Alex Oxlade-Chamberlain and Shkodran Mustafi in close attendance... passing to a teammate looked like the most sensible option... but Hazard had other ideas. With a shimmy to the left and a jink to the right, he set off on a mazy run leaving the Gunners trailing in his wake. 'Tough-guy' Arsenal midfielder Francis Coquelin then ran at... and bounced off the comparatively diminutive-looking Blues man... that was funny... funnier still in the YouTube replays watched endlessly without boredom later on. 'Go on my son!' I shouted, leaping maniacally out of my seat and clenching my fists as he ran past me and my cohorts gathered at the juncture of the East Stand and Gate17. Right in front of us now, Hazard weaved back inside towards the D of the Arsenal penalty area and rinsed Koscielny once again. The Gunners defence looked like a bunch of flabby drunks running for (and missing) the last bus... Mustafi gave up and laid down on the floor! Just Cech to beat now... Goaaaaaaaaaaaaaaal!!!!!!

I've seen a lot of special goals at Stamford Bridge in my time of watching Chelsea... right then, at that moment, as I celebrated wildly with my mates, I was convinced I'd maybe just seen the best... I wasn't alone, and the feeling would linger long after the final whistle. (Hazard would later pick up the goal of the month award for this strike and surely it had to be a cast-iron contender for goal of the season.)

Predictably, as befitting such a 'worldy', the goal knocked the complete bollocks out of Arsenal. Good!

Better still, with five minutes left, substitute Cesc Fabregas, who'd been abused by the Arsenal away contingent gathered in The Shed as he was warming up in advance of entering the fray, rounded off the scoring taking advantage of a poor Cech clearance by lobbing the ball back over the keeper into the net. Classy, unlike the fans that once revered him, Fabregas didn't celebrate scoring against the club where he made a name for himself. Chelsea's exultant supporters did it for him with a rousing rendition of *Fabregas is magic, he wears a magic hat...*

There was still time left for Olivier Giroud to score for Arsenal what I believe is still referred to as a consolation goal... but the majority of visiting Gunners fans had already departed accompanied by the mirth-inducing chant *you're fucking shit, you're fucking shit, you're fucking shit.*

Chelsea were excellent value for their 3-1 win. This victory was the Blues ninth in a row at home with the aggregate score standing at 27-4 in favour of Antonio Conte's team. Talking of aggregates... a Gooner mate of mine texted me shortly after the final whistle to advise me that although Chelsea had won 3-1... the aggregate score for the season was 4-3 in Arsenal's favour... I didn't bother replying... the text went a long way to explaining the mentality at the Emirates where it looked like the Fourth Place trophy would be heading once again.

Conte's summary after the game encapsulated the flavour of his achievements as Blues boss to date. "In four days we have had two games against two great teams. I think we are showing we deserve to stay on top of the table. I am very pleased for my players. In every session they show me great attitude and great will to fight and win this league."

Spot on Antonio. Oh and the way he celebrated Chelsea's goals with Blues supporters in the East Stand adjacent to the technical area showed exactly what the club's current success meant to him personally... Proper Chels!

5 February

That Hazard goal didn't lose any of its intricate, shimmering beauty after a goods night sleep.

6 February

There were still 14 games left to play this season... and while complacency would be as big a fools errand as printing t-shirts and scarves with Premier League Champions writ large on them a la Liverpool in 2014, the portents looked as favourable for Chelsea as their remaining fixtures.

At Stamford Bridge, the Blues still had to entertain Swansea, Watford, Crystal Palace, Manchester City, Southampton, Middlesbrough and Sunderland. Road trips would take Conte's side to Burnley, West Ham, Stoke, Bournemouth, Manchester United, Everton and West Brom. Of those fixtures, the games against the Manchester clubs stood out and potentially posed the biggest threat... but as with the recent Arsenal game, they also presented a significant opportunity to assert authority.

It's true Man City now had Jesus on their side and he'd been working miracles for Pep Guardiola since arriving at the Etihad in January, but similarly to Man U and the rest of Chelsea's rivals the fixture schedule didn't do them any favours.

City, like United, Arsenal and Tottenham would return to European competition later in February. Guardiola's side also still had to play United, Liverpool and Arsenal. United meanwhile also had to play Spurs and Arsenal and the latter two still had to play each other. Keeping Liverpool in the equation, with Spurs looming on the horizon and Arsenal to play in March... the Reds also had the rigours of a Merseyside derby with Everton to come.

The schedule made it impossible for Chelsea's rivals not to drop points when facing each other, a factor which could prove decisive in the run in. Conte would of course have been well aware of this, however such was the Italian's steely resolve and pedigree that there was zero chance of anything resembling self-righteousness creeping into the Stamford Bridge dressing room. There was a remarkable set of statistics concerning Conte that backed this likelihood up. His managerial record in league games for Juventus and Chelsea combined currently read Played 138, Won 102, Lost 10.

Phenomenal. Relentless even.

It's true that in football unless an outcome is a mathematical certainty anything can happen, but as far as Chelsea were concerned, given their vastly superior points and goal difference melded with consummate desire, ability, consistency, favourable fixtures… and Conte the alchemist weaving his magic 3-4-3 spells… it really was becoming difficult to see anything other than a Blues title win. I was cautiously optimistic.

8 February

Ah Diego Costa. Right now, Conte needed Costa's goals to spearhead Chelsea's title challenge… but the Blues boss had to already be planning ahead for next season, a campaign which whether the league was ultimately won or not would surely include European football once more. Whether or not Costa, currently contracted to Chelsea until 2019, featured in those plans was a question that had continued to feature prominently in many related discussions and for now only Conte knew the answer.

Notwithstanding the £33 million paid to Marseille for Michy Batshuayi, a fee which made the Belgium international Chelsea's second most expensive signing after Fernando Torres, Conte's continued sparing use of the 23-year old even when Costa had been unavailable suggested the Italian's mind might be on another Belgian of similar age when it came to strikers.

Last summer, Chelsea had a £58 million bid for Romelu Lukaku rejected by Everton but in the wake of the prolific centre-forward's spectacular four-goal haul against Bournemouth at the weekend stories resurfaced linking the player with a move back to Stamford Bridge. On a day when Costa blanked as Chelsea routed Arsenal 3-1, Lukaku's goals saw him leapfrog the Brazil-born Spain international to become the Premier League's leading marksman with 16 goals.

Lukaku's current stats in the English top flight made compelling reading. To date, the Belgium international had featured in 172 games scoring 76 goals. Prior to being sold to Everton in July 2014 during the ill-fated second reign of José Mourinho, Lukaku had already found the net 32 times in Premier League matches during loan stints with the Merseyside club and West Bromwich Albion.

Lukaku had yet to sign a new Everton contract his agent Mino Raiola spoke of as being '99.9% done' in December. Irrespective of that piece of paperwork, the temptation of a return to SW6, the lure of Champions League football and a salary likely to be double the £100k Everton were reported to be offering would surely make a move back to Chelsea a no-brainer for Lukaku and I for one was with the lad in spirit.

Such was Lukaku's form, that the £70 million price tag currently being touted in the media might rise markedly if the striker continued to find the net for Everton and, injury permitting, there was no reason to suggest this might not happen. Last year, Manchester United paid a world record fee of £89 million to Juventus for the services of Paul Pogba. Chelsea could easily eclipse that if Conte persuaded Roman Abramovich that Lukaku's goals could bring Champions League glory to Stamford Bridge once more. Having been money shy at the Goodison Park transfer table last summer, this time around surely Abramovich would not hesitate making funds available for the signing.

Even if Chelsea were asked to pay £100 million for Lukaku, a player whom the London club returned a profit of at least £10 million on when selling him to Everton, in real terms, the deal for a world-class player with a minimum of eight years of his best football ahead of him wouldn't actually cost Abramovich that much given the Blues coffers were brimful with cash from the recent sales of Oscar and Patrick Bamford and would be further swelled if Costa were sold.

I'd always thought that Lukaku might be the player to come somewhere near to challenging Sir Frank Lampard's goalscoring record at Chelsea. To be honest, I'd like Lampard's record to remain intact for the rest of my natural, but then if Lukaku did come back to the Bridge and beat it, it would only mean one thing… more glory for the Blues. Let's see how that one pans out then.

12 February

Premier League
Burnley 1 Chelsea 1
Turf Moor
Attendance: 21,744
Referee: Kevin Friend

Chelsea (3-4-3): Thibaut Courtois, Cesar Azpilicueta, David Luiz, Gary Cahill (c), Victor Moses, N'Golo Kante, Nemanja Matic (Cesc Fabregas 67), Marcos Alonso, Pedro (Michy Batshuayi 87), Diego Costa, Eden Hazard.
Scorer: Pedro 7

THE ITALIAN JOB

Booked: David Luiz 75, Fabregas 90

Burnley (4-4-2): Heaton; Lowton, Keane, Mee, Ward, Boyd, Barton, Westwood, Brady (Arfield 64), Barnes, Gray (Vokes 82).
Scorer: Brady 24
Booked: Westwood 68, Lowton 77, Barton 88

Liverpool beating Tottenham 2-0 at Anfield the previous day meant Chelsea had a temporary chance to open up a 12-point gap at the top of the table by beating Burnley at Turf Moor… but it wasn't to be.

Pedro's 7th minute opener was cancelled out by a well-taken Robbie Brady free-kick 15 minutes later, and that pretty much was that. Coming away from 'fortress' Burnley (at the time the Clarets boasted the third best home record in the league after Chelsea and Spurs) with only a point after a scrappy game in trying conditions wasn't the worst eventuality that could have befallen the Blues… although the nappy-shitters, out in force on social media, painted a picture so bleak you'd have thought Conte had blown the title. A draw was better than a loss, and Chelsea still headed the Premier League by ten points although this could be cut to eight should Manchester City defeat Bournemouth in the final fixture of the game-week the following day.

Animated amidst the Turf Moor snow flurries, Conte cut an increasingly frustrated figure in the Chelsea technical area as he watched his side fail to build on the advantage Pedro's well-executed early goal had provided and subsequently create little in the way of chances to re-take the initiative after Burnley equalised.

Diego Costa's goals that helped power Chelsea to the top of the league had dried up. A third successive blank against Burnley, a game in which Costa managed just two shots, both of which were easily blocked, was a cause for concern, and Conte, given the apparent lack of trust in the capabilities of Michy Batshuayi, didn't appear to have a compelling Plan B. Was that me shitting my nappy as well just there?

As Chelsea toiled against obdurate opponents, wing-backs Marcos Alonso and, to a somewhat lesser extent, Victor Moses were less effective than they had been in previous games and as a consequence Costa didn't enjoy the type of service he had been used to in the past. That said, the Blues striker did compensate for this by linking up well with Pedro and Eden Hazard but he still failed to self-generate the type of chances he was converting earlier in the season.

Conte's use of substitutes, Cesc Fabregas replacing Nemanja Matic in the 67th minute and Willian replacing Moses in the 72nd minute brought with it a switch to 4-2-4 with Pedro playing wide left and Willian wide right. It was an admirable change of tactics and might have borne fruit had the Italian made the adjustments earlier in the game. Half-time could have been a productive call and might have caught Burnley out before they had time to adjust, because as it transpired Clarets centre-back Michael Keane was in no mood to concede an inch to Costa and co. nor were his fellow defenders.

The late introduction of Batyshuayi who replaced Pedro in the 87th minute, told it's own story as Conte persisted with Costa to the dour end. It was now 329 minutes since the striker had scored the last of this season to date's 15 Premier League goals, and the question the Blues boss had to be asking himself was what would happen to Chelsea's points advantage over their rivals if the drought continued?

If Costa's dip in form was just a blip that all strikers went through now and again, then perhaps there was nothing to be worried about… but the nagging doubt remained that last month's brouhaha might have had a damaging psychological effect on the player.

Costa's last clear-cut chance to score was the penalty he'd taken against Liverpool which was saved by Simon Mignolet. Had he beaten Mignolet, Chelsea would almost certainly have won the game 2-1 and Costa would have taken the plaudits. Whatever may or may not have been playing on the striker's mind about the future would have been forgotten in an instant. Costa's was a big game player and that would have been a big game goal. In the Arsenal match that followed, for all Chelsea's superiority as they coasted to a 3-1 victory, Costa had noticeably faded from view in the second-half… that vital spark was missing and it remained the case against Burnley.

Next on the fixture list was an FA Cup tie with Championship side Wolverhampton Wanderers. Typically Conte would be expected to rotate heavily with Costa likely to be 'rested' as Batshuayi got another chance to impress. Perhaps Conte might consider playing Costa from the start or giving him a decent 30 minutes off the bench. A striker needs goals, and the Wolves match might present Costa with an opportunity to rediscover his mojo ahead of a home league game with rejuvenated Swansea City. The flip side of course was that Batshuayi might power a hattrick in the cup game… a feat that could convince Conte to give him some serious game time in league matches.

Fortunately for the Chelsea manager, with Pedro now finding the net regularly and Hazard looking back to his best, the Blues did have goals elsewhere in them so the concern over Costa wasn't a crisis just yet!

15 February

Chelsea's Under-18s progressed to the semi-finals of the FA Youth Cup by beating Leicester City 1-0 at the King Power Stadium. Ike Ugbo scored the only goal of an edgy game in which manager Jody Morris persisted with the more traditional 4-3-3 set-up that had served him well in the preceding round.

17 February

"I like to win every competition in every season. For sure, it won't be easy in the league or the FA Cup," said Conte with believable conviction ahead of the Wolves game. "If you ask me if I want to try to win both competitions? Yes for sure. We must have this winning mentality. When you are a Chelsea coach or player you must have the ambition to win every competition you play."

With the top-flight teams still in the competition all facing lower league opposition, it was going to be an interesting weekend. Would any of the 'giants' be killed? If Chelsea, Man City, Man U, Arsenal, Spurs, Burnley, Middlesbrough and Leicester City all prevailed, then the quarterfinal draw would likely see some heavyweights paired together.

There were hopes in some quarters that Millwall might cause an upset and beat struggling Leicester… and then draw Chelsea. That would be one hell of a day for the daydreamers on social media who still masturbated while watching endless reruns of *The Football Factory* … but would no doubt come up with a catalogue of excuses as to why they couldn't attend the game should it materialise.

From a personal point of view, I was hoping my local non-league team Sutton United could cause the upset of the century and beat Arsenal at their wonderfully anachronistic Gander Green Lane home. They'd already seen off once mighty Dirty Leeds of the Championship on their 3G 'plastic' pitch and with the Gunners giddy from a 5-1 midweek Champions League hiding by Bayern Munich was the impossible a possibility?

I'd be watching with interest on Monday night and listening out for my favourite Sutton chant which had a degree of familiarity for Chelsea supporters who reside in my North Surrey manor. *Forever and ever, we'll follow our team. We're Sutton United, we rule supreme. We'll never be mastered, by those Carshalton bastards, We'll keep the yellow flag flying high. U's U's U's U's U's!*

18 February

FA Cup Fifth Round
Wolverhampton Wanderers 0 Chelsea 2
Molineux
Attendance: 30,193
Referee: Jonathan Moss

Chelsea (3-4-3): Asmir Begovic, Kurt Zouma, John Terry (c), Nathan Ake, Victor Moses, Cesc Fabregas, Nathaniel Chalobah, Pedro (Cesar Azpilicueta 72), Willian (N'Golo Kante 80), Diego Costa, Eden Hazard Hazard (Ruben Loftus-Cheek 85).
Scorers: Pedro 64, Diego Costa 89
Booked: Pedro 48

Wolverhampton Wanderers (4-2-3-1): Ikeme, Coady, Batth (c), Hause, Doherty, Price, Saville (Saiss 83), Costa, Edwards, Weimann (Wilson 74), Bodvarsson (Ronan 83).
Booked: Saville 20, Weimann 32

Chelsea booked their place in the quarterfinals of the FA Cup via a laboured 2-0 defeat of Wolves at Molineux where the attendance for the visit of the Premier League leaders was the highest for 36 years. After a turgid first-half in which the Blues failed to assert any kind of authority over the struggling Championship side it appeared that the game was headed for stalemate and a replay, but Pedro whose appetite for goals in this season's competition seemed insatiable had other ideas.

In the 64th minute, a wonderful triangular passage of play in the Wolves penalty area saw Eden Hazard pass to Willian and the Brazilian loft a perfectly flighted ball for Pedro to head Chelsea into the lead. The Spaniard, deployed very effectively from an attacking perspective at left-wing-back by Antonio Conte, had darted undetected behind the home defence and was perfectly placed to score. Four goals, two assists and counting... would Pedro's cup form continue? He was certainly worth backing in the anytime goal scorer markets for those who liked a flutter.

Seeing fellow Premier League sides Burnley and Leicester City suffer ignominious defeats to lowly opposition in the respective guise of non-league Lincoln City and League One Millwall earlier in the day, and Manchester City held to a draw by Championship outfit Huddersfield Town may have convinced Conte to start Diego Costa up front... the striker's selection was definitely a surprise.

Whether it was planned from the outset or not, once again the Blues boss made the right call as Costa, who'd proved a handful for the Wolves backline throughout the game, finally unshackled his markers a minute from time to seal victory for Chelsea. After 413 blank minutes it was a big plus from a confidence point of view for the player who validated his inclusion in the side. Poor Michy Batyshuayi though... I wondered what the kid must be thinking. The previous week I'd drunkenly tweeted him my support, never expecting a reply … but I got one saying 'thanks'... decent that to be fair.

Nathaniel Chalobah and Cesc Fabregas paired in the midfield engine room played well together. Chalobah had by now definitely edged ahead of his academy graduate rivals as the kid most likely to establish himself in Chelsea's first team. Whether or not that would actually happen remained to be seen, but the 22-year old did his credentials no harm at all with another robust performance. As for Fabregas, he simply oozed class... but I doubted it would lead to anything other than a place on the bench when Chelsea returned to Premier League action against Swansea the following week.

The 2-0 win did mask a few areas of concern. An alien-looking back three of Kurt Zouma, John Terry and Nathan Ake lacked the cohesiveness and understanding of regular trio Cesar Azpilicueta, David Luiz and Gary Cahill while Hazard didn't look remotely interested for much of the contest. Would Chelsea have had more of a cutting edge earlier on had Conte opted to play one of the younger players with a point to prove, Ruben Loftus-Cheek or Batshuayi for example? We'll never know... and of course the result ultimately meant it didn't matter.

The aftermath of the match saw Antonio Conte provide an intriguing insight into the thinking behind his selection process for FA Cup games. "If the player deserves to play I am pleased to give them the opportunity, but not because there is sentiment," explained the Italian. "The right way is to give every single player what they deserve."

So presumably Batshuayi deserved nothing. Harsh... but I wasn't going to rail against Conte's reasoning.

"Don't forget our target is to win, not to try to make all the players happy," continued the Blues boss. "The right choices are important and, for example, I thought for Diego it was very important to play and to score. For me it was very important to find a new solution with two wingers as wing-backs. It is important to always find the best solution."

It all made sense. Conte made sense... and the result... well there you go.

19 February

At around 6.30pm the draw for the quarterfinals of the FA Cup was made. Chelsea's ball, number 6, was the first out of the velvet bag. I swear the collective intake of breath among Blues supporters caused trees to bend in China as I stood in front of the TV in my kitchen... Sunday dinner preparations put on hold momentarily. Was it really going to be number 8, Millwall? God help us! No, instead it was number 3, Manchester United. Brilliant! José back at the Bridge again. Given the 4-0 hiding his Red Devils' team received when he'd returned earlier in the season, the Special One would be desperate to avoid a repeat... it would make for an interesting contest in more ways than the obvious one.

20 February

Arsenal shocked the football world by beating Sutton United 2-0 at Gander Green Lane. The Gunners reward for this remarkable feat, a home quarterfinal tie against fellow giant-killers Lincoln City.

23 February

Antonio Conte took time out from his regular football routine to meet with Eddie Jones the head coach of the England rugby union team. In similar fashion to Conte, Jones had transformed England's fortunes with his side currently on a 16-game winning streak. "Eddie is a winner and he is transferring that mentality on to the team," said a clearly impressed Conte. "It is important for me to compare my work and experience with another sport to gain inspiration and tactical ideas for the future."

Interesting stuff. Rather than resting on his laurels, Conte was pushing the boundaries in a way that set him apart from his peers.

What next? Well how about this!

THE ITALIAN JOB

"When your name is Chelsea, you must always fight to win,' advised Antonio Conte, speaking later in the day at a special dinner held in his honour which had been organised by the Chelsea Pitch Owners. How could any Blues supporter not love this fella?

Meanwhile, Leicester City decided to sack manager Claudio Ranieri the man who had guided them to the Premier League title the previous year. Shades of Chelsea dispensing with José Mourinho in 2015 six months after he won the title. But whereas I didn't feel massively sorry for Mourinho who was the architect-in-chief of his own misfortune, Ranieri perhaps deserved better. Unfortunately, there was little or no sentiment in the majority of football club boardrooms these days.

24 February

"He reached a dream to win the title. I'm disappointed as a friend and as a coach," said Conte when asked about Ranieri's sacking at his weekly press conference. "I was already sacked this season by the bookmakers," joked the Chelsea manager when asked if he was concerned about being sacked after winning the title.

25 February

Premier League
Chelsea 3 Swansea City 1
Stamford Bridge
Attendance: 41,612
Referee: Neil Swarbrick

Chelsea (3-4-3): Thibaut Courtois, Cesar Azpilicueta, David Luiz, Gary Cahill (c), Victor Moses (Kurt Zouma 84), N'Golo Kante, Cesc Fabregas, Marcos Alonso, Pedro (Nemanja Matic 75), Diego Costa, Eden Hazard (Willian 84).
Scorers: Fabregas 19, Pedro 71, Diego Costa 84
Booked: David Luiz 74

Swansea (4-3-3): Fabianski, Naughton, Fernandez, Mawson, Olsson, Carroll (Ayew 75), Fer, Cork (c), Routledge (Narsingh 80), Llorente, Sigurdsson.
Scorer: Llorente 45+1
Booked: Naughton 34, Olsson 35, Fer 79

A 10th consecutive home victory in the Premier League (a club record-equalling 12 in all competitions) provided a welcome reminder of Chelsea's formidable title credentials. Cesc Fabregas marked his 300th appearance in the English top flight by scoring the opening goal in the 19th minute and moments later, with the Blues crowd still singing about his famous magic hat, the Spaniard might have bagged another had a fierce drive which struck the Swansea crossbar been a couple of inches lower.

Buoyed by the recent appointment of one-time Chelsea assistant manager Paul Clement who had brought in Blues legend Claude Makalele as his second in command, prior to this fixture, the Swans had won four of their last six league games and hauled themselves up from the relegation basement to 15th place... clearly they were not going to lie down easily.

Against Burnley, a blundering Nemanja Matic foul had resulted in a free-kick from which Robbie Brady powered the ball past Thibaut Courtois for the Clarets equaliser. Conte would have had words about that and of course we all knew that Chelsea would be ill advised to ignore set-pieces against Swansea who in Gylfi Sigurdsson had a master of the dark arts when it came to addressing a dead ball.

How about a bit of déjà vu then?

In first-half stoppage time, the Blues defence probably thought there was little risk in Sigurdsson taking a free-kick inside the centre circle. What a fool's errand that turned out to be. The Iceland international floated a wonderful ball that was met perfectly by the head of Fernando Llorente. Goal! 1-1.

So that was Llorente then. The 32-year old journeyman Spaniard, who played for Antonio Conte at Juventus and whose full name, Fernando Javier Llorente Torres, carried Chelsea connotations, had been a rumoured January transfer target for the Blues. Conte wouldn't have been too happy with what he had just witnessed... it probably made him wish he'd signed the player!

After his recent meeting with England rugby union supremo Eddie Jones, Conte had spoken of gaining tactical ideas. Now rugby is about ball handling skills... and early in the second-half Cesar Azpilicueta, under pressure from Sigurdsson (who else), appeared to have switched codes. The penalty area in front of The Shed is fair old distance from where I sit, but it certainly looked like an Azpi handball. Fortunately, referee Neil Swarbrick thought differently. Siggy protested, as did the Swansea fans at that end of the ground... Swarbrick gave nothing and suddenly Chelsea were in the ascendancy again.

Former Arsenal goalkeeper Lukasz Fabianski had made several important saves and blocks before living up to his old 'Flappyhandski' nickname in the 72nd minute when Pedro, neatly played in by man-of-the-match Fabregas, fired a speculative curling shot at goal. The ball somehow squirmed through Fabianski's grasp and into the net. 2-1

In an irresistible vein of form, Pedro had been directly involved in 10 goals in his past nine games for Chelsea in all competitions (seven goals, three assists). Good stats... there was only going to be one winner now, and six minutes from time after some excellent skills from Eden Hazard, Diego Costa fired home his 16th league goal of the campaign to give the final score a more emphatic feel about it. 3-1

Chelsea may have scored three goals and won the game, but the biggest cheer of the day came at half-time when club legend Frank Lampard walked on to the pitch to be greeted by the sight of a wonderful large banner paying tribute to him which was unfurled in the centre circle. *Super, Super Frank...* sang the crowd in unison.

When the chant died down, 'Sir' Frank said a few words that epitomised his spirit and highlighted the shared regret that he hadn't been able to say a proper farewell to Blues supporters at the time he's left the club. "I didn't get the chance to say goodbye properly last time, and I always regretted that. I want to thank all of you," he told a hushed crowd. "All my special memories of this place... and I'm thinking of them right now... I couldn't have done it without you. We couldn't have done that without you."

Goosebumps!

Another one of those special Chelsea memories to be filed away and recalled at some point in the future.

26 February

As expected, Manchester United won the first trophy of the season beating Southampton 3-2 EFL Cup final at Wembley. Much was made by the media of it being the first piece of silverware secured by José Mourinho for the Red Devils, but it was 35-year old two-goal 'hero' Zlatan Ibrahimovic who really stole the headlines. The duo were portrayed as the saviours of Man U... I was left savouring the prospect of Conte and Co. putting them firmly in their place in the FA Cup in a couple of weeks time… hopefully!

As I watched United labour to victory, I wondered if Mourinho might be thinking he needed more creativity and industry in the middle of the park? Having signed Willian for Chelsea back in 2013, come the summer transfer window would the Portuguese be back in for the 28-year old Brazil international who had been rendered bench fodder by the form of Pedro? A horrible thought came into my mind… Man U fans bastardising the Willian chant for their own purposes.

If Conte did decide Willian was surplus to requirements, I hoped that Chelsea would have the common sense to transfer him abroad rather than be seen to be strengthening a rival Premier League club and giving their supporters club the type of ammunition they could fire back at us with venom. Mind you, I then laughed at the fact that Harry Kane had scored hattrick for Tottenham Hotspur earlier in the day in a 4-0 rout of Stoke. Imagine the fun to be had if Chelsea signed Kane in the summer.

27 February

@chucklescabbie posted on twitter to say that he had just picked up Antonio Conte in his taxi. London's finest black cab driver admitted serenading the Chelsea manager with a one man version of *Antonio, Antonio, Antonio* but did not divulge any further details which left him open to some merciless leg-pulling at the cfcuk stall for the remainder of the season.

MARCH 2017

2 March

Reports bubbled up in the Italian media that Antonio Conte was homesick and mulling over a return to Serie A where Inter Milan, flush with cash thanks to, yes you can guess, new Chinese owners, were reported to be willing to offer him a contract worth £10 million per year. The funny thing about this story was that Conte's wife Elisabetta and his daughter had already planned to move to London in the summer.

Later in the evening Conte was presented with the Manager of the Year award at the London Football Awards held at Battersea Evolution. Nice to win, but what short year's these people have! Also recognized on the night was Chelsea midfielder N'Golo Kante (Player of the Year) and Frank Lampard who received the Outstanding Contribution to London Football Award.

6 March
Premier League
West Ham United 1 Chelsea 2
London Stadium
Attendance: 56,984
Referee: Andre Marriner

Chelsea (3-4-3): Thibaut Courtois, Cesar Azpilicueta, David Luiz, Gary Cahill (c), Victor Moses (Kurt Zouma 77), N'Golo Kante, Cecs Fabregas (Nemanja Matic 64), Marcos Alonso, Pedro, Diego Costa, Eden Hazard (Willian 74).
Scorers: Hazard 25, Diego Costa 50.
Booked: Fabregas 45+2

West Ham (4-3-3): Randolph, Kouyate, Fonte, Reid (Byram 64), Cresswell, Noble (c) (Fernandes 77), Snodgrass, Obiang, Feghouli (Ayew 64), Carroll, Lanzini.
Scorer: Lanzini 90+2

Ahh the joys of Monday night football. Despite Sky disturbing the usual pre match tension equilibrium of a regular weekend to further their aims of televisual domination, it was business as usual for Chelsea at the London stadium where goals from Eden Hazard and Diego Costa sealed a 21st top-flight victory of the campaign for the Blues. Manuel Lanzini's stoppage-time goal made for a slightly jittery final few seconds, but in the end it was scant consolation for the home side who were properly mastered in their new back yard by the Premier League leaders.

Antonio Conte kept faith with the same starting XI that saw off Swansea meaning that Cesc Fabregas retained his place in the side ahead of Nemanja Matic, and the Italian also got his tactics spot on to nullify the aerial threat of West Ham's 6ft 4in striker Andy Carroll with Gary Cahill and Victor Moses in particular deserving credit in this respect.

On their own patch, in what was fortunately a much calmer environment for visiting Chelsea supporters than it had been for the EFL Cup tie earlier in the season, West Ham enjoyed a bright opening spell keeping possession but failing to break down the Blues well-drilled rear-guard.

When it came, midway through the first-half, there was an air of inevitability about Chelsea's first goal… a counter-attacking gem initiated by a deep-lying N'Golo Kante who was perfectly placed to read and intercept an attempted pass by Hammers midfielder Robert Snodgrass. Kante fed Hazard who surged forward, played a delightful one-two with Pedro and then teased West Ham keeper Darren Randolph into committing himself before slotting the ball into the net. 1-0, let that be a lesson to you.

The goal silenced the home crowd. *You're not West Ham anymore* chanted a buoyant Blue army, a barbed reference to the Hammers leaving Upton Park for the vacuous London Stadium and the recent news that Chelsea would be remaining at their ancestral Fulham home.

Earlier in the day Mayor of London Sadiq Khan had given his approval to Chelsea's new stadium declaring his confidence that it would be "a jewel in London's sporting crown". Careful use of 'a' rather than 'the', but looking once more at the drawings… and West Ham's folly… 'the' would not have been wide of the mark.

The taunts didn't stop there either. West Ham lacked Chelsea's creativity, clearly missing the mercurial skills of France international Dimitri Payet who has been sold in the January transfer window following a player power, hero to zero-style spat. *He left cos your shit* was a damming indictment of a club that had failed and continued to fail its loyal fans who deserved better.

Chelsea's second goal was a far simpler affair. A poorly defended Cesc Fabregas corner five minutes after the break was thighed in by Costa for his 17th Premier League goal of the campaign. *Antonio, Antonio, Antonio* chirruped Chelsea supporters joyfully.

Taking no risks, Conte soon withdrew Pedro bringing on Matic and adjusting his set up from 3-4-3 to 3-5-2 with Hazard joining Costa up front. The duo worked well together and Costa might have added to his tally when teed up by his teammate but Randolph pulled off a fine save. Chelsea continued to dominate and Fabregas might also have given the score a more emphatic look if a fizzing shot had dipped a little lower.

There was an unnecessary scrappy carelessness about Lanzini's goal, the build-up to which saw Andre Ayew allowed the freedom of a by now 4/5 empty London Stadium… but criticism would be harsh on Chelsea. That said, Thibaut Courtois looked furious about losing the clean sheet… maybe it affected the Belgium international's bonus?

After the game, Courtois' annoyance was put into plain English by Conte. "I think we played a good game. We controlled the game," said the Italian. "It's just a pity for the goal we conceded at the end. To give away a clean sheet at the end is not good. We must improve in this situation. But I'm pleased. We showed great concentration and commitment and will to win."

*****

With 11 games remaining, the Blues current 10-point advantage at the top of the table was beginning to look unassailable, but with that came an element of concern.

Given the always evident commitment and winning mentality that manager Antonio Conte displayed which he had so clearly instilled in his players, there was zero chance of complacency creeping into the Chelsea dressing room and the Italian continued to nip any growing sense of self-entitlement in the bud by constantly playing down his team's position. Of course it was the right thing to do, but given the current scenario Blues supporters were struggling to keep a lid on the urge to chant *we're gonna win the league*.

There was no doubt that Conte was the originator of Chelsea's inexorable revival from last season's shambles. Tactical master class had followed tactical master class with every member of the team displaying a complete understanding of their manager's gameplan. It was a joy to watch.

Throughout the campaign, every player that had featured regularly in the side had earned praise and all of it had been well justified. When it came to week-in-week-out consistency though none could match the qualities of midfielder N'Golo Kante who was without doubt the crucial cog in Conte's Chelsea machine.

There was a joke doing the rounds on social media after the West Ham victory that Leicester City bought the Premier League title for £5.6 million and sold it to Chelsea for £32 million… the reference of course being Kante. The funny thing was though, that it did appear to be more than coincidental… and even funnier for Blues fans was the fact that Kante twice resisted the overtures of Arsenal manager Arsene Wenger preferring to join Conte's Chelsea revolution instead.

Prior to arriving in England, Kante had spent two seasons with unfashionable France Ligue 1 side Caen… who notably were in Ligue 2 when he'd joined them from Boulogne in August 2013 and won promotion in his first season with the club.

Arriving at Leicester under the radar in August 2015, Kante gradually began to gain acclaim as Claudio Ranieri's side started defying their 5000/1 title odds… that said, it was teammates Riyad Mahrez and Jamie Vardy whose goals grabbed the headlines. As the Foxes won the title, Mahrez, Vardy and Ranieri picked up various end of season awards, while Kante had to make do with being named in the PFA Team of the Year.

Would Leicester have won the title without Kante's 175 tackles and 157 interceptions (more than any other player in the league)? It's a question that could be answered with a big retrospective No! Since Kante left the King Power Stadium for Stamford Bridge last July, Leicester's form, despite retaining the services of Mahrez, Vardy, and up until his recent dismissal, Ranieri, had collapsed. Conversely, Chelsea benefited markedly from having the diminutive powerhouse in their ranks. Kante may stand just a fraction over 5ft 6in… but what the 25-year old lacked in height he made up for in boundless box-to-box energy.

Against West Ham, goals from Eden Hazard and Diego Costa may have sealed victory for Chelsea, but it was Kante's stealth and determination that smoothed the passage to another precious three points and it had been the same story throughout the season. Understated could be Kante's middle name. It was incredible to think that the Paris-born player's talent went unnoticed by the France international set-up for so long. Kante did not feature in any of his country's junior sides and had only earned his first cap just over a year ago. (26 March 2016 Netherland 2 France 3)

Recognition comes in many guises… and for Kante, hopefully last week's London Football Awards Player of the Year award would be eclipsed next month by the PFA Player of the Year award and a bevy of other similar gongs. If Chelsea did go on to win the league, Kante would become the first player to win back-to-back titles since his France countryman Eric Cantona achieved the feat with Leeds United in 1992 and Manchester United the following season… and the stage would be set for him to take a maiden bow in the Champions League.

Conte would almost certainly strengthen his squad in the summer as he made a bid for European glory. Some players places in his current side may well come under threat, but Kante's wouldn't be one of them with first-name-on-the-team-sheet status unlikely to change.

7 March

As Chelsea's stock continued to rise under the guidance of outstanding manager Antonio Conte, across London rivals Arsenal were experiencing a downturn in fortune that had an unsettling look about it for the Emirates club and was proving to be a source of amusement for Blues supporters.

Having lost 5-1 to Bayern Munich at the Allianz Arena in the first leg of a Round of 16 tie, Arsenal were defeated by the same remarkable score at the Emirates. "Imagine losing 10-2 to Bayern in the last 16 instead of doing them in their own stadium to win the whole competition" tweeted @HarrisCharles5 Charlie had a point. Maybe Chelsea could profit from the debacle unfolding in London N5.

A lot had happened in the six months since Arsene Wenger's team raced into that horrible 3-0 first-half lead against Conte's shell-shocked troops. The Italian's change of tactics soon catapulted Chelsea to the top of the Premier League table while Wenger had gone from hero to zero as Arsenal lost their way. That 10-2 mauling by Bayern had amplified the Frenchman's problems as did recent stories of a training ground bust up with star player Alexis Sanchez who was subsequently dropped for the recent game with Liverpool (which also ended in defeat) and remained in a state of contract limbo having yet to agree terms on a new deal.

The Sanchez scenario was redolent of the drama that had enveloped Chelsea striker Diego Costa in January when the Blues forward rowed with a fitness coach and was also had his head turned by a phenomenal £30 a year salary offer to decamp to the Chinese Super League. Conte had taken that situation by the scruff of the neck and dropped his top scorer and soon after it had been business as usual with Costa finding the net regularly again as Chelsea's relentless pursuit of title glory continued.

Like Sanchez, Costa was also haggling over a new contract however it had been reported that the striker was now close to signing a five-year deal worth £57 million. Arsenal meanwhile were allegedly some £100k adrift of their prize asset's £300k-a-week demands and with a huge question mark against the future of Wenger and success proving elusive, the sale of Sanchez who would have just a year left on his current deal at the end of the campaign looked a real possibility.

Sanchez to Chelsea was a story that had already done the rounds, and notwithstanding Arsenal's stance that they would not sell the player to a domestic rival, Blues owner Roman Abramovich, with his mind already on a return to the grand European stage, wouldn't hesitate opening his wallet to sign the 28-year old should Conte make a case to him to do so.

With the Chile international able to play any of the front three positions, the mouth-watering prospect of Eden Hazard, Sanchez and Costa lining up together drew parallels with the potent Barcelona triumvirate of Luis Suarez, Lionel Messi and Neymar who were about to make a telling contribution to the Catalan club's record-breaking Champions League Round of 16 recovery against Paris Saint-Germain.

Sanchez it was who had opened the scoring against Chelsea in that 3-0 rout at the Emirates last September. Taking advantage of a mistake by Blues defender Gary Cahill, the Arsenal forward had charged away with the ball and beaten Thibaut Courtois with a composed finish. The Chilean had scored 20 goals in all competitions for the Gunners so far this season and netted 62 times across 128 appearances since his arrival from Barcelona in July 2014. Decent stats eh Mr Abramovich?

Sanchez's versatility as a striker, and his willingness to tackle-back made him an ideal proposition for Conte's tactical template that typically started with 3-4-3 and shifted to 3-5-2 when the time came to close out a game. What was also compelling about his potential acquisition was it becalmed concerns about Hazard being wooed by Real Madrid, a rumour that had been doing the rounds for almost two seasons. Similarly, should the sometime surly Costa throw another tantrum that irked Conte then Sanchez would make for an ideal replacement.

Interestingly enough, although Arsenal made lots of noises about their reluctance to sell Sanchez to a top-flight rival, when it came to Chelsea there was a history of high-profile deals between the two clubs which suggested that if the money was right a player could be moved on.

Current Arsenal keeper Petr Cech spent over a decade at Stamford Bridge before moving to the Emirates for £10 million in June 2015. While Chelsea supporters were initially annoyed at the deal, their anger soon dissipated. The same could not be said for their Arsenal counterparts in 2006 when Gunners left-back Ashley Cole failed to agree terms on a new deal and signed for Chelsea in a cash plus player deal that involved William Gallas. Arsenal fans never forgave Cole for his perceived mercenary treachery, but it was water off a duck's back for the England star who'd smiled in the face of the taunts whenever he faced his old club and typically turned in a five-star performance.

Should Sanchez sign for Chelsea a flurry of 'Alexis 7' Arsenal shirt burning could be expected from irate Gunners fans accompanied by an hysterical meltdown on their fans TV channel which had already provided plenty of hilarity since its inception. Putting the value Sanchez would bring to Conte's team to one side for a moment, from a Blues' supporter perspective it would be worth Abramovich making the player his marquee signing of the summer to see just the reactions of those who once idolised him.

*****

The build up to the Manchester United cup tie… Monday night football again Grrr… was always going to be about José Mourinho more than anyone or anything else. Writing in the season ticket renewal letter that went out to Man U fans, Mourinho had been gushing about their support and the club in general… well he would be… best club, best fans, best atmosphere… yeah, yeah… never kid a kidder José eh?

Truthfully, Mourinho's track record of slating the supporters of the club's he'd managed was as impressive as his record of winning silverware. Earlier in the season he'd dug out Man U fans for not creating a buzz at Old Trafford, and he'd done the same in his last stint as Chelsea manager when he'd described the atmosphere at Stamford Bridge as "not very hot" following a 2-2 draw with West Bromwich Albion in November 2013. A couple of years later he'd admitted to being 'embarrassed' when those same supporters, whom he described as 'unbelievable', chanted his name, and continued to do so, when he lost the plot not long after winning the title. Fickle? Ha ha Football's a fickle business and Mourinho a fickle businessman... he was hardly going to write that Man U fans lacked passion in a document aimed at getting them to part with several hundred pounds.

A genuine curio associated with the tie and indeed all FA Cup quarterfinals was football's governing body once again pandering to the whims of the television companies by announcing that for the first time there would be no replays at this stage of the competition should any match end in a draw. At Stamford Bridge, should José decide to park the bus (remember that shit?) extra time and then penalties would ensue. Not only that, but if a manager had made all three substitutions available to him in normal time, a fourth sub could be made in extra time. Whatever next?

13 March
FA Cup Quarterfinal
Chelsea 1 Manchester United 0
Stamford Bridge
Attendance: 40,801
Referee: Michael Oliver

Chelsea (3-4-3): Thibaut Courtois, Cesar Azpilicueta, David Luiz, Gary Cahill (c), Victor Moses (Kurt Zouma 88), N'Golo Kante, Nemanja Matic, Marcos Alonso, Willian (Cesc Fabregas 81), Diego Costa (Michy Batshuayi 90+4), Eden Hazard.
Scorer: Kante 51
Booked: Diego Costa 87

Man Utd (4-4-1-1): De Gea, Jones, Smalling (c), Rojo, Darmian, Valencia, Herrera, Pogba, Young (Lingard 81), Mkhitaryan (Fellaini 37), Rashford.
Sent off: Herrera 35 (second yellow)
Booked: Herrera 20, Young 78

There was no need for extra time, no need for extra men (though Man U could have done without losing one) and no need for penalties as a solitary goal from Chelsea's man-of-the-moment N'Golo Kante proved to be the Blues match-winner in what was a predictably feisty encounter under the Stamford Bridge floodlights.

THE ITALIAN JOB

As expected (no need for Mystic Meg's crystal ball with this one), José Mourinho ended up dominating the headlines for all the wrong reasons and the angst the Portuguese generated deserved a few paragraphs of its own… but first the football.

In the three preceding rounds of this season's FA Cup competition that Chelsea had contested, Antonio Conte had rotated his squad and given fringe players and the youth a chance to prove what they could do. Fine against lower league opposition. The question on many Blues supporters lips pre-match at the cfcuk stall was would Conte up the ante against Man U or would he go the same way as before given the news that illness, injury, and the suspension of leading scorer Zlatan Ibrahimovic?

@chucklescabbie was convinced John Terry was going to start, I wasn't too sure myself. There was a general air of confidence about Chelsea's chances which @MIBIAL and myself shared which made us apprehensive slightly as being long-in-the-tooth, we recognised this hadn't been advisable in the past… but there you go. I fancied 2-0 with Pedro to finding the net to maintain his record of scoring in every round. I placed my bet on the Spaniard to score and waited for @chucklescabbie to read out the team news when it was announced one hour before kick-off.

Ha ha, well Conte surprised us there then. No Terry and no Pedro. In fact the Italian made only two changes from the side that won at West Ham last time out. Amusingly, United's line-up featured young Marcus Rashford up front. The prodigious striker had been reported as being 'ill' and not fit to play earlier in the day. Maybe Mourinho was trying to trick Conte into fielding a more experimental line-up as opposed to his big guns? Epic fail!

The atmosphere inside the Bridge was rocking. 6,000 noisy Mancs in The Shed played their part in the moments before kick-off, and the lights down, *Liquidator* did the rest. The early exchanges were measured, and United's fans continued to make a racket. It was good to see the underdogs enjoying themselves… just like Peterborough and Brentford's supporters had… smile.

Eden Hazard had Chelsea's first big chance shortly after the quarter-hour mark. A balletic turn saw him bamboozle Chris Smalling and off he went on one of those mazy runs of his… we were out of our seats. Here we go, that goal against Arsenal all over again. But no! United keeper David De Gea tipped Hazard's flashing low drive around the post for a corner which Willian took, and the Spain international stopper had to be at his best again to deny Gary Cahill a certain goal when the Chelsea centre-back jabbed the ball towards the net.

It was all Chelsea, all Hazard. The Blues creative midfielder was certainly getting some stick, and Ander Herrera soon found his way into Michael Oliver's notebook for an ungainly block that sent the Chelsea man sprawling to the grass. Phil Jones too was in the thick of the skulduggery, playing a hefty-booted version of *me and my shadow* with Hazard.

10 minutes before the break, Man U were down to 10 men. Having had words with Jones about another clunking tackle on Hazard, moments later Oliver took umbrage with Herrera when the United man tripped the same Chelsea player from behind. Enough was enough. Red card Herrera. Hazard, evidently the Mourinho-orchestrated target for bully-boy tactics, would also later fall victim to cynical fouling from Antonio Valencia and a stamping touch of actual bodily harm courtesy of Marcos Rojo.

On the touchline, Mourinho and Conte jousted and kept fourth official Mike Jones occupied. In the stands some chanted *Fuck off Mourinho*. A song United's fans once sang with gusto… now it was coming from the Chelsea sections. Harsh!

The second-half was barely five minutes old when Kante scored a rare but precious goal. Having lost the attentions of countryman Paul Pogba on the edge of the United penalty area, the France international took a couple of steps to his right and fired the ball low and hard beyond the despairing reach of De Gea and into the back of the net. Delirium!

Amusingly, before the game, I'd filmed a mystery man in a Kante mask singing a tribute to the Chelsea midfielder (worth a look if you have five minutes to peruse the video selection on the *gate17chelsea* YouTube channel). He started off with a simulated trumpet sound to the Johnny Cash tune of *Ring of Fire*, and then began to sing…

He covers every inch - N'Golo Kante.
Of every football pitch - N'Golo Kante.
Covers every blade of grass - N'Golo Kante.
And he'll leave you on your arse - N'Golo Kante.
£32 million pounds - N'Golo Kante.
Drives his mini to the ground - N'Golo Kante.

I wished everybody knew the song and could have burst into it after Kante scored… all those people pretending to be trumpets would have been brilliant. Would it catch on later in the season maybe?

THE ITALIAN JOB

United's response to Kante's goal was to almost immediately equalize as Smalling took the ball on and found Rashford who turned Cahill inside out before forcing a brilliant save out of Thibaut Courtois. Close but no cigar. The football gods were definitely on Chelsea's side tonight.

Diego Costa and Willian both had chances to increase the Blues advantage, but the goal-action was over. Oliver's final whistle was the cue for a rabble-rousing *One Step Beyond...* Chelsea were through to the semi-finals of the FA Cup. Wembley, here we come. The draw made shortly after the game finished paired the Blues with Tottenham Hotspur with Arsenal facing Manchester City in the other tie.

Speaking after the game Conte heaped praise on Eden Hazard. "He showed great character, strong character," said the Italian. "We want to play football and for the first 25 minutes it was impossible for Hazard to play because he got a lot of kicks."

Mourinho meanwhile... well where do you start?

In the days leading up to the Man U cup tie someone had asked me how I felt about Mourinho these days given the way things were at Chelsea now with meraviglioso Antonio Conte at the helm.

I'd scratched my head and given it plenty of thought. The best analogy I could come up with was that José was like a bunny boiler of an ex-girlfriend that I'd always had brilliant sex with who kept on turning up trying to ruin my perfect marriage. I'd loved her deeply, but she'd had to go because she was a proper roll and butter. Yeah, a nutter! One slate short of a roof! Two tacos short of a combination platter! Three carrots short of a casserole! Four clowns short of a circus! Barking mad! Dangerous even!

It was the best thing for both us... well for me anyway... to split up. I thought it would be easy... but I ended up having to get a restraining order... it got that bad. Of course in the end, it all calmed down. She met a millionaire, moved to Florida... and that was that.

So anyway... back to José.

When the FA Cup draw paired Chelsea with Man U there was every chance that irrespective of the outcome Mourinho would somehow find himself caught up centre-stage in a vortex of controversy.

Having won seven major trophies including three Premier League titles in two stints as Blues boss, statistically-speaking José was without any shadow of doubt Chelsea's greatest manager… a fact he was swift to remind the small section of home supporters who'd taunted him during the Red Devils 1-0 defeat at Stamford Bridge.

Cries of *Judas* and worse emanating from the normally sedate East Stand behind the technical area where Mourinho spent an increasingly agitated 90 minutes were countered irately by the 54-year old with a three-fingered reference to the league titles won and post-match comments that until this record was broken "Judas is number one".

Predictably, this led to an apocalyptic meltdown on social media where Mourinho had become an increasingly divisive figure among Chelsea supporters since he took the Old Trafford job.

Although there was plenty of evidence to suggest that the man once revered as the Special One by Blues fans the world over was the architect of his own downfall at the Bridge when he was unceremoniously sacked midway through last season, in general Mourinho had retained the respect, loyalty and love of the Chelsea populous to whom he had brought so much joy.

When Antonio Conte was appointed as his full time successor, few, Mourinho included probably, could have imagined the remarkable impact the Italian would have… not only in terms of resurrecting Chelsea's fortunes, but also by way of re-inventing the way football was played in the English top-flight.

The Blues were only two games into that Premier League record-equalling 13-match winning streak when Mourinho had returned to the Bridge for the first time as Man U manager. A cordial reception with no trace of malice from the home crowd and it was down to the business on the pitch. Let any arguments be settled there… 11 v 11.

Of course the fine detail is covered off earlier in this book. Chelsea steamrollered United 4-0. A breath-taking performance that made a bold statement about Conte's new regime. The Italian's unbridled touchline passion for the game and winning had already secured him the affection of Blues fans, and with his team beaten out of sight it got to the United boss who had words with his successor about over-celebrating. It seemed like a case of sour grapes. That and hearing the home fans repeatedly chanting *Antonio, Antonio, Antonio* must have been chastening for Mourinho, but that's football. Just as in real life, the world moves on.

THE ITALIAN JOB

Rather than leaving it at that and focussing on his job as Manchester United manager, for some reason unbeknown to anyone but himself, from time to time since that defeat Mourinho had made slyly veiled digs at Chelsea. For example… the supposed, in his opinion, 'defensive' style of play Conte apparently advocated, the fixture schedule, or the quality of support at the Bridge. Such remarks were water off a duck's back for many Blues fans who recalled his sledging style when he was the lord of SW6 and put it down as 'typical José ' pandering to his new audience… but like rust bubbling away beneath a bright shiny surface, for many others there was a corrosiveness about his demeanour these days which was starting to tarnish his outstanding legacy.

The Premier League table which at this time saw Chelsea top by 10 points and 17 points clear of sixth placed Man U didn't lie, nor did the fact that it was the Blues and not the Red Devils that had progressed to the semi-finals of the FA Cup. Surely this should be enough for Mourinho to give up the goading and realise that until he could get the better of Conte it made him look foolish, but sadly this seemed unlikely to happen. With Chelsea due at Old Trafford for a league fixture in a few weeks there would no doubt be more vituperation and associated supporter squabbling.

Conte had the ability and desire that suggested he could surpass Mourinho's notable feats as Chelsea manager… but he had yet to win a trophy with the Blues. Mourinho had already won the EFL Cup for Man U, but he knew he had to deliver more… and he would forever be beyond desperate to put one over his former employers.

How would it all end? That's an interesting question which to date has only been partially answered.

The truth is, like all grand love affairs that finish there can be a bittersweet element to the association. And, continuing the analogy, in the fullness of time, perhaps when Mourinho departed Man U and England for good, Chelsea supporters might unify once more to reminisce fondly about their love for the Special One and the silverware-lined glory of his madness.

Right now though, it was all about Conte… a new passion, a new true love. Un grande amore… as they say in Italy. And true love conquers all including Mourinho and Manchester United.

Antonio, Antonio… Antonio, Antonio, Antonio.

14 March

Any Chelsea victory over Tottenham Hotspur is welcome, and the Under-18s 2-1 win away at White Hart Lane in the First Leg of the FA Youth Cup was very well received indeed. Manager Jody Morris went with 3-4-3 and Reece James and Ike Ugbo provided the goals to give the Blues the edge in the tie.

18 March

Premier League
Stoke City 1 Chelsea 2
bet365 Stadium
Attendance: 27,724
Referee: Anthony Taylor

Chelsea (3-4-3): Thibaut Courtois, Cesar Azpilicueta, David Luiz, Gary Cahill (c), Victor Moses (Cesc Fabregas 70), N'Golo Kante, Nemanja Matic (Ruben Loftus-Cheek 82), Marcos Alonso, Willian (Kurt Zouma 88), Diego Costa, Pedro.
Scorers: Willian 13, Cahill 87
Booked: Costa 17, Fabregas 90+1

Stoke (4-4-2): Grant, Bardsley, Shawcross, Martins Indi, Pieters, Ramadan (Crouch 90+2), Cameron, Allen, Arnautovic, Walters, Berahino (Diouf 61).
Scorer: Walters 38
Sent off: Bardsley 90+3
Booked: Bardsley 40, Pieters 65, Martins Indi 65, Cameron 90

Chelsea's seemingly relentless march towards the Premier League title continued at the bet365 Stadium where a late Gary Cahill goal gave the Blues a 2-1 victory over Stoke City in a predictably feisty but thoroughly enjoyable to watch encounter.

A lively first-half saw Willian open the scoring for the visitors with a deft free-kick and the home side equalise via a debatable Jonathan Walters penalty conceded by Cahill.

Referee Anthony Taylor had his work cut out to keep on top of some brutish Stoke tackling with Chelsea striker Diego Costa involved in skirmish after skirmish, but in the end skill won the day and the Potters concluded the game with 10 men when Phil Bardsley was sent off for a second bookable offence.

Shorn of the services of Eden Hazard, Chelsea proved they could function admirably without their gifted playmaker and Cahill stepped up to the mark in true John Terry 'captain, leader, legend-style fashion. The defender's lion-hearted performance epitomised the never-say-die spirit of Antonio Conte's side.

Hazard, who'd been the victim of repeated actual bodily harm perpetrated by Man United's hatchet men on Monday, was reported to have succumbed to a muscle injury in training... just as well probably because his body might not have been able to withstand the thuggish challenges meted out by Stoke.

It's a curious fact that Mark Hughes' side got their reputation as being cloggers, a Sunday league pub side... etc etc during the two reigns of former manager Tony Pulis (whose new club West Brom had amusingly beaten Arsenal 3-1 earlier in the day), but this version of Stoke were worse than anything Pulis had ever presided over.

'Sparky' Hughes was popular in his time as a Chelsea striker and indeed is known to be a Blues fan... maybe he never got over the fact he missed out on the manager's job at Stamford Bridge when his star as a gaffer was in the ascendancy. Every time a Hughes-managed team had faced Chelsea... starting with over physical Blackburn Rovers and followed by Manchester City, Fulham, Queens Park Rangers and now Stoke it had been the same story... kick, grapple, maim... be horrible.

Once again, Antonio Conte deserved huge credit for his tactical approach to the game and overcoming the challenges that presented themselves as it unfolded. There was an interesting statistic that was bandied about online later in the day that highlighted the fact that Conte was the only manager in the top flight to have used all the substitutions available to him so far this season, and once again he did so to great effect against Stoke.

Having struggled to get the required cut through with his template 3-4-3, with the game mired at 1-1 and seemingly heading for a draw, Conte's introduction of Cesc Fabregas and the attendant switch to 4-2-3-1 gave Chelsea the added impetus they needed and later on the fresh legs of Ruben Loftus-Cheek and Kurt Zouma gave the Blues energy when they needed it to close out the match.

From a goal-scoring point of view Costa might have benefitted from the earlier introduction of Fabregas… that said, the Chelsea striker was too busy enjoying his duels with Ryan Shawcross, Bruno Martins Indi and Bardsley. Such skulduggery saw him booked as early as the 17th minute, but he continued with his battles and importantly drew attention away from creative teammates.

Handed a rare league start in place of Hazard, Willian served up a typical piece of Samba-style wizardry when tricking the Stoke defence and keeper Lee Grant into thinking he was going to cross a free-kick instead of firing at the goal. The ball squirmed past Grant who would have writhed with embarrassment later when watching replays of the goal.

There was no doubt at all who Chelsea's man of the match was… skipper Gary Cahill. Leading by example and putting a robust shift in in defence, Cahill had to be considered unlucky when Walters went to ground far too easily under his 'challenge' in the incident that led to the penalty from which the Stoke man scored. It was disappointing. The Blues defender was clearly gutted. But not for the first time in his Chelsea career he dug deep… determined to atone for his 'error'. The 'bingo' moment came in the 87th minute when a lose ball following a Fabregas corner found Cahill in space in the Stoke penalty area. Boom! Back of the net! An epic goal from an immense player who still continued to attract unnecessary criticism from social media trolls and keyboard warriors. Show 'em your medals Gary…

Travelling Blues supporters behind the goal understandably went mental as Chelsea's players ran to them and celebrated. Not to be outdone, Conte punched the air and then turned and swung chimp-like on the roof of the dug out behind his technical area. Quality!

We're gonna win the league chanted the Blues crowd. Even those of us who erred on the side of caution couldn't find a reason to disagree. *We're gonna win the league. We're gonna win the league. And now you're gonna believe us, and now you're gonna believe us… and now you're gonna be…lie…ve us… We're gonna win the league!*

Of Chelsea's nearest rivals, only second-placed Tottenham Hotspur managed a win that weekend beating Southampton 2-1 at White Hart Lane. The result kept Spurs in 'contention'… 10 points behind. At the Etihad, third-place Manchester City came from behind to draw 1-1 with fourth-place Liverpool. City manager Pep Gaurdiola bizarrely called the event "one of the proudest days of my coaching career"… what a weirdo! The Citizens were now a distant 12 points behind Chelsea… and Klopp's Liverpool, if they could still be counted as a genuine threat were 13 points adrift.

10 games to go… catch us if you can. Conte subsequently advised that "we have to take 21 points to win the title otherwise we risk to lose". Decent maths that. Once again the Blues boss spoke about the "winning mentality" of his players. "It is a great team and we must play always to win. In this game we showed from the start until the end the will to win the game, not to come here for only one point."

Importantly also, Conte heaped praise on Cahill. "Gary can play also as a centre-forward," he joked. "He has good quality, acrobatic qualities, and he's very good, very strong during the corners and set-pieces. I'm pleased for him because we conceded a penalty after the referee saw a little push by Gary and then he found the solution to score the second goal to win."

So now there followed the two-week tedium of an international break and associated concerns about key players getting injured… fingers crossed that wouldn't happen. When Chelsea returned to action they would have two successive home games in four days. First against Crystal Palace… and then Manchester City.

Conte had been right in highlighting that the Blues needed to win seven games to be sure of the title… but that wasn't taking into account the likelihood of the chasing pack dropping points. Looking at the remaining fixtures, there was a hope that Chelsea might stand a chance of winning the title at Old Trafford when they played Manchester United there on 16 April.

Much as it would be spitefully wonderful to make Mourinho suffer (I was sort of feeling sorry for him by now having calmed down after the FA Cup tie), that match would come too soon. If it were to happen, winning the title and all that… I figured the home game with Middlesbrough (6 May) who had recently sacked manager Aitor Karanka and drifted down into the relegation zone could be the opposition who would get rolled over the day Chelsea won the league. Time… as ever would tell.

*****

Later in the day, a crowd well in excess of 3,000 were at Stamford Bridge to watch Chelsea's Under-18 demolish Tottenham Hotspur 7-1 in the second leg of their FA Youth Cup semi-final. Another 3-4-3 masterclass from Jody Morris' side brought Ike Ugbo a hattrick with Trevor Chalobah, Dujon Sterling, Callum Hudson-Odoi and Juan Castillo also rippling the Spurs net.

A 9-2 aggregate victory over Tottenham… oh, that felt nice. A shame that Spurs' first team wasn't to be had quite so easily!

22 March

Gary Cahill was recognized for his sterling endeavours as Chelsea skipper this season by being made captain for England's friendly international fixture against Germany in Dortmund. The match (which England lost 1-0) was an irrelevance compared to the horrific events that transpired during the day in London where five innocent people had been murdered and 50 more injured by a spiteful, selfish lunatic who brought carnage to the Capital.

27 March

As expected the international break brought with it a few nerve-jangling moments for Chelsea supporters. Hotshot striker Diego Costa and in-form goalkeeper Thibaut Courtois suffered injury scares while star player Eden Hazard became the subject of intense transfer speculation.

Costa had developed a foot and ankle problem while training with the Spain international team at the weekend. Fortunately X-rays revealed the forward was ok and he was subsequently passed fit by doctors from the Spanish Football Federation.

Courtois meanwhile had developed a hip problem while playing for Belgium in a World Cup qualifier against Greece. Having played the full 90 minutes, the keeper was now undergoing treatment at Chelsea's Cobham training facility.

Courtois' countryman Hazard was withdrawn from the Belgium squad as a precaution by the London club's medical staff as the 26-year old was still recuperating from the calf complaint which had kept him out of his side's recent win at Stoke City.

While it's true that Chelsea managed to defeat a brutish Stoke team without the services of Hazard, the fact is that shorn of the mercurial skills of their playmaker in chief the Blues laboured and it took that late Gary Cahill goal to seal victory.

This was Hazard's fifth season as a Chelsea player. Since signing from France Ligue 1 side Lille for £32 million in June 2012 his stock had risen markedly so much so that La Liga giants Real Madrid were reported as being in 'negotiations' to take him to the Bernabeu in the summer.

To date in his Chelsea career, Hazard had made 237 appearances scoring 66 goals and providing a phenomenal 50 assists. Accolades had come in the form of PFA Young Player of the Year (2014), PFA Player of the Year (2015), Chelsea Player of the Year 2014 and 2015 and this season he looked set to add to his collection of winners medals which included Premier League, League Cup and Europa League gongs.

Yes, 2015-16 was a campaign to forget for the Belgian, but so it was for many of his teammates and Chelsea as a whole. Under Antonio Conte, the world had moved on. Hazard may have cut a dispirited figure last season and was indeed linked with a move to Paris Saint-Germain, but Conte sorted out the mixed up jigsaw puzzle and presented us once more with the player we knew and loved… and what a player.

11 goals and five assists so far this season coupled with fully embracing Conte's do-or-die philosophy had won back the ardour of Chelsea fans whose patience had been tried last term by Hazard's apparent attitude problem and any still wavering about his commitment and value to the Blues cause were won back over by the Belgian's incredible solo goal against Arsenal in February.

Among the millions applauding Hazard's genius would have been Real Madrid manager Zinedine Zidane whom if the latest stories were to be believed had worked out a way to accommodate the player's technical artistry at Real and wanted to make him a Galactico.

Earning £200,000 per week, Hazard whose current deal was set to expire in 2020 was Chelsea's highest paid player… and the interesting thing regarding the Real rumour was that unless Conte had devised a strange plan for the Blues next season that didn't include the Belgian there was zero chance of the deal happening. This of course didn't stop the media going large on Hazard to leave the Bridge angled stories.

Talk of Real president Florentino Perez testing Chelsea's resolve with a world record bid for Hazard seemed futile though. Blues billionaire owner Roman Abramovich didn't need the money. Under Abramovich's watch, while it's true the London club had sold many top players for big money… among them Oscar (£52 million Shanghai SIPG), David Luiz (£50 million to PSG), Juan Mata (£37 million to Manchester United) … the transfers had gone through with the relevant manager's blessing.

Somewhere in the middle of the Hazard rumour had to be his agent and the likelihood was that Abramovich would rebuff the financial overtures of Perez but find himself signing off a significant pay rise for the player. That's the way football worked and Barcelona's Lionel Messi was the example to follow. It was true that at 29-years of age Messi's time at the Camp Nou might be coming to an end, but the Catalan club had managed to keep the Argentine goal machine throughout the best period of his career… resisting along the way the temptation to sell to cash-rich club owners… like Abramovich.

Right now, Hazard was at the peak of his powers. With Conte at the helm, Chelsea represented one of the best clubs for a world-class player to continue to develop and win silverware. Coupled with this, an imminent return to the Champions League stage and a World Cup to look forward in 2018 made the upheaval and pressure that would come with a move to Real nonsensical for Hazard whose wife and young family were settled in England.

All of that said, Chelsea's limitless capacity to surprise meant that the thought of Hazard leaving didn't completely go away. The main thing was, he wasn't going anywhere for the remainder of the season and hopefully he would be fit for the Blues home game with Crystal Palace at the weekend.

APRIL 2017

1 April

Premier League
Chelsea 1 Crystal Palace 2
Stamford Bridge
Attendance: 41,489
Referee: Craig Pawson

Chelsea (3-5-2): Thibaut Courtois, Cesar Azpilicueta, David Luiz, Gary Cahill (c), Pedro, N'Golo Kante, Nemanja Matic (Willian 59), Marcos Alonso, (Michy Batshuayi 74), Eden Hazard, Diego Costa, Cesc Fabregas (Ruben Loftus-Cheek 90+7).
Scorer: Fabregas 5
Booked: Diego Costa 50, Cahill 79, David Luiz 83

Crystal Palace (4-2-3-1): Hennessey, Ward, Tomkins (Dann h/t) (Delaney 60), Sakho, Schlupp, Cabaye, Milivojevic, Puncheon (c), Zaha, Townsend (Kelly 60), Benteke.
Scorers: Zaha 9, Benteke 11
Booked: Benteke 68, Milivojevic 73

Boom! April Fool! There it was in its purest, unadulterated, most devastating form. Yes! Glorious unpredictability! When it was least expected, Chelsea contrived to snatch defeat from the jaws of victory… against Crystal Palace. Palace! For God's sake!

Bathed in balmy Spring sunshine, the denizens of Stamford Bridge had been in a relaxed mood as the teams took to the pitch. The presence of a couple of hundred boisterous, black-shirted, Palace 'ultras' in the top tier of the away section of the Shed End provided a source of amusement to the home crowd. Fair play to them to be quite honest, a bit more stirring than the 'stripey Nigel's of old that used to follow the club.

Referee Craig Pawson got the game under way, and Chelsea were soon into their regular stride bossing the early exchanges. The Palace 'ultras' incessant racket was muted in the fifth minute when a raking Cesc Fabregas pass set Eden Hazard in motion down the right flank. Hazard jinked his way through the visitors defence and fired the ball into the five-yard box where Fabregas was now perfectly place to turn the ball into the net. 1-0. The perfect start.

Fabregas is magic he wears a magic hat and all that and everything. Cue excited chatter about how many Chelsea were going to score and winning the title etc. And why not? What could possibly go wrong? The pre-match banter at the cfcuk stall had been more about the impending midweek game with Manchester City, currently in third place, and the challenges that match presented rather than anything Palace might offer.

@chucklescabbie had read out the team news one hour before kick-off as per usual. Victor Moses who'd picked up a calf strain in the FA Cup victory over Manchester United had failed to recover in time. Pedro was deputising at right wing-back. That was fine. The Spaniard had done that in earlier rounds of the cup… and scored to boot. Moses' absence and the switch in role for Pedro presented manager Antonio Conte with the opportunity to accommodate Fabregas in his starting XI albeit that this meant switching to 3-5-2 from his successful 3-4-3 template. But that would be okay wouldn't it? It's only Palace and Big Sam, they probably wouldn't even notice.

Truth was as it happened. Palace were all over it. Far from lying down and being rolled over when they went a goal down… and that's what we thought was going to happen… the Eagles fought back and exposed the imbalance in Conte's revised strategy. They did it quickly too.

Just four minutes after Fabragas had given Chelsea the lead, and with chants of *Antonio, Antonio* still bubbling around the Bridge, Palace winger Wilfred Zaha equalised. It was a goal Hazard-esque in its quality as Zaha held up the ball beautifully just inside the Blues penalty area before drilling it past Thibaut Courtois. Boom! A thunderflash was let off by the Palace pyromaniacs in The Shed. Game on.

Moments later Palace turned the match on its head. Carving Chelsea's right side open with worrying ease, Christian Benteke and Zaha swapped passes before Benteke lofted the ball over Courtois. 2-1. Boom! Another thunderflash in The Shed. The sound-wave shocking Blues supporters out of the paralysed state of disbelief they suddenly found themselves in.

THE ITALIAN JOB

This wasn't in the script.

What followed wasn't glorious or unpredictable. The growing sense among us was that it was going to be one of those days. Chelsea would deliver an astonishing 35 crosses into the box and have 24 shots on goal forcing Palace keeper Wayne Hennessey into a remarkable 11 saves. Diego Costa infuriatingly missed chance after chance... well at least three absolute sitters.

In a bid to find a way back into the game, Conte tweaked his set up. Pedro played as a winger, and then Willian entered the fray on the hour mark and Chelsea shifted to 4-2-4. Late on, the increasingly versatile Spaniard then found himself at left-back as Marcos Alonso was replaced by under-utilised striker Michy Batshuayi. It would have been great for the kid's morale to have made his mark on the game by scoring, but it wasn't to be. Not even a desperate-ish-looking 2-4-4 bombardment could breach the stout Eagles defence.

10 minutes of added time at the end of the match, a consequence largely of an injury to Scott Dann which saw the Palace defender stretchered off following a lengthy spell of treatment, brought with it opportunity... but Chelsea couldn't find a way through. All out attack at the end of the game saw Courtois lumber forward to challenge at a set-piece... nothing, nada, niente, niet.

Can we play you every week taunted the Palace rabble.

Having repeated last season's feat of winning 2-1 at the Bridge, the Eagles it seemed had become Chelsea's bogey side. Coincidentally, Craig Pawson had refereed that game as well.

You couldn't have faulted the Blues for effort. Yes with hindsight, Conte might have stuck with 3-4-3. Yes, David Luiz had a bit of a nightmare. Yes, Costa was pretty crap. My summary was the game had the look and feel of a bad day at the office. Shit happens and it had just happened. Chelsea would have to rewind and come again on Wednesday.

The loss to Palace and the fact that second-placed Tottenham Hotspur had won 2-0 away at Burnley thereby reducing Chelsea's lead at the top of the table to seven points predictably sent sections of Twitter in a nappy-filling meltdown.

The last thing I saw before I switched off my social media feeds for the day was a tweet from an armchair Arsenal mate of mine @pazzer36 "Better delay that book launch bruv!!" he advised. I'd gone public with the cover of *The Italian Job* earlier in the week. It made me smile. My God! though. Imagine if the unthinkable happened. I'd actually felt physically sick at the prospect.

I wanted to see what our main man Antonio Conte had to say about what had happened.

"I think today we deserved at least a draw," said the Blues boss. "I don't want to say a win, but at least a draw. We created many chances to score, we dominated the game against a very strong team with really good players. It's a pity but it wasn't our day."

It's a pity but it wasn't our day
It's a pity but it wasn't our day
It's a pity but it wasn't our day

Exactly. I repeated Conte's humble words to myself as I nursed a San Miguel… and then another one… and one more.

I reminded myself of the Italian's statement following the 2-1 loss at home to Liverpool back in September that I had repeated a few times. They resonated deeply once more.

Pay attention and be focused
Pay attention and be focused
Pay attention and be focused

4 April

Antonio Conte marked the first anniversary of his appointment as Blues manager with a chuckleworthy statement about title rivals Spurs. "I think the difference between Chelsea and Tottenham is this: if you stay in Chelsea and win it's normal. If you stay in Tottenham, if you win it's great, great, but if you lose it's not a disaster because you find a lot of situations to explain a good season."

Surely not mind games from Conte? "In this season, us and Tottenham stay in the same level," he continued. "Chelsea were underdogs at the start of the season, but now we are top and we want to keep this position."

Too right. And with Manchester City next up, the big question was…

given the unexpected Palace debacle... would the Blues manager change anything? "If you win or if you lose or draw, it doesn't change our idea, our philosophy or our method, it's the same," advised Conte although he was clearly still reviewing who would make his starting XI. "I have to check a couple of situations and make the best decision." One being Pedro playing at right wing-back which he noted... the other? Hmmm. Would Conte make an adjustment to his backline for the visit of City?

I went to bed thinking I'd take a dreary 1-0 Chelsea win... but creeping forth from the back of my mind were goals, lots of them. @walterotton was predicting 5-3 on Twitter... that would make for a trouser-browner of a game. May the good lord have mercy on our true Blue souls.

5 April

Speaking on the wireless ahead of the City game former Chelsea player and coach Ray Wilkins suggested that Antonio Conte wanted to bring in former Italy and Juventus star Andrea Pirlo as part of his coaching team at Stamford Bridge once Steve Holland departed to assist England manager Gareth Southgate at the end of the season.

"I know for a fact he (Pirlo) has been around Stamford Bridge on a number of occasions this year," said Wilkins in an enthusiastic manner. "He's the one that Antonio Conte would like."

That would make for an exciting appointment, though the general consensus was that Chelsea would steer Conte in the direction of hiring in a home-grown coach to take over from Holland. "I do believe if he pulls off this Premier League win that he should be able to bring in who he wishes," concluded Wilkins. Fair point to be honest.

5 April (continued)

Premier League
Chelsea 2 Manchester City 1
Stamford Bridge
Attendance: 41,528
Referee: Mike Dean

Chelsea (3-4-3): Thibaut Courtois, Kurt Zouma (Matic h-t) David Luiz, Gary Cahill (c), Cesar Azpilicueta, N'Golo Kante, Cesc Fabregas (Willian 81), Marcos Alonso, Pedro, Diego Costa, Eden Hazard (Ruben Loftus-Cheek 90).
Scorer: Hazard 10, 35
Booked: Kante 90+3

Man City (4-2-3-1): Caballero, Navas, Stones, Kompany (c), Clichy, Fernandinho, Delph; De Bruyne (Sterling 79), Silva (c), Sane (Nolito 85), Aguero.
Scorer: Aguero 26
Booked: Clichy 52, Delph 77, Kompany 83

Good fortune returned to favour Chelsea as they beat Manchester City 2-1 in a nerve-shredding game that could quite easily have gone either way. Pre-match at the cfcuk stall there had been an edgy sense of anticipation among the great and the good that tarried to share some banter. The accord was that the Blues had to win to reassert their title credentials… it was that simple.

@chucklescabbie broke the team news at 7pm. Antonio Conte had shuffled his pack to try and address the right wing-back issue created by the continued absence of Victor Moses who wasn't quite ready to return to first team action. Cesar Azpilicueta was to assume the role instead of Pedro with Kurt Zouma coming into the side at centre-back for his first Premier League start in over a year. Pedro would be deployed in an advanced role. It made sense. We were all pleased to see Zouma get a chance. The 22-year old had the mobility and physicality to stand up to the test likely to be provided by Man City hotshot Sergio Aguero.

Inside Stamford Bridge, the atmosphere was apprehensive. Chelsea needed to find the net early to ease the tension in the crowd… and they did just that, although almost immediately the reminder was there that they done the same against Crystal Palace and that hadn't worked out too well!

THE ITALIAN JOB

Eden Hazard, at his livewire best, opened the scoring for the Blues in the 10th minute when Man City goalie Willy Caballero fluffed his lines... here we go! 1-0 And then, oh no! Here we go again. 16 minutes later it was the turn of Chelsea keeper Thibaut Courtois, on his 100th appearance for the club, to make a fool of himself and gift Sergio Aguero a somewhat undeserved equaliser.

Was this going to be Palace all over again? Keeping an eye on the 'live-score' feed on my phone, I was encouraged by the news that Swansea City had taken an early lead against Tottenham Hotspur at the Liberty Stadium... a match which had kicked-off 15 minutes earlier than the Chelsea / City game. Clearly, it was ridiculous to be hoping for the Swans to do the Blues a favour by beating Spurs... but we were all living in hope. That's football for you.

Down in the technical area, Chelsea manager Antonio Conte and his City counterpart Pep Guardiola cut animated figures. Both gesticulating wildly, Conte in particular looking like a deranged marionette. What was going through his mind?

10 minutes before half-time Man City midfielder Fernandinho put Pedro on the floor in the penalty area. Referee Mike Dean had no hesitation in pointing to the spot. The Chelsea crowd held their breath as Hazard stepped up. Noooo!!! The Belgium international's penalty was lame... saved by Caballero. But the City keeper would have been wiser to tip it round the post than parry it into to the Chelsea player's path. In a flash, despair turned to joy as Hazard buried the ball in the net to restore the Blues lead.

The scoring was done... but of course none of us had any idea that would be the case. Half-time came, and at the break Conte decided that Chelsea would have a better chance of keeping City at bay with Azpilicueta, who'd done an excellent job at wing-back and provided the assist for Hazard's opener, dropping back to his more familiar recent role in the back three. Somewhat unfortunately, Zouma was withdrawn in favour of Nemanja Matic while Pedro was shunted out onto the right wing.

Nobody argued against the decision, and ultimately Conte was vindicated as Chelsea hung on grimly in a pulsating second-half. Man City had the better of the early exchanges and created some gilt-edged chances, but the Blues rode their luck and had the woodwork and some smart keeping from Courtois who denied Aguero to thank for maintaining their advantage.

Hazard might have had a hattrick but scooped a shot over the bar and as he did so, my phone vibrated to alert me to the fact that Spurs had scored a late equaliser at Swansea. It kept vibrating. 2-1 Spurs. 3-1 Spurs. Full time at the Liberty! There were still 15 minutes to play at the Bridge… and City were in the ascendency. It was horrible to watch to be honest. Time never ending. Purgatory! "Come on ref! Blow your whistle!"

Up at The Shed end, Man City defender John Stones squandered a glorious chance to equalise somehow sending the ball over the bar when it had to be easier to score. "Please ref, blow!" Stamford Bridge was a cacophony of whistles, I swear if Conte could have joined in, he would have done.

Peep, peep, peep… there it was. Three shrill notes. Thank you Mr Dean! Almost immediately, the heavy, heavy monster sound of *One Step Beyond* by Madness pumped out of the stadium Tannoy… job done!

Speaking after the game, Conte mused, "My look is tired because I feel like I played it tonight with my players. I suffered with them." The Chelsea manager's words echoed the sentiment of every Blues supporter in the ground and countless millions around the globe who had tuned in to watch the match. We were all exhausted and emotionally drained.

Explaining his half-time changes Conte advised, "I think Kurt played a really good game but the substitution was tactical because in the first-half we were suffering a lot in midfield and they were finding spaces between the lines, so I wanted to reinforce the midfield with Matic, bring Azpi into his position and play Pedro as wing-back." His summary that "It was more offensive because your wing-back is more of a winger than a defender" was correct, though the observation that Chelsea "had more balance" and "controlled the game well" I wasn't too sure about and what about Diego Costa? On the missing list again!

"We must be focused and try to win six games and take three points. If we are able to do this, we will win the title," concluded Conte, avoiding the Costa issue. Decent maths once again from the Italian. I struggled to get to sleep that night, the adrenaline buzz of being at the game just wouldn't wear off. I wondered if Conte had the same problem? He'd spoken earlier in the season about having sleepless nights, but back then Chelsea were labouring. At least now they were in control of their own destiny.

With eight games to go, the Blues advantage over Spurs remained seven points. Catch us if you can… but please don't.

THE ITALIAN JOB

8 April

Premier League
Bournemouth 1 Chelsea 3
Dean Court
Attendance: 11,283
Referee: Andre Marriner

Chelsea (3-4-3): Thibaut Courtois, Cesar Azpilicueta, David Luiz, Gary Cahill (c), Victor Moses (Kurt Zouma 90+2), N'Golo Kante, Nemanja Matic, Marcos Alonso, Pedro (Willian 87), Diego Costa, Eden Hazard (Cesc Fabregas 84).
Scorers: Smith o.g. 17, Hazard 20, Alonso 68
Booked: Moses 8, Kante 58, Pedro 74

Bournemouth (4-4-2): Boruc, A Smith, Francis (c), Cook, Daniels, Fraser (Gradel 84), Arter, Wilshere, Pugh (Ibe 71), Afobe (Mousset 77), King.
Scorer: King 42
Booked: Arter 38, Gradel 90

Chelsea took a giant stride towards the Premier League title beating Bournemouth 3-1 at sun-drenched Dean Court. After an edgy start, the champions elect scored twice in quick succession, Adam Smith's 17th minute own goal being swiftly followed by a masterful piece of finishing by man-of-the-match Eden Hazard.

Josh King gave the home side hope scoring just before the break, but Marcos Alonso restored Chelsea's two goal advantage midway through the second-half with a deft free-kick, and from that point on there was only going to be one outcome.

Having no doubt watched title rivals Tottenham Hotspur demolish Watford 4-0 in the day's early televised fixture, Antonio Conte and his players knew they had to beat Bournemouth to ease any pressure being felt that if Spurs continued on their winning streak, dropped points would allow the Lilywhites to reel them in.

Blues supporters who had chuckled for a while at Spurs' fans ridiculous chant, *Chelsea rent boys we're coming for you* (a 'clever' variation of their *Leicester City we're coming for you* ditty from the previous campaign that hadn't quite worked out for them) came up with the witty riposte *Tottenham Hotspur we're waiting for you*. With one game to go before the Wembley FA Cup semi-final between the clubs, there were a couple of ways to view the chant. Rivalry redefined. It would be one hell of a day... whatever happened.

The key positive for Antonio Conte against Bournemouth was the return of Victor Moses to his now customary right wing-back position. Moses restored much-needed equilibrium to Conte's template 3-4-3, and his inclusion permitted the Italian to field the starting XI that had catapulted Chelsea to the top of the league earlier in the season.

The 3-1 score line may have suggested that this was a routine win for the Blues, but it was far from easy and had goalkeeper Thibaut Courtois not been at his outstanding best early on to prevent David Luiz shanking a poor attempted clearance into his own net the result might have been different.

Once again, playing at the top of his game, Eden Hazard's marauding runs terrified Bournemouth's backline. The Belgium international took his goal superbly, latching onto N'Golo Kante's pass and showing deft control to tease Cherries keeper Artur Boruc before sliding the ball into the net.

If Hazard was displaying the type of mercurial trickery that unlocked defences and won matches the same could not be said of his teammate Diego Costa who toiled in vain to find the net. The striker did however play a significant part in two of Chelsea's goals. The Blues opener came from a wild Costa shot that was going well wide before being turned in by Adam Smith and the forward drew the foul that led to the free-kick from which Alonso scored.

Maybe Costa was saving himself for that FA Cup semi showdown with Tottenham? Personally, on the basis that I was by now convinced that his slipshod form was down to the fact that mentally he'd already left Chelsea, I wouldn't mind if he never scored again for the Blues... with the exception that is of netting the winner against Spurs.

Conte who looked like he was shedding a few kilos doing his regular technical area workout in the sunshine was as cool as a cucumber after the game. "It's normal to have a pressure," he beamed. "We started the game very well with great attention and focus. Then we conceded the goal and we lost a bit of confidence." With regards to crowing cockerels he had the following pearls of wisdom to share. "When you have this type of opponent, Tottenham, who is in good form and wants to catch you, it is important to have a good answer. This (beating Bournemouth) is a good answer."

THE ITALIAN JOB

The Costa conundrum didn't seem to faze Conte one bit. "He fought a lot for the team and he is important, said the Blues boss. "It is important for the team that we won against a strong team. Now it is important to rest and restart and prepare for the game against Manchester United."

The concern remained however that Costa wasn't finding the net. With just three top-flight goals to his name since the turn of the year, the striker had been bypassed by Hazard (five) and left wing-back Marcos Alonso (four) and there has been plenty of supporter chatter on social media regarding the 28-year olds continued selection. The point was laboured once more that Costa hadn't looked the same player since January and the twin dramas involving his spat with a Blues fitness coach that led to him being dropped and the big money offer from China.

Given the complete clarity that Conte didn't see Michy Batshuayi as a viable alternative… against Bournemouth, had the Italian opted to play Hazard as a false 9 flanked by Willian and Pedro, it would have been acceptable to Blues fans. Given the fact that the Chelsea manager had chosen this strategy which yielded an emphatic victory against Leicester City (the game he dropped Costa for) it was reasonable to suggest the same winning outcome could have been achieved against the Cherries.

Talk of Conte going with a false 9 has been accompanied by jokes that Chelsea were currently playing with a false 19, a reference to Costa's shirt number and his dearth of goals. Harsh!

On Twitter @danlevene took the prize for the wittiest observation about poor Diego's failings. "If this Diego Costa were put on firing-squad duties, there would be no need to campaign against the death penalty."

In his Chelsea managerial career to date, Conte had displayed a ruthless streak when it came to team selection, and this had indeed included dropping Costa. Right now however, the Blues boss was giving every indication that he intended to persist with his misfiring striker in the hope he would rediscover his touch and, starting at Old Trafford against Man United, score what would be his 50th Premier League goal… and a few more to boot.

Given the impressive way Conte had transformed Chelsea's fortunes this season he currently could do no wrong in the eyes of Blues supporters. Team selection and tactics had remained almost completely criticism-free since last October when the Italian switched to 3-4-3 in the wake of those catalytically significant defeats to Liverpool and Arsenal.

Football fans are a notoriously fickle bunch though, and should Chelsea somehow lose the initiative in the title race to Tottenham, which for 99.9% of Blues supporters would represent a fate worse than death, the love for Conte might dissipate quickly... particularly if more Costa profligacy in front of goal was at the root of the failure.

Scary thoughts to be having!

Seeking reassurance, I wanted to hear what was Conte saying?

"We have shown great character all season and great desire and will to fight for the title. We started this season and nobody thought Chelsea could fight for the title. Instead, we found the right motivation together."

Of course he wasn't speaking to me personally, he was speaking to the world... but I drew comfort from his words and those of the true Blue massive who had serenaded the Chelsea team off the pitch at Dean Court with the chant *We shall not be moved!*

10 April

Crystal Palace beat Arsenal 3-0 at Selhurst Park. Looking at the Premier League table it was remarkable to think that six months previously the Gunners had beaten Chelsea by the same score, a result which had seen Arsene Wenger's side move up to third, three points ahead of the Blues who slumped to eighth. Antonio Conte's team were now an astonishing 21 points ahead of Wenger's who were now languishing in sixth.

Remarkably, both Palace and Arsenal were due to play Tottenham in the title run in. In an ordinary season, it might have been the Gunners you'd have thought might be able to do Chelsea a favour, but right now it was Big Sam's Eagles who had recently dented Blues fans pride and hopes who looked more capable of taking something from their game with Spurs.

13 April

Eden Hazard and N'Golo Kante were among the nominees on the PFA Players' player of the year shortlist. Also nominated, Zlatan Ibrahimovic of Manchester United. I was hoping the towering Swede wouldn't be adding to his tally of 17 goals for the Red Devils on Easter Sunday when he led the Man U line against Chelsea.

THE ITALIAN JOB

14 April

Chelsea's game with Manchester United at Old Trafford had a season-defining aspect to it for both clubs that guaranteed a global television audience likely to be measured in billions… and that was before the José Mourinho factor was added into the equation.

Seven points clear of Tottenham Hotspur with seven games to go, irrespective of how Spurs fared at home to Bournemouth on Easter Saturday, and they were expected to win comfortably, should Chelsea beat Man U it would emphatically underline the Blues Premier League title credentials and give Antonio Conte's side a huge psychological advantage over their nearest rivals.

The recent slip-up against Crystal Palace was reason enough to take nothing for granted, but Chelsea's run-in after the trip to Old Trafford… Southampton (h), Everton (a), Middlesbrough (h), West Brom (a), Watford (h), Sunderland (h) … suggested that protecting a possible seven point advantage shouldn't prove too taxing for Conte's team.

United went into the game four points adrift of a berth in next season's Champions League competition. A loss to Chelsea would make qualification via the Premier League route look like a forlorn hope for the Red Devils whose best bet of a return to Europe's elite competition lay with winning the Europa League.

Competitions and league positions aside, the Mourinho factor made the fixture compelling… a must watch for football supporters of all allegiances. As Man U manager, the Portuguese had come up short in two encounters against the club where he won seven major trophies in two stints as boss.

A 4-0 hammering in the reverse league fixture at Stamford Bridge earlier in the season and a 1-0 FA Cup quarterfinal loss at the same venue last month would have rankled deeply with Mourinho who'd be desperate to avoid a hat-trick of defeats.

At Old Trafford, Conte would in all probability name the same starting XI that carved United open at the Bridge. Thibaut Courtois, Cesar Azpilicueta, David Luiz, Gary Cahill, N'Golo Kante, Nemanja Matic, Victor Moses, Marcos Alonso, Pedro, Eden Hazard and Diego Costa looked set to line-up in the Blues boss' now familiar 3-4-3 and Mourinho would need no reminding of the potential threat they posed.

The FA Cup game saw Conte make just one change to this XI with Willian coming in for Pedro. The match was a much tighter affair... in truth a brutish ugly contest which saw Hazard kicked from pillar to post. One kick too many for referee Michael Oliver resulted in Man U midfielder Ander Herrera being dismissed before half-time a decision which provoked a predictable touchline meltdown from Mourinho whose subsequent spat with an always animated Conte ended with the feisty duo being pulled apart by fourth official Mike Jones.

Bobby Madley would be the man in the middle for the Old Trafford clash with Oliver the appointed fourth official tasked with keeping Mourinho and Conte apart should events on the pitch provoke a coming together.

So what did the dynamic duo make of it in their respective pre-match pre-ambles?

"You say it's emotional but, for me, it's a game. It's one more game. No different for me. Not at all." José Mourinho

"It's only a sporting competition between him (Mourinho) and me. There is a game of football. I want to try and win with my team. He wants to try and win with his team." Antonio Conte

Who was kidding who?

Man U were on an unbeaten league run of 21 games although the fact that 10 of these matches had ended in a draw makes the sequence less impressive. United had drawn again in their Thursday night Europa League quarterfinal first-leg tie with Anderlecht, and with the all-important second-leg to come four days after their game with Chelsea would Mourinho be conscious of fatiguing key players and rest some of his big names? Against any other team, quite probably... against the Blues? No chance!

15 April

As expected, Tottenham Hotspur thrashed Bournemouth. Spurs 4-0 rout of the Cherries cut Chelsea's lead at the top of the Premier League to four points and gave the Lilywhites a +6 goal difference advantage over the Blues. The Man U game suddenly had a pivotal feel about it.

THE ITALIAN JOB

16 April

Premier League
Manchester United 2 Chelsea 0
Old Trafford
Attendance: 75,272
Referee: Robert Madley

Chelsea (3-4-3): Asmir Begovic, Cesar Azpilicueta, David Luiz, Gary Cahill (c), Victor Moses (Cesc Fabregas 54), N'Golo Kante, Nemanja Matic (Willian 67), Kurt Zouma (Ruben Loftus-Cheek 83) Pedro, Diego Costa, Eden Hazard.
Booked: Diego Costa 33, Cahill 47, Fabregas 90.

Man United (3-5-2): De Gea, Bailly, Rojo, Darmian, Valencia, Fellaini, Herrera, Pogba, Young (c) (Fosu-Mensah 90+3), Rashford (Ibrahimovic 83), Lingard (Carrick 60).
Scorers: Rashford 7, Herrera 49.
Booked: Herrera 73, Rojo 75

Chelsea slumped to a disappointing 2-0 defeat against Manchester United at Old Trafford, a result that had plenty of supporters and critics alike questioning if the Blues had the staying power to win the title.

Goals from Marcus Rashford and Ander Herrera sealed what was a deserved victory for the Red Devils despite the fact the match officials missed Herrera's blatant hand ball in the build up to Rashford's 7th minute opener. For the record, Chelsea didn't have a single shot on goal... shots on goal typically being a key requirement for winning any football game.

It's true that Antonio Conte's preparations for the game had been thrown out of kilter, firstly by goalkeeper Thibaut Courtois infuriatingly sustaining an ankle injury while filming a promotional basketball video for Chelsea, part of the club's commercial duties with the NBA, and secondly by Marcos Alonso succumbing to 'illness' during the warm-up... but it would have been lame to use the changes enforced on Conte as an excuse for the Blues lacklustre performance. The theory that the Chelsea squad had been exposed to a virus via a meal consumed on a team-bonding night the previous Thursday cut no ice. Victor Moses and Diego Costa had also been reported as feeling below-par... maybe Costa had been eating at the same restaurant every week for the past month!

Orgasmic Vibe is an anagram of Asmir Begovic, but Chelsea's

replacement keeper, making his first Premier League start of the campaign, was functional as opposed to sexy and unfortunately there was nothing he could really do about either of Man Us goals. Would the result had been any different had Courtois played? Probably not. Hopefully though, the Belgium international would be fit to face Spurs prolific attack at Wembley the following weekend.

Similar to when regular right wing-back Victor Moses had been absent recently through injury, the late loss of Alonso's proved problematic for Chelsea… it also raised questions regarding common sense more so on the part of the player rather than the manager. Perhaps if the Spaniard had been more forthcoming about the extent of his problem then Conte could have made a contingency plan. The hurried inclusion of Kurt Zouma as a late replacement for Alonso appeared to lack genuine thought.

The Blues boss shunted Cesar Azpilicueta out to left wing-back and deployed Zouma as a centre-back and Chelsea were on the back foot from the kick-off as United manager José Mourinho paired youthful-looking duo Rashford and Jesse Lingard up front and played a high line with Herrera man-marking Eden Hazard and Eric Bailly and Marcos Rojo shackling Diego Costa.

In a nutshell, Mourinho won the tactical battle hands down. At the final whistle as the Portuguese smugly pointed at the Man U crest on his gilet, an act which extinguished the final flickering flame of love I had for him.

Conte meanwhile bore the look of a man who knew that this time around he'd got it all wrong. Despite this, the Italian would have drawn comfort from the travelling Blue and White Army who defiantly and repeatedly chanted *we're top of the League*. Football is about belief and Chelsea's away-day match-going supporters could always be relied on to back the team 1000%.

Thinking about it, I felt sorry for Zouma mainly because after showing so much promise prior to picking up that horrible knee injury he had struggled to re-capture the form which had made him a firm favourite with supporters and a first team regular. Conte hadn't really fancied him this season and having started him in the recent 2-1 win against Manchester City, the Chelsea manager had subbed him at half-time.

Logic suggested playing Pedro at left wing-back, keeping Azpi in the back three and starting Willian was the way to go… but Conte's ideas were different. Similarly, Cesc Fabregas might have offered more than Nemanja

Matic from a creative point of view, but the Spaniard was only given a run out when it was too late. Hindsight eh.

Chelsea's cause wasn't helped much either by Diego Costa who offered nothing and was bossed by Bailly and Rojo. Conte's continued persistence with his misfiring striker who inexplicably was afforded the full 90 minutes despite his failings was an increasing source of concern. Was the Blues boss simply praying to God for divine intervention and a goal from the 28-year old, or did he have a hitherto unknown plan to restore him to the peak of his devastating powers? If it were the latter, it wasn't working and the natives were getting very restless.

If there was a silver lining to the big black cloud that darkened Easter Sunday for Chelsea supporters everywhere it was the fact that Antonio Conte was man enough to humbly admit the defeat was his fault.

"We didn't play a good game and United deserved to win the game," said the Blues boss contritely. "They showed more desire, more ambition, more motivation. In this case the fault is of the coach." Conte concluded he had not been able to "transfer the right concentration, desire, ambition to win…"

Imagine Mourinho ever admitting such a thing? No, he would have been risking the wrath of the FA for calling referee Bobby Madley blind for not spotting Ander Herrera's handball or ear-bashing Gary Cahill for helping Jesse Lingard to his feet later on when Herrera's shot deflected in off the unfortunate Zouma.

So that was that. Twitter predictably went into one of its famous meltdowns. Two camps appeared. Those relaxed about the fact that Chelsea were still four points clear of Tottenham with six games to play, and those soiling themselves that in the space of three weeks a 10 point lead had become seven points and was now four points. The media were loving the fact that the title race was back on.

My nerves were starting to jangle, but for now I was still in the relaxed camp. The title was still Chelsea's to lose… God forbid… and next on the fixture list… well, well, well… a break from the Premier League agenda… Spurs in the FA Cup semi-final. I had a feeling that the outcome of that game might have a psychological effect on the winners and losers that would in some way determine the destination of the title.

17 April

A joint announcement from Chelsea and John Terry that our legendary captain would leave at the end of the season came as no surprise to Blues supporters who had become accustomed to the London club calling time on the playing careers of its stalwarts while they still had a season or two of football left in them.

At 36-years of age JT was at the veteran stage of a phenomenal career which to date had seen him make 713 appearances for Chelsea. Although first team opportunities had been scarce this season under Antonio Conte, it's fair to say that an injury early on in the campaign coupled with a lack of European competition had limited his opportunity for game-time.

With a return to Champions League football all but assured next season, a fit John Terry might have expected to play in the group stage games as well as the early rounds of the League Cup and be there as back-up for top-flight fixtures, but clearly Conte had his own plans for the future and given Chelsea's success under his stewardship there was no case to argue that Terry should have walked straight back into the first team when he regained fitness.

There were of course plenty of Blues fans who had been hoping that their icon might have stayed on at Chelsea either as a squad member or as part of the coaching staff, but Terry himself stated that he was "eager to carry on playing".

Conscious of what happened when another venerable club legend Frank Lampard left the Bridge and ended up joining Manchester City and indeed scoring against Chelsea, those same supporters were nervous about where Terry might end up and what impact he might have at a new club.

There had been recent speculation that Terry could join West Bromwich Albion in the summer. Baggies manager Tony Pulis favoured experienced heads in his stout defence with 37-year old Gareth McAuley a prime example. McAuley had at this point in the season made 30 appearances at centre-back for West Brom scoring seven goals… JT must have been thinking, I'll have some of that.

Chelsea director Marina Granovskaia advised during the statement that the club and Terry himself were looking ahead at the possibility of him returning to the Bridge at some point in the future in a non-playing capacity and the cordial aspect to the announcement made this plausible.

THE ITALIAN JOB

Terry advised he was committed to helping Chelsea for the remainder of this season, and with the Premier League and FA Cup Double still a very real prospect his influence particularly at the moment when the club's title aspirations had taken a bit of a knock would prove invaluable… hopefully!

Should Chelsea get back on track, the chance remained that they could secure the title with a game to spare. That being the case it would be a wonderful gesture by Antonio Conte to afford JT one last start in the final league match of the season against Sunderland at Stamford Bridge.

Terry of course would bring the curtain down on a glittering career that had brought him 14 major honours as well as 78 England caps by scoring the winning goal with a trademark towering header before being the first to hold aloft the Premier League trophy to make it 15 major honours.

What is football without dreams? Nothing. Terry had surely realised his, but this last one would be something special for man and his legion of supporters. How was it going to turn out? I was beginning to make myself nervous again.

18 April

For the third season in succession, Chelsea's Under-18s contested the final of the FA Youth Cup with Manchester City. A pulsating 1-1 first leg draw at City's Academy Stadium gave little indication as to which of these great young sides would ultimately win the trophy.

Blues boss Jody Morris and his Citizens counterpart Lee Carsley followed the tactical lead of their respective senior side mentors Antonio Conte and Pep Guardiola, Morris going with 3-4-3 and Carsley 4-3-3 and it was first blood to Chelsea when Ike Ugbo scored his ninth goal of the competition just before the break. Phil Foden levelled for City on the hour mark and despite the home side taking the initiative in the latter stages of the game they were unable to score a second goal meaning Morris' side had the psychological edge and an away goal going into the second leg which would be played the following week at Stamford Bridge.

To be honest though, while watching Chelsea's 'kids' doing their thing on television, my mind kept drifting and thinking about the forthcoming FA Cup semi-final with Tottenham Hotspur. PMT Pre Match Tension on a Tuesday night ahead of a game on Saturday… that was a novelty. I wondered if Marcos Alonso, Victor Moses and Diego Costa would be recovered from the mystery virus that had afflicted them at Old Trafford. I wondered if Antonio Conte was contemplating dropping Costa. I wondered what I would do (drop him). I wondered…

21 April

Friday morning. Pre Match Tension I tweeted, wondering if others felt the same way? @chelseapep Me too-big style … @julio25 Me three. Sick …

There could only be one winner of the FA Cup semi-final … and right now it felt almost like the actual final itself didn't matter… just beating 'them'. Maybe the day-early PMT was down to the fact that although winning the Premier League was a different kettle of fish altogether… everything seemed thrown together. *Chi dorme non piglia pesci* as they say in Italy… those who sleep don't catch any fish. I'd tried blotting out that 'fate worse than death' scenario that not catching any fish represented, that somehow Chelsea's title bid would collapse… but it kept coming back.

A recurring nightmare… bad-karma time.

As you sow, so shall you reap.

I shouldn't have laughed at Spurs last season, or Liverpool in 2014… that Gerrard slip… or the Aguerrrrrrrooooo goal thing when Man City pipped Man United for the 2012 title. But that's football. That's how we roll. *Don't worry about a thing, cos every little thing is gonna be alright…* right?

*****

News broke that former England, Aston Villa and Middlesbrough defender Ugo Ehiogu had died at the age of 44. The Tottenham Under-23 coach had suffered a cardiac arrest at Spurs training centre the previous day. Ehiogu was married with a young family.

Concerns about Chelsea were firmly put into perspective.

Antonio Conte opened his pre-match presser with a sympathetic statement. "Before starting the press conference, I want to send my and the players' and the club's condolences to Ugo's family. When there is this sad news it's never good. When this type of situation happens football is not important."

So true.

Conte went on to advise that Thibaut Courtois had recovered from the ludicrous basketball injury that had kept him out of the Man U game, the inference being he would play against Spurs... he also hinted that Gary Cahill, who'd taken ill during the week and been hospitalized, was a major doubt though his condition wasn't serious. No Cahill! *Gulp*

I thought about perspective again.

#RIP Ugo

22 April

**FA Cup Semi-final
Chelsea 4 Tottenham Hotspur 2
Wembley
Attendance: 86,355
Referee: Martin Atkinson**

Chelsea (3-4-3): Thibaut Courtois, Cesar Azpilicueta (c), David Luiz, Nathan Ake, Victor Moses, N'Golo Kante, Nemanja Matic, Marcos Alonso, Willian (Eden Hazard 60), Michy Batshuayi (Diego Costa 60), Pedro (Cesc Fabregas 74).
Scorers: Willian 5, 43 pen, Hazard 75, Matic 80
Booked: Alonso 45+3, Kante 90+2

Tottenham Hotspur (3-4-3): Lloris, Dier, Alderweireld, Vertonghen, Trippier, Wanyama (Nkoudou 80), Dembele, Son (Walker 68), Eriksen, Kane, Alli.
Scorers: Kane 18; Alli 52
Booked: Alderweireld 4, Alli 73

Chelsea crushed Tottenham 4-2 in a drama-filled FA Cup semi-final at Wembley. Set piece specialist Willian twice gave the Blues the lead, first with a free-kick, and then with a penalty... but Spurs levelled on both occasions, initially via Harry Kane and then Dele Alli. The Lilywhites looked to be in the ascendency but were undone by goals from Eden Hazard and Nemanja Matic, the latter's thunderous strike serving as a signal for a fire drill to evacuate the Spurs end of the ground.

Chelsea manager Antonio Conte once more proved his mettle with an outstanding coaching masterclass which melded tactics and psychology and left highly-regarded Tottenham boss Mauricio Pochettino realizing that he still had a lot to learn.

The result must have felt like a dagger to the heart for Spurs supporters who genuinely believed that this was their year. A seventh straight FA Cup semi-final defeat made an unwanted new record for the White Hart Lane outfit and led to a few gags that chairman Daniel Levy should get their new stadium sponsored by Viagra so they might stand a chance of getting more than a semi.

Joking aside, it remained to be seen whether or not, as was being suggested in many pre-match preambles, there would be a knock-on psychological effect on the semi-final losers in respect of challenging for the Premier League title.

Heading into Wembley, Chelsea supporters had every right to feel slightly unnerved by the rumours on social media spreading virally like the illness in the Blues dressing room that Conte wasn't going to start with either Eden Hazard or Diego Costa. The Costa thing, well that was a case of 'be careful what you wish for', plenty of fans had grown tired of his profligacy… still though, it was a big call. Hazard on the other hand… madness! Surely not?

4.15pm… one hour before kick-off, all was revealed. The rumours were true. No Costa… and no Hazard! The duo were consigned to the bench as Conte made five changes to the side that had been well beaten by Manchester United at Old Trafford the previous weekend.

Thibaut Courtois returned in goal… that was expected. Nathan Ake was preferred to Kurt Zouma as a replacement for Gary Cahill. It was a third FA Cup start of the season for Chelsea for Ake who had impressed in the first-half of the season while on loan at Bournemouth but had been unable to get into the Blues first team for league matches. Willian came in for Hazard, and forgotten striker Michy Batshuayi replaced Costa. Cesar Azpilicueta took the skipper's armband for the first time from the absent Cahill.

It was a massive call by Conte and immediately led to thoughts that the Italian was prioritizing the league over the cup. Maybe, after all, the penny hadn't dropped about the importance of beating Spurs. Ha ha, of course it wasn't like that. It had nothing to do with priorities. Conte had picked the team he believed could do the job on the day.

Fresh legs. Fresh impetus. Fresh ambition…

Know how.

THE ITALIAN JOB

Conte knows best!

Pochettino for his part, tried to compete on the surprise tactical front by curiously deploying in-form goal machine Heung-Min Son at left wing-back. The gamble failed, and worst still for Spurs it was Son who brought down Victor Moses for the crucial penalty which allowed Willian to restore Chelsea's lead just before the break. Pochettino also chose to 'rest' Kyle Walker and Ben Davies. To be fair though, before kick-off I didn't really think about the significance of the Argentine's team selection... I was more concerned about how Chelsea's new-look starting XI would fare.

A minute's applause for Ugo Ehiogu served as a timely reminder about how precious and fragile life was...

Referee Martin Atkinson got the game underway, and as expected the pace was frenetic. Atkinson's first big decision was to award a free-kick to Chelsea just outside the Tottenham penalty area when Toby Alderweireld floored Pedro. There was no debate about it to be honest. Who was going to take the kick though? It was David Luiz's birthday, and earlier in the day I'd had a bet on the Blues center-back to mark the occasion with a goal. I quickly thought about that free-kick against Liverpool... boom! Then there was Marcos Alonso... he could bang them in. Then of course there was Willian...

According to the popular chant Willian hates Tottenham, whether the Brazilian actually does or not is immaterial... but Spurs fans probably think he does and rue every time they see him lining up against them in the Blue of Chelsea that they were gazumped in their endeavours to sign the player.

Willian flighted his kick perfectly, curling it beyond the desperate clawing hand of Hugo Lloris in the Tottenham goal. 1-0

The goal settled early nerves.

Antonio. Antonio.

A plane flew overhead trailing a banner with the simple reverential message for the Blues boss. Fantastic! But was it too early? Possibly! Five minutes later, Spurs were level. Assist-master Christian Eriksen teed up Harry Kane who deftly headed the ball beyond Courtois. That took the jam out of our collective donuts. 1-1

Game on!

Worryingly, Tottenham then started to assert themselves in key areas. Eriksen in particular proved to be a thorn in Chelsea's side. Possession doesn't win football matches though, goals do.

A couple of minutes before half-time, N'Golo Kante led a Blues counter attack and picked out Victor Moses who had waltzed into the Spurs penalty area inviting a clumsy challenge from Son. Down went Moses. Atkinson pointed to the spot. Lilywhites players protested vigorously… Willian stepped up… and beat Lloris again. 2-1

Phew!

Half-time came and went. Back underway, Chelsea sat back and allowed Tottenham to come on at them which was probably not the wisest thing to do. Another piece of perfect pin-point passing wizardry from Christian Eriksen brought Spurs level again. The Denmark international picked out Dele Alli who had got away from David Luiz sufficiently to blast the ball home from ten yards out. 2-2

Game on again! Nerves jangled. The atmosphere crackled with an intensity that made the hairs on the back of my neck stand on end. This is what football was all about. Expectation. Hope. Fear. Yeah… that possession thing again. Spurs were having too much of it.

What would Conte do?

Send on Eden Hazard and Diego Costa just after the hour mark, that's what. Genius or a no brainer? Genius to be able to have such crown jewels on the bench to be able to execute such a double substitution. Willian and Michy Batshuayi made way. The former looked slightly peeved, the latter, well he'd put a shift in… good on the kid.

Shortly after, Pochettino fiddled with his defence replacing Son with Kyle Walker… and not long after that Conte replaced Pedro with Cesc Fabregas. The substitutions would have a pivotal outcome on the result of the game. Moments after coming on, Fabregas delivered what was Chelsea's only corner of the game into the Spurs penalty area, Walker might have done better with his clearance… the ball bobbled out to Hazard on the edge of the box… a couple of touches were followed up by a fizzing shot. 3-2

Tottenham to their credit didn't give up, but Chelsea, with Fabregas and Hazard looking as fresh as Spring daisies were an altogether different proposition now. Conte had got it just right… again! With 10 minutes to go the dynamic duo combined to carve open the Spurs defence. Hazard then ran with the ball away from goal and found Nemanja Matic 25-yards out… Boom! The Serbia international didn't deliberate too long about what the best course of action was delivering a net-bursting volley that crashed into the top of the net. 4-2

Game over!

Watching the highlights back on TV later that night, the reaction of Kurt Zouma to Matic's goal summed up the day. Zouma's unbridled joy was a beautiful sight to behold. It may have only been 22 April, but for me, and thousands of others I expect… it felt as if Christmas had come early.

Antonio Conte rightfully got the post-match plaudits with glowing appraisals of his game plan. A week's a long time in football eh.

"During the season there is a moment as a coach you must take a strong decision," said the Blues boss after the match. "You have to take a risk. If you win the plan worked, if you don't the responsibility is on you. I think today our plan worked very well."

Succinct as ever from Conte who now had a couple of days to prepare a new plan this time to defeat Southampton. I slept well and dreamed of winning the Double… and why not? It had been one hell of a day!

23 April

Arsenal came from behind to beat Manchester City 2-1 at Wembley in the weekend's other semi-final. Alexis Sanchez, continually linked with a move to Stamford Bridge in the summer, scored the winner to set up an all-London final on 27 May.

N'Golo Kante rounded off a perfect couple of days by picking up the PFA Player of the Year award at London's Grosvenor Hotel. There were no dissenting voices heard that this was in some way an injustice. Well done N'Golo!

25 April

Premier League
Chelsea 4 Southampton 2
Stamford Bridge
Attendance: 41,618
Referee: Lee Mason

Chelsea (3-4-3): Thibaut Courtois, Cesar Azpilicueta, David Luiz, Gary Cahill (c), Victor Moses (John Terry 86), N'Golo Kante, Nemanja Matic, Marcos Alonso, Cesc Fabregas (Pedro 76) Diego Costa, Eden Hazard (Willian 89).
Scorers: Hazard 5, Cahill 45+1, Diego Costa 53, 89.
Booked: Kante 40, Fabregas 49

Southampton (4-2-3-1): Forster, Soares, Stephens, Yoshida, Bertrand, Romeu, Davis (c), Ward-Prowse (Long 82), Tadic, Boufal (Redmond 68), Gabbiadini (Rodriguez 86).
Scorers: Romeu 24, Bertrand 90+4
Booked: Romeu 60, Tadic 73

Chelsea returned to Premier League action and continued where they left off at Wembley with another resounding 4-2 victory this time over Southampton.

As expected, Antonio Conte restored Eden Hazard, Diego Costa and fit again skipper Gary Cahill to the Blues starting XI and the trio responded by providing all Chelsea's goals in an action-packed game.

Hazard opened the scoring early on. Cesc Fabregas, deployed in an attacking role, picked out a re-energized Costa who had darted forward and got behind the Southampton defence. The Chelsea striker held the ball up confidently before knocking it back to Hazard who swept the ball across the box and into the bottom left corner of Fraser Forster's goal. It was the Belgium international's 15th Premier League strike of the season, his best return since joining Chelsea in June 2012.

Hazard might have doubled the Blues advantage 10 minutes later, but a curled shot whistled over the bar. Southampton battled back to equalise through a scrappy goal from former Chelsea player Oriol Romeu who prodded home a loose ball from close range after Thibaut Courtois had parried a shot from Manolo Gabbiadini into his path.

THE ITALIAN JOB

Romeu didn't celebrate, but his teammates did. Squeaky bum time. The goal gave the Saints heart. Thoughts turned back to the Palace home game in which Chelsea had surrendered an early lead and ended up losing. Stamford Bridge was bouncing though. The Shed End, whose pre-match banners display had been particularly impressive, were leading the *Chelsea, Chelsea* chants. Surely lightning wasn't going to strike twice?

It took a captain's goal from Gary Cahill on the stroke of half-time to settle nerves and restore Chelsea's lead. N'Golo Kante latched onto a cleared corner ball and floated it to the edge of the box finding Marcos Alonso who headed it into the middle of the area. From my Gate 17 vantage point at the other end of the ground it looked like Diego Costa had powered the ball into the net via an overhead kick. We celebrated wildly then watched the replay and saw that it was Cahill who had nipped in and headed the ball beyond Forster.

The second-half was all about Diego Costa.

Having failed to score in five successive Premier League games, Costa's 30-minute FA Cup cameo off the bench against Spurs had given little indication of the man-of-the-match display that would follow against Southampton... indeed a woefully misdirected header simply served to underline the thoughts of many Blues supporters that the striker's useful time as a Chelsea player had come to an end. Conte of course had other ideas, thankfully.

Costa's first goal came in the 53rd minute. Cesc Fabregas and Eden Hazard combined for a short corner which saw the Spaniard precisely pick out Costa who got his head to the ball and directed into the net. His second was a thing of beauty. A minute from time, Costa worked a one-two first with Hazard and then with substitute Pedro before shifting the ball from foot to foot and drilling it home. Wonderful! *Diego, Diego, Diego.*

It had been a while!

Costa may have failed to find the net of late, but against Southampton he brought his league tally for the season to a still impressive 19 and significantly his first goal was his 50th in just 85 games. A noteworthy strike-rate to reach the landmark that bettered by five matches Harry Kane's feat of reaching 50 league goals for Tottenham achieved earlier in the season.

Whether or not Costa would still be a Chelsea player next season was immaterial in respect of the current campaign. The striker had the between his teeth again and would be eyeing the Blues favourable run of fixtures with a smile on his face.

The biggest cheer of the evening had come a few minutes before Costa's second goal when John Terry came on as a late substitute for Victor Moses. Remarkably, it was Terry's first Premier League appearance since the 2-2 away draw with Swansea in September when he'd picked up the injury which would cruelly shape his final season as a Chelsea player.

Terry was cheered every time he touched the ball and made a couple of telling interceptions, but he could do nothing about Southampton's cheeky second goal deep in stoppage time which saw Ryan Bertrand, a Champions League winner with Chelsea, head home a Jay Rodriguez cross.

He's won more than you. He's won more than you. Ryan Bertrand, he's won more than you, we chanted with smiles on our faces.

Referee Lee Mason blew the full time whistle. It felt like an important victory. Assuming that Tottenham were going to beat Crystal Palace the following night, Chelsea, with five games remaining, would still be four points ahead of their rivals and needing four wins to be champions.

Blues supporters had played their part in the stirring victory over Southampton and Conte was swift to acknowledge this fact after the match. "It's important to stay together and understand this moment, to be ready to push our team in the right way," he said grittily. "For this reason I want to say thanks to our fans because they showed great passion."

26 April

Watching Chelsea's Under-18s took precedence over the voyeuristic opportunity to see if Tottenham Hotspur might come unstuck against Crystal Palace at Selhurst Park. Roman Abramovich, Antonio Conte, John Terry and Frank Lampard, thought the same, all four of them enthusiastic spectators looking on as the Blues beat Manchester 5-1 in the second leg of the FA Youth Cup Final at Stamford Bridge to register a 6-2 aggregate victory and win the trophy for a sensational fourth year in succession.

Trevor Chalobah, Ike Ugbo, Callum Hudson Odoi, Dujon Sterling and Cole Dasilva scored for Chelsea showing there were goals right through Jody Morris's young side. How far would these kids end up going with their careers at Stamford Bridge? Ah the perennial question. Morris too was showing great promise as a coach. What would the future hold for the former Blues midfielder who had come through the junior ranks at the Bridge and become the youngest player to play in the Premier League for the club as a 17-year old back in February 1996?

Meanwhile…

Crystal Palace 0 Tottenham Hotspur 1

The next round of fixtures had a pivotal feel about them. Said before I know. But this time… yes, this time… Chelsea's trip to Goodison Park to face Everton a couple of hours before Tottenham 'entertained' Arsenal in a north London derby at White Hart Lane looked like a pair of matches the results of which could shape the title run in.

Three points for Conte's men at Goodison in the early afternoon game and what happened at the Lane would be just a sideshow. Anything other than a Chelsea victory on Merseyside and nerves would start fraying again. Surely Arsenal would turn up against Spurs? The Gunners still had an outside chance of securing a top four Champions League slot and even if they didn't they had to be motivated to help kill off their deadly rivals' title ambitions?

Forget about Tottenham.

Chelsea just had to do their job.

I thought about Conte's mantra…

Pay attention and be focused
Pay attention and be focused
Pay attention and be focused

30 April

Premier League
Everton 0 Chelsea 3
Goodison Park
Attendance: 39,595
Referee: Jonathan Moss

Chelsea (3-4-3): Thibaut Courtois, Cesar Azpilicueta, David Luiz (Nathan Ake 81), Gary Cahill (c), Victor Moses, N'Golo Kante, Nemanja Matic, Marcos Alonso, Pedro (Cesc Fabregas 81), Diego Costa, Eden Hazard (Willian 84).
Scorers: Pedro 65, Cahill 78, Willian 86
Booked: Cahill 34, Azpilicueta 39, Costa 56, Hazard 74

Everton (4-3-3): Stekelenburg, Holgate, Williams, Jagielka (c), Baines, Gueye, Davies, Barkley, Valencia (Kone 71), Lukaku, Calvert-Lewin (Mirallas 71).
Booked: Calvert-Lewin 37, Valencia 57, Gueye 77

Chelsea paid attention and remained focused at Goodison Park where a 3-0 victory enabled them to take the Premier League title race by the scruff of the neck. After an edgy, goalless first-half Antonio Conte's side played like Champions elect scoring three times without reply. Pedro broke the deadlock in the 66th minute with a world class strike, Gary Cahill doubled Chelsea's lead shortly after, and substitute Willian put the game beyond Everton's reach late on.

Having seen a ten-point lead at the top of the table whittled down to just four points by second-placed Tottenham Hotspur, anything other than a win at Goodison would have seen Chelsea reeled in further by Spurs as the Lilywhites beat Arsenal 2-0 at White Hart Lane later the same afternoon. Irrespective of the Tottenham result, psychologically, beating Everton had the feeling of being the pivotal win the Blues needed.

Passion and perception had become impressive cornerstones for Conte. Against Everton, as per usual, the Italian lived and breathed every kick of the ball and yet again he made the right call with his starting XI... and the timing of his substitutions, excepting the forced replacement of Luiz? Impeccable!!

Conte made just one change to the side that had triumphed over Southampton earlier in the week, Cesc Fabregas dropping to the bench to accommodate Pedro. It was half expected. Frustrating maybe for Fabregas, but despite his restricted game time during the course of the season the Spaniard's unerring contribution to Chelsea's cause continued to prove invaluable as did that of his fellow Barca old-boy Pedro and both players would have a huge say in determining the outcome of the game.

There was a tenacity about Ronald Koeman's Everton side in the first-half that unnerved me. Toffees trio, Dominic Calvert-Lewin, Enner Valencia and Romelu Lukaku proved a handful to contain and Calvert-Lewin striking the post in the first minute saw me having to retrieve my heart from my mouth. And what of Lukaku? Was he going to hurt and haunt? He certainly looked in the mood, and David Luiz was at times struggling to cope with the pacey, hulking Belgian.

Sometimes in football though, it takes a stroke of genius to break the resolve of an opposing team, and at Goodison Pedro provided that moment of virtuosity. 25 yards out from goal, the Spaniard latched onto a pass from Nemanja Matic, glided past Everton defender Phil Jagielka... and unleashed a left-foot thunderbolt which flew past Toffees keeper Maarten Stekelenberg into the roof of the net. 1-0 to Chelsea!

In an instant the complexion of the game changed.

A little over 10 minutes from time, Everton midfielder Idrissa Gaye who'd attached himself to Eden Hazard for much of the contest, chopped down the Belgium international. Hazard got up, dusted himself down and swung the resultant free-kick goalwards. Stekelenberg made a poor error of judgement and parried the ball weakly onto the knee of onrushing Gary Cahill. Goal! 2-0 Chelsea! Scrappy maybe, but it still counted and that's what counted.

Cahill, making his 150th Premier League start led the jubilant celebrations mirrored by travelling Blues supporters gathered in the Bullens Road Stand. The Chelsea skipper, robust as ever in defence now had eight goals in all competitions this season. A captain and leader in the mould of legend John Terry, Cahill was continuing to silence the critics that had sought to undermine his position in Conte's side.

The game was now over as a contest. Everton folded and stacked their cards... but there was still time for Chelsea to make the result look more of a rout than perhaps it was. With what I'm sure was his first touch, Willian, on as an 86th minute sub for Hazard, sped into the Toffees penalty area and ran onto a superlative Cesc Fabregas pass. Fabregas himself, not long on the pitch in place of Pedro had been played in by Diego Costa and proved himself to be the Blues assist-king once again as Willian swept the ball into a gorgeous, inviting, empty net. 3-0 Chelsea!

Referee Jonathan Moss, whose decisions along the way had seen seven players among them Cahill, Azpilicueta, Costa and Hazard yellow-carded eventually got round to blowing the final whistle. Was it Jon Moss the Premier League ref that had been in charge of the game or Jon Moss the Culture Club drummer? What's in a name? At the end of the game, it didn't matter. What did was the result and the three points that went with them. As the Blues players' made their way over to salute the ecstatic away support they were met with a rousing rendition of *We shall not, we shall not be moved* sung with hearty conviction.

We shall not, we shall not be moved. We shall not, we shall not be moved. Just like a team that's going to win the football league. We shall not be moved.

Antonio Conte's football philosophy had been a revelation from the day he signed on the dotted line to become Chelsea's manager. More sage-like words tumbled from his mouth after this critical victory. "I think we must continue this way… to play game by game and take three points in every game. We know every win in this part of the season is very important," he said calmly after his customary shower. "The road is long so we need to rest and prepare in the right way."

MAY 2017

4 May

Diego Costa possibly moving to China was back in the news with Tianjin Quanjian reported to have reached a pre-contract agreement worth a staggering £25 million a year to the 28-year old striker. Chelsea apparently were being offered £75 million for their player. If I were Antonio Conte I would offer to drive Costa to the airport myself. With that sort of money swelling the Stamford Bridge coffers, a deal to bring Lukaku 'home' could easily be put together if that's what the Blues boss genuinely wanted.

The Chinese Super League club managed by Italy legend Fabio Cannavaro were also rumoured to be interested in signing John Terry. Now that's one deal I could never see happening... not for all the tea in... ahem err China!

Conte didn't seem too concerned when pressed about the 'news'. "I am not worried about this. I see my players every day, at this point of the season," he said with a smile. "You have the fantastic position to reach a great target and win the Premier League and reach the final of the FA Cup. These are two big targets and are the most important thing for us. Speculation, is not important for me."

5 May

West Ham United 1 Tottenham Hotspur 0 ... Boom! An unexpected Friday night result that meant Mauricio Pochettino's side remained four points behind Chelsea having played a game more. Indeed, should Conte mastermind victory over Middlesbrough on Monday night and follow it up with another win away at West Bromwich Albion on the Friday, the title will be won before Spurs had the chance to kick another ball. Sky had perhaps been trying too hard when manipulating the fixture list for their own selfish purpose.

It's happening again, It's happening again. Tottenham Hotspur it's happening again, happy Hammers fans had chanted at the London Stadium as they ground out a 'famous' victory over Spurs. It was a reference of course to Spurs once more falling short when it mattered in the title race. Last season it was Leicester City, this time around it was going to be Chelsea.

Laugh? It was hard not too. It's fair to say the remainder of the weekend was blanketed by a very pleasant alcoholic haze. Boro, down among the dead men, would be relegated if they lost at the Bridge. Surely they couldn't put a spanner in the works a la Palace? I thought briefly back to the ridiculous two-legged relegation / promotion play off that Chelsea lost out on aggregate to Middlesbrough in May 1988. Shocking! A shiver ran down my spine. Calm yourself Marco. Trust Conte. Have another drink. I did. I felt confident and convinced myself that the only question that needed answering wasn't whether or not the Blues would beat Boro… just by how much?

Pay attention and be focused
Pay attention and be focused
Pay attention and be focused

7 May

There had been plenty of rumours doing the rounds since early March that Inter Milan were trying to lure Antonio Conte back to Italy, to be expected really. However, the latest tittle-tattle to bubble up in the media on the day I chose to renew my season ticket left me wincing with apprehension.

It was no secret that Barcelona manager Luis Enrique was set to depart the Camp Nou at the end of the season, and no real surprise to hear that the Catalan club were apparently also interested in Conte. Where the worry lay with this story was that unemployed former CSKA Moscow and Russia national team coach Leonid Slutsky, a close personal friend of Chelsea owner Roman Abramovich and a regular at Stamford Bridge this season, was suddenly being touted as a replacement for Conte should he leave!

I thought about the last time a friend of Roman's suddenly found himself cast in the role of Blues boss and broke out in a cold sweat. Now as it happened, the manager in question, Avram Grant, was a lovely fella who remarkably came for a drink with a few us in what used to be known as the So Bar just across the road from the Bridge shortly after he'd been sacked in May 2008… but in truth, Grant should never have got anywhere near the Chelsea job… and wouldn't have had it not been for his close connection

THE ITALIAN JOB

with Abramovich.

A non-story maybe, but as we all know... anything can happen when it comes to Chelsea Football Club!

8 May

Premier League
Chelsea 3 Middlesbrough 0
Stamford Bridge
Attendance: 41,500
Referee: Craig Pawson

Chelsea (3-4-3): Thibaut Courtois, Cesar Azpilicueta, David Luiz (John Terry 84), Gary Cahill (c), Victor Moses, Cesc Fabregas, Nemanja Matic, Marcos Alonso, Pedro (Nathaniel Chalobah 81), Diego Costa, Eden Hazard (Willian 71).
Scorers: Costa 23, Alonso 34, Matic 65

Middlesbrough (4-3-3): Guzan, Fabio, Chambers, Gibson (c), Friend, De Roon, Clayton, Forshaw (Leadbitter 57), Traore (Bamford 57), Negredo (Gestede 83), Downing.
Booked: Fabio 60, Bamford 89

Touching distance! Chelsea did what they had to do in front of an expectant Stamford Bridge crowd beating Middlesbrough and extending their lead at the top of the Premier League to seven points over Tottenham Hotspur with three games left to play. Goals from Diego Costa, Marcos Alonso and Nemanja Matic secured victory for Antonio Conte's side who ended the match knowing that victory away at West Bromwich Albion on Friday would secure the title.

The result confirmed Middlesbrough's swift relegation back to the Championship, and for older supporters like me there was a sugar-coated sweetness to this aspect of the evening that made it just perfect. Almost 30 years previously, May 1988, Boro had prevailed in a two-legged play-off which condemned Chelsea to a season in the old Second Division so this was payback time.

Pre-match was notably marked with an excellent display of banners in The Shed which had been getting more and more visually creative and vocal as the season progressed. Just before kick-off as the familiar sound of *Liquidator* was booming out of the stadium PA system, six banners dropped down from the top tier. Alternating in blue and white the words KEEP THE BLUE FLAG FLYING HIGH. A huge THE SHED banner depicting Chelsea's lion rampant regardent was unfurled and held in position. It look great from my vantage point over in Gate 17. (My seat is in the Upper Matthew Harding Stand on the wrap-around section with the East Stand.) The Lower Matthew also made a visual mark with the expansive PRIDE OF LONDON banner being unfurled and passed overheads from east to west.

The scene was set. Chelsea just needed to get on with the business of winning the game and in truth, despite the edgy opening, the result was never in doubt.

Diego Costa broke the deadlock in the 23rd minute slotting the ball close in between Boro keeper Brad Guzan's legs. Staying or going to China at the end of the season looked like the last thing on Costa's mind as he celebrated his 20th league goal of the season.

Cesc Fabregas, who had already made several statements of intent tickling the visitors tummies with some precision passing, sent in a diagonal ball from the left-hand side of Boro's penalty area which was a visiting defender helped on it's way to Costa. 1-0

The sense of relief was palpable.

Are you watching White Hart Lane reverberated around the ground.

Fabregas was in his element bossing proceedings from midfield. Crazy to think that the 30-year old was only starting the game because N'Golo Kante, who had just been named the Football Writers Association Footballer of the Year, a prestigious accolade to match the PFA Player of the Year award recently collected, had failed to recover from a muscle strain.

When @chucklescabbie had broke the team news at 7pm at the cfcuk stall, Kante's absence had been met with indifference by those gathered round, me included. At face value this might seem strange given the high degree of influence the France international had in propelling Chelsea to the title and FA Cup final, indeed at any other club his absence might have caused a mild panic… but not at the Bridge… principally because Conte had Fabregas in reserve to replace him.

Conte had used Fabregas sparingly this season. The arrival of Kante last

THE ITALIAN JOB

summer and the Italian's preference to partner the France international with Nemanja Matic in Chelsea's midfield engine room meant the 30-year old Spaniard suddenly found himself on the periphery of the first team. Benched for the majority of league games, cameo substitute appearances had been the name of the game with first XI starts mainly coming in the domestic cup competitions. A lack of European football also proved restrictive.

Crazy to think that a player who would be among the first names on the team sheet of many Premier League managers and be an ever-present to boot could find himself marginalised in such a way. Understandably, before Christmas, rumours had surfaced that Fabregas might leave in the January transfer window... obviously he didn't... and the stories continued with plenty suggesting he may depart at the end of the campaign.

In the midst of all this, the former Barcelona and Arsenal star had, to his eternal credit, got on with the job and, when given the opportunity as he was against Boro, showcased his supreme talents. There would be no shortage of suitors for his services should Conte allow him to leave.

Randomly, my thoughts turned to Wembley, the FA Cup final and the prospect of securing the Double. Fabregas' former club Arsenal would provide the opposition, and Gunners fans had been increasingly vocal in their disdain of their former hero when he'd previously lined up against them for the Blues. What chance of him playing then, to really get their collective goat?

There was no guarantee Conte would start Fabregas against Arsenal. In the 4-2 semi-final triumph over Tottenham Hotspur, the midfielder had come off the bench with a little over 15 minutes left and the score at 2-2 with Spurs in the ascendancy. He transformed the game almost immediately, first taking the corner which would lead to Eden Hazard scoring Chelsea's crucial third goal, and then combining superbly with the Belgium international in the build-up to Matic's wonder-strike which sealed victory.

Whatever part Fabregas played in the final, and I felt certain he would, there was a definite sense among Blues supporters that his contribution would be significant. A goal? An assist? The set-up for Matic against Boro had made him the first player in Premier League history to provide 10 assists in six different seasons. I chuckled at the thought it must take a special kind of person to compile all these weird nerdy statistics that have become a part and parcel of the way the modern game is reported. You'll note there are no 'heat maps' in this book!

It's true that Fabregas certainly hogged the limelight on this particular night, my man-of-the-match for sure and deservedly so... however, for me personally, his countryman Marcos Alonso ran him a close second. Alonso's surprise acquisition on transfer deadline day was met with many furrowed brows among the Chelsea brethren, but playing at left wing-back the Spaniard proved to be nothing short of a revelation.

Against Boro, Alonso's lightning quick pace and ability to continually get in behind a pedestrian defence brought a sixth league goal of the campaign. Cesar Azpilicueta, making his 150th top-flight appearance for Chelsea, found Alonso with a raking pass and from the tightest of angles the 26-year old found the net as Guzan diverted the ball over the line. The Boro goalkeeper who'd made a spectacular save from Alonso was understandably distraught. 2-0. Game effectively over.

The floodgates could have opened, but they didn't. The second-half brought one more goal which that man Fabregas was instrumental in creating for Matic. A rousing rendition of *Fabregas is magic* was followed by *Tottenham Hotspur it's happened again,* amusing this as it was the past tense version of West Ham's chant from the previous Friday when they'd defeated Spurs. The Chelsea crowd were in a jubilant *Antonio, Antonio, Antonio* mood. Where it not for the fact that the game was being played on a Monday night there would have been plenty of hangovers the next day.

Not for the first time this season, the biggest cheer of the 90 minutes came late on when David Luiz was withdrawn and John Terry took to the field. Every time Chelsea's captain, leader, legend touched the ball he was applauded from the stands. Given the current scenario, if the Blues did indeed win the title at West Brom on Friday it would give Antonio Conte the opportunity not only to rest key players for the cup final but give Terry a full game or maybe (preferably) two which would enable supporters to give him the fitting send off his long service and outstanding achievements deserved.

Chelsea Football Club hadn't exactly covered itself in glory in this respect... the most prominent memory being the uncelebrated and untimely departure of Frank Lampard though there had been plenty more in my time of following the club. Now, barring a disaster of biblical proportions, they would have the opportunity to appease Blues fans by celebrating the phenomenal career of John George Terry where he and they would like it... on the Stamford Bridge pitch after he'd played his final competitive game. I made a note to myself to have a bet on JT scoring. That would be the icing on the cake.

After the game Antonio Conte was understandably happy. "We must be pleased. It was a great performance, my players showed commitment and work-rate for three important points," said the Italian, his eyes gleaming with pride. "At this stage it was important to win and exploit Tottenham's defeat. Now, another step to the title. We have to rest well and prepare for West Brom."

From the very first time Conte addressed the media as Chelsea manager, it was clear that he had a very personable side to his character that became more and more endearing as this rollercoaster ride of a season got going. At the final whistle, the Blues boss had showed his class by acknowledging and saluting the Middlesbrough supporters who unlike their team had turned up on the night. It would be a long journey back to Teeside for them. A time for reflection, a time to contemplate and hope that Boro chairman Steve Gibson might be able to find someone with the same qualities as Antonio Conte to restore their club's ailing fortunes.

11 May

"Tomorrow's game is the most important for us. It's a final. We are always thinking in this way," said Antonio Conte addressing the press the day before the West Brom game. "My players are totally focused on the moment. We are in a good position but we need three more points to make this target."

Pedro meanwhile deservedly picked up the April goal of the month award for his spectacular deadlock-breaking strike against Everton. It was the second time the Spaniard had won the award during the course of the season. Who'd have thought it last summer? Another Conte success story!

12 May

Premier League
West Bromwich Albion 0 Chelsea 1
The Hawthorns
Attendance: 25,367
Referee: Michael Oliver

Chelsea (3-4-3): Thibaut Courtois, Cesar Azpilicueta, David Luiz, Gary Cahill (c), Victor Moses (Kurt Zouma 86) Cesc Fabregas, Nemanja Matic, Marcos Alonso, Pedro (Michy Batshuayi 75), Diego Costa, Eden Hazard (Willian 75).
Scorer: Batshuayi 82

West Brom (4-1-4-1): Foster, Dawson, McAuley (Wilson 64), Evans, Nyom, Fletcher (c), Brunt, Livermore, Field (Yacob 51), McClean (Chadli 59), Rondon.
Booked: McClean 20, Field 36, Wilson 71.

Singing, singing, Chelsea are the champions!
Singing, singing, Chelsea are the kings!

A 1-0 victory at the Hawthorns over a dogged West Brom side ensured the Blues secured the Premier League title with two games to spare. Substitute Michy Batshuayi, yet to start a top-flight game for the London club, scored the goal that mattered inside the last 10 minutes to seal the deal for Antonio Conte's team who were tenacious throughout a contest they thoroughly deserved to win.

One season in the Chelsea job and Antonio Conte had made a serious case with Blues supporters to be recognised as the greatest manager the club has ever had. From tactical know-how to personable qualities and everything in-between, the Italian ticked every box in a way that had never been done before. Having the Midas touch helped as well. Against West Brom, with 15 minutes left and the score seemingly stuck for perpetuity at 0-0, Conte rolled the dice and replaced flagging duo Eden Hazard and Pedro with Willian and Batshuayi and it was the underutilised Belgium international who stepped up to score the goal which brought with it victory, three points and the title.

Expectation had been mounting throughout the day with the whole of planet Chelsea in a buoyant mood. In the West Midlands, West Brom's modest ground played host to the champions elect and the Blues travelling

THE ITALIAN JOB

support gathered in the 2,800 capacity Smethwick End Stand and a few other less advisable vantage points were in fine voice from the start despite the local stewards preventing them from taking banners into the stadium.

The Baggies had long since stopped claiming that they rinsed reggae instrumental *Liquidator* through their stadium PA before Chelsea and indeed their local neighbours Wolves. The sound of the Harry J Allstars classic was welcomed though and set the scene for what was to follow.

Conte retained the same starting XI that had dealt comfortably with Middlesbrough on Monday meaning valorous and fit again midfielder N'Golo Kante found himself on the bench. No real surprise there really given the majestic form Cesc Fabregas had displayed against Boro.

Tony Pulis' teams never lie down and make things easy for the opposition, and as usual it was a case of his brawn against our brain with Chelsea having to be at their tenacious best to eventually get the result they needed. Indeed West Brom might have scored early on when Salamon Rondon got past David Luiz to get a goal-bound header away. Fortunately Thibaut Courtois was able to make a crucial save and immediately the Blues started to up the ante.

Eden Hazard had a predictably tough evening though as West Brom defenders Craig Dawson, Allan Nyom and Chris Brunt ensured he would be counting the number of bruises on his legs the following morning. Hazard still managed to provide Chelsea with incisiveness and on another night might have questioned Conte about why he was substituted.

Victor Moses, a constant thorn in West Brom's side, was denied a goal just before the break when Baggies keeper Ben Foster kept out his rasping drive. Unfortunately for Moses, he too was given the Tony Pulis Sunday pub team treatment with James McClean the main culprit. The Blues wingback was too good though for the Baggies player who would eventually be booked for his trouble and replaced on the hour mark.

There was a curious Chelsea-esque air of inevitability that Batshuayi would be the man to find the back of the net when he came on for Pedro in the 75th minute. The 23-year old striker may have felt neglected along the way this season, but despite being marginalised by Conte for the bulk of the Blues top-flight campaign he'd always remained motivated and had a cheerful disposition that was endearing. I thought back to his first couple of league appearances of Chelsea. He'd come off the bench in the season-opener against West Ham and teed up Diego Costa for the late winner, and in the next match as a late substitute at Watford he'd scored his first goal. Why not more of the same now? It would be proper Chels if it happened.

And so it came to pass…

The Blues had kept West Brom on the ropes for a long period before they scored. Just one break that was all that was needed. Marcos Alonso first nodded the ball to Gary Cahill who sensing perhaps the opportunity to write himself into the history books fired off a shot from outside the Baggies penalty area. That wasn't going to do it GC. Chelsea needed to be more clinical. The ball fell loose though to Cesar Azipilicueta on the edge of the six-yard box and the Spaniard squared the ball to Batshuayi who put the ball past Ben Foster. 1-0.

For Azpilicueta, simply outstanding throughout the game, capping a five-star performance with a well-crafted assist would earn him plenty of man-of-the-match plaudits. An ever-present to date in Chelsea's title-winning campaign, Azpi once more proved his versatility both as a defender and cutting edge chance creator. Surely one of the most underrated players in the Premier League, the 27-year olds contribution to the Blues glory story needed to be highlighted more.

We'll just call you Dave, we'll just call you Dave. Azpilicueta we'll just call you Dave.

The chant would be heard soon enough, but right now Chelsea fans behind the goal had erupted in an orgiastic frenzy of delirium. Simultaneously, Antonio Conte wheeled round in his technical area and charged to his backroom team and bench to celebrate. Meanwhile at the other end of the ground scuffles broke out as Blues supporters who'd acquired tickets in the home sections blew their cover by cheering. Referee Michael Oliver halted the game momentarily while the trouble was brought under control and a couple of fans were removed from the pitch. There was always a chance of such an eventuality occurring given the news that West Brom followers had been selling their own tickets at inflated prices to cash in on the game's significance. Fortunately, matters didn't get out of hand and Oliver was able to restart proceedings and the match played out to its favourable conclusion.

The jubilant celebrations at the final whistle and beyond were magnificent. Chelsea players swan-dived on the pitch in front of rapturous Blues supporters who serenaded each and every one of them with their own chant while Antonio Conte was hoisted up and thrown into the air (and caught of course).

Championes… Campeones… Campione (take your pick, personal choice the latter as it's Italian) *Olé, Olé, Olé* sang the Chelsea crowd after bouncing for a minute.

And the Celery Moment as my mate Chidge likes to refer to the defining happening of a matchday on his excellent Chelsea Fancast show… Willian singing the Willian song! *He hates Tottenham, he hates Tottenham…*

Post-match comments underlined the belief that it was Conte's ethos that had sparked Chelsea's spectacular renaissance after the debacle-laden departure of José Mourinho.

"People have written us off as a team and individually and this has shut them up," announced Gary Cahill. "We are champions. It's another one in the cabinet."

"These boys have been on the field doing it week in week out. It's been a delight to sit and watch, a different perspective," added John Terry. "The togetherness was shown from day one."

Michy Batshuayi's emoji and emotion-laden tweet summed things up perfectly.

@mbatshuayi Don't worry I got this yall. God Loves unexpected heroes. Very happy tonight enjoy the title FAM!!! #CFC #KTBFFH #Neversurrender

Cesc Fabregas won the prize for the most astute observation of the evening. "The beauty of football, a player who didn't play a lot scores the winning goal for the championship," said the man with the magic hat. "Football is fucking unbelievable," he concluded.

Too right Cesc! Glorious unpredictability and all that.

The final words had to go to Antonio Conte, and what priceless jewels they were once again. "Every game I feel like I have played with my players! I show my passion and my will, my desire to stay with my players in every moment of the game. This is me, I am this," said the Italian exuberantly. "In the present, in the past, I stay with my players in positive and negative situations. We won this title together."

Beautiful! Simply beautiful!

*****

Chelsea's first team may have grabbed all the headlines on Friday 12 May but it would be remiss not to mention the achievement of the Blues Under-18 side managed by Jody Morris who as a result of beating Reading 3-0 at Cobham earlier in the day won the Under-18 Premier League. The triumph paired with the FA Youth Cup success represented a first league and cup double for Chelsea's youth side since 1961.

15 May

Premier League
Chelsea 4 Watford 3
Stamford Bridge
Attendance: 41,473
Referee: Lee Mason

Chelsea (3-4-3): Asmir Begovic, Kurt Zouma, John Terry (c), Nathan Ake, Cesar Azpilicueta, N'Golo Kante, Nathaniel Chalobah (Cesc Fabregas 77), Kenedy (Ola Aina 74), Willian, Michy Batshuayi (Pedro 83), Eden Hazard.
Scorers: Terry 21, Azpilicueta 35, Batshuayi 48, Fabregas 88
Booked: Ake 29, Chalobah 57

Watford (3-4-2-1): Gomes (c), Mariappa, Prodl, Holebas, Amrabat, Behrami, Doucoure, Janmaat, Cleverley, Capoue (Deeney 90), Niang (Okaka 70).
Scorers: Capoue 23, Janmaat 50, Okaka 73
Sent off: Prodl 90+1
Booked: Holebas 3, Amrabat 10, Prodl 82, Deeney 90+4

Chelsea's first game since winning the Premier League title had circus feel to it as the Blues ran out winners by the odd goal in seven against Watford. Antonio Conte made nine changes to his starting XI from the side that beat West Brom on Friday and one of his 'fresh' faces, John Terry, making his first top-flight start since September, opened the scoring with what was Chelsea's 100th goal in all competitions this season.

Moments later though, Watford were level when JT had a rush of blood to the head and presented Etienne Capoue with a gilt edged opportunity to equalize... which he did. Man of the match Cesar Azpilicueta, redeployed at right wing-back by Conte, restored Chelsea's lead before the break and when Michy Batshuayi made it 3-1 shortly after the restart it looked like the Blues might run away with the game.

Watford were far from done though. Daryl Janmaat pulled a goal back on 50 minutes and with barely 10 minutes left substitute Stefano Okaka, a player with the physical attributes of lower league legend Adebayo 'the beast' Akinfenwa, trundled forward to level the score at 3-3.

Chelsea didn't win the Premier League by chance. Persistency and playing to the final whistle had served Conte's troops well time and again and not for the first time this season it was a late goal that brought victory. Super sub Cesc Fabregas entered the fray on 77 minutes and scored the winner with three minutes left. Stamford Bridge understandably erupted breaking into an enthusiastically noisy rendition of *That's why we're Champions…*

Referee Lee Mason who'd had his work cut out policing what for reasons unknown evolved into a bad-tempered encounter… with Watford largely the culpable party… finally saw red and sent Hornets defender Sebastian Prodl off for a second yellow offence in injury time.

Pre-match banter at the cfcuk stall had concerned itself with Antonio Conte potentially resting maybe three or four players. David Luiz, Eden Hazard and Diego Costa were viewed as the likely lads and so when @chucklescabbie announced the team at 7pm, he'd had to hold his phone out for all to see the screen as many thought he'd been drinking. That was some rotation from the Blues boss, but nobody was fazed by his decision. The inclusion of John Terry was very well received and immediately led to Dave Johnstone and myself scouring bookmaker sites for the best odds on our captain, leader, legend to ripple the net. That proved profitable!

The Chelsea massive gathered inside Stamford Bridge we're understandably in a celebratory mood and it was The Shed once more who provided the most visually stimulating display pre kick-off with drop down banners from the upper tier spelling out C H A M P I O N S. A simple message that conveys everything it needs to especially to Tottenham Hotspur supporters who were coming for us, but never quite reached us. *Are you watching White Hart Lane?*

How much fun can you have with your clothes on? Plenty when Chelsea have just won the league and deprived Spurs from doing just that. *Champions of England, you'll never sing that.*

As the game got underway the crowd had unified for a banging rendition of *Antonio, Antonio, Antonio* and Don Conte applauded the four stand sections of the Bridge. Unbeknown to us, his wife Elisabetta Muscarello was among us, and photos emerged later of her overcome with emotion and wiping away tears as she witnessed the reverential love for her husband. Such adoration would surely smooth a path to living in London next season for Elisabetta and daughter Vittoria who had been at the Middlesbrough game the previous week and held up a canvass which depicted a cartoon graphic of her Dad and his players and bore the slogan The Confather.

The Confather – not too sure if that worked for me personally. Conte is nicknamed 'il martello' (the hammer) in his native Italy… now that is far more evocative isn't it! Shame that hammers have an association with West Ham otherwise we could have got all over that.

Conte's team selection owed more to the fact the Italian, with the FA Cup final in mind, was resting the majority of his preferred first XI rather than displaying a great desire to 'play the youth'. Nevertheless, it was great to see the likes of Kenedy, Nathaniel Chalobah, Nathan Ake all start. Chalobah once again caught my eye. I thought once more about that Twitter meme from the Man City away game before Christmas that showed a photo of Chalobah standing over Sergio Aguero captioned *everyone's a gangster until a gangster walks in the room.* Funny that. Chalobah certainly looks like he has what it takes to be a proper Chelsea player, but then we've all said that so many times about so many players haven't we. So let's wait and see.

Among those rested was Gary Cahill. Along with Cesar Azpilicueta, Cahill had been Chelsea's only ever-present to date this season… now it was just Azpi… perhaps the most underrated player in the Premier League if not world football. I'll come back to this observation in more detail in the review section at the end of the book.

Given so many changes, Conte's decision to play Eden Hazard for the full 90 minutes given the physical abuse the Belgium international has endured for much of the campaign seemed somewhat strange. Would Hazard feature in the final game of the season against Sunderland? Had he just played his last full game as a Chelsea player at Stamford Bridge? The rumours were doing the rounds again that Real Madrid were clearing the decks at the Bernabeu and preparing a world record bid for the 26-year old. I hoped it was just the usual poppycock.

THE ITALIAN JOB

I can't rightly recall which goal, John Terry's opener, or Cesc Fabragas' winner received the mightiest cheer. Terry's probably. We were still celebrating it and counting our winnings when he made an error of judgment at the other end of the pitch which resulted in Watford's equalizer. Still it didn't matter really. *Double, Double, Double, John Terry has won the Double...* JT probably wouldn't get a game in the FA Cup final against Arsenal, but that wouldn't matter because if Chelsea won his special chant would be augmented with the word 'again'.

The final whistle brought with it fireworks, streamers and ticker-tape. Conte and his players circled the pitch exchanging applause with supporters, the Italian and John Terry taking turns to wear a decent-looking inflatable gold crown. This was great. The final game would surely eclipse it.

I wondered what Antonio made of the match?

"For sure, at this stage of the season, I like to see this type of game because it's funny to watch a game and see both teams scoring four and three goals," he explained. "Above all, once you have won the League you can allow these situations."

19 May

Antonio Conte's presser ahead of the final league game of the season with Sunderland saw the Blues boss quizzed about a starting role for JT. Irrespective of what was decided, Terry would lift the 15th major trophy of his career after the Black Cats match and there was no doubt that the man himself would have wanted his 717th appearance to come from the starting whistle rather than the subs bench.

Conte was inscrutably cryptic with his answer saying, "John is a champion and he deserves the best. It will be a surprise. It's important to make the best decision and to find the best solution for him, for his career. He's a legend for this club and in this season he has been very important to win this title. For this reason I think I have to take my time and to make the best decision for him."

All of that translated to me as meaning Terry was going to start. One way or another it was going to be emotional. I thought about the fact that Conte had sanctioned a one-year extension to Chelsea's captain, leader, legend at the start of the season... I knew what his decision was going to be...

21 May

Premier League
Chelsea 5 Sunderland 1
Stamford Bridge
Attendance: 41,618
Referee: Neil Swarbrick

Chelsea (3-4-3): Thibaut Courtois, Cesar Azpilicueta, David Luiz, John Terry (c) (Gary Cahill 26), Victor Moses, N'Golo Kante, Cesc Fabregas, Marcos Alonso, Willian, Diego Costa (Michy Batshuayi 62), Eden Hazard (Pedro 70).
Scorers: Willian 8, Hazard 61, Pedro 78, Batshuayi 90, 90+2.
Booked: Costa 39

Sunderland (3-5-2): Pickford, Jones (Gibson 88), O'Shea (c), Lescott, Manquillo, Rodwell (Gooch 62), Cattermole, Larsson, Oviedo; Januzaj, Borini.
Scorer: Manquillo 3
Booked: Jones 48

Champions Chelsea thrashed relegated Sunderland 5-1 at Stamford Bridge and in doing so a new Premier League record of 30 wins in a season. The centre-piece of an emotion-packed afternoon was fabled captain, leader, legend John Terry, making his final home appearance for the London club, being afforded a superb tribute as he was substituted in the 26th minute, mirroring the shirt number he has worn with distinction throughout his career.

This was the 'surprise' that Antonio Conte had alluded to a couple of says previously. Terry left the pitch via a guard of honour from his teammates and a standing ovation from the supporters. It looked theatrical and stage-managed, but nobody on planet Chelsea cared. Of course there were a clutch of dissenting voices led by a couple of BBC pundits. Former Tottenham Hotspur player Garth Crooks told viewers he was "uncomfortable with it" while Alan Shearer somewhat pompously suggested that the "integrity of the game" had somehow been "undermined".

Other predictable sections of the media joined in. A journalist whose name is an anagram of Wasted Thyme, and who had decided shortly after John Terry had announced his departure from Stamford Bridge that his playing career would be defined as 'moral cowardice', described the tribute as 'toe-curling' and advised that it had presented an opportunity to scam bookmakers. This latter observation was based on analysis of the Twitter feed of visionary Chelsea supporter and cfcuk fanzine maestro David Johnstone aka @onlyapound who had predicted the event and tweeted "John Terry starts today and will be substituted in the 26th minute #CaptainLeaderLegend #WeWillAlwaysLuvYa". (Bookmaker Paddy Power honoured two inspired bets placed at odds of 100/1 that JT would be subbed in the 26th minute. Cost to bookie £3,500... hardly the betting scam of the century.)

When the storm in a teacup subsided it transpired that the stunt had been John Terry's idea, executed with the full blessing of Antonio Conte and indeed Sunderland manager David Moyes who agreed to have his side put the ball out of play so the substitution could take place.

Waxing lyrical after the game, Conte said of Terry's guard of honour, "He deserved this. He's a legend of this club, not just this club but one of the best defenders in the world." The tributes to JT had started before kick off with The Shed putting on a superb visual display comprising two large banners, one unfurled in the upper tier which depicted Terry with the wording 'PROPER CHELS' at the foot and a second which draped down to the lower tier and read 'Thank you for everything.' The banners were set off with blue and silver foil. It looked stunning and the whole end participated, kudos to all involved. Not to be outdone, the Matthew Harding Stand unfurled a giant 'Captain, Leader, Legend' flag which moved slowly over thousands of appreciative heads from the East Stand side to the West. *He's won it all* chanted the stadium in unison.

A huge banner which read 'Thank you – Grazie' pulled tight across the hotel was visible from Gate 17. I wasn't sure if this was a tribute to John Terry and Antonio Conte or just Conte... and, to be perfectly honest, as *He's won it all* morphed into *Antonio, Antonio* it didn't really seem to matter.

In the midst of such celebrations it was easy to forget that there was a football match to be played. The reminder of that came in the 3rd minute when Sunderland had the temerity to take the lead that muted what had been a very enthusiastic chant of *Champions of England we know what we are.*

With the exception of Terry, this was Conte's first choice defence and the Italian was less than impressed when Chelsea failed to clear their lines having conceded a sloppy free-kick. Javier Manquillo picked up a loose ball and volleyed home at the far post. Better to get such carelessness out of the way now rather than at Wembley in the cup final I thought to myself.

Despite this setback, it was clear from the off there was only going to be one winner. The Blues laid siege to the Black Cats goal and in the end gave them a mauling. Willian soon equalized with a fizzing low drive and the visitors had excellent young goalie Jordan Pickford and the woodwork to thank for keeping the scores level for the remainder of the first-half which of course was punctuated by the Terry tribute.

It was great to see David Luiz looking fit and reenergized after being rested by Conte while Cesar Azpilicueta who chalked up another impressive 90 minutes to give him an exceptional 100% appearance record Chelsea's league campaign was as effective as ever.

Chelsea upped the ante in the second-half and in the end blew Sunderland away. Shortly after the hour, Eden Hazard, who'd survived the close up and personal attentions of Billy Jones and Jack Rodwell, put the Blues in front with his 17th goal of the season. 10 minutes later, conscious of preserving Hazard's physical wellbeing as much as anything, Conte replaced the Belgium international with Pedro who duly obliged by scoring and providing an assist for fellow substitute Michy Batshuayi who had earlier replaced the somewhat ineffective Diego Costa. Batshuayi ended the match with a brace, not a bad return from the bench for Chelsea's expensive and underutilized striker.

Once again, Conte's substitutions had worked a treat. The 5-1 final score underlined Chelsea's worthy status as champions and the party started in earnest. Amusingly, with pretty much the entire Blues congregation hanging around to see the Premier League trophy presented, MC Neil Barnett announced that Arsenal defender Laurent Koscielny had been sent off against Everton and would miss the cup final. The Gunners beat the Toffees 2-1, but results elsewhere, notably Liverpool's 3-0 victory over Middlesbrough, meant Arsenal had failed to qualify for the Champions League for the first time in 20 years. *Arsene Wenger we want you to stay* chanted the Chelsea massive in unison… now that was funny.

Barnett also took the trouble to mention the fact that one of Chelsea's greatest ever players and a former outstanding manager to boot, Eddie McCreadie, was present. The previous evening Eddie had attended a celebration evening in his honour held at Stamford Bridge, an event tied to the publication of *Eddie Mac Eddie Mac*, a book (shameless plug here for another Gate 17 title) which chronicles the spritely now 77-year olds time as Blues boss.

John Terry's emotional send off may have grabbed the headlines, but it

THE ITALIAN JOB

would be remiss not to mention another Proper Chels farewell tribute this time to Steve Seymour the Gate 17 steward who had kept order in our section since the infill area between the main Matthew Harding stand and the East Stand first opened almost 20 years ago. With just a few minutes of the game remaining, wearing his high visibility jacket signed by many of our number, Steve was saluted and then led a rip-roaring rendition of *Zigger Zagger* which was followed up by everyone nearby singing *You're getting sacked in the morning* ... a chant which confused plenty of supporters in nearby blocks who weren't aware of what was going on.

Back with Terry... who else? After 717 appearances (would their be another at Wembley?) lifting the 15th trophy of his 22-year Chelsea career was bypassed by sentimentally when the 36-year old addressed supporters.

After acknowledging departing first team coach Steve Holland, he announced, "Today is one of the most difficult days of my life..."

It really did feel like the end of a defining Chelsea era for me and everyone around me...

JT's subsequent sentences were punctuated with ripples of applause, cheers... and tears.

"I've been very fortunate to work with some unbelievable players and managers throughout my career. I'm thankful to every single one of them."

"We all have to thank Roman Abramovich. I'd like to thank him and all the board. He's the best owner in world football."

"I'd like to thank my wife and my kids for supporting me in this amazing journey I've had."

"You are the best supporters in the world, without a shadow of a doubt. You've given me everything. You picked me up when I was down, sung my name when I had a bad game and disappointed you."

"I'll come back here one day, supporting the team for years to come."

It was stirring, it was great, it was Chelsea! Snidey comments from elsewhere reeked to high heaven of jealousy to be honest. Plain and simple.

John Terry, John Terry, John Terry.
John Terry, John Terry, John Terry.

John Terry, John Terry, John Terry
JOHN TERRY,... JOHN TERRY!!

(A detailed personal tribute to JT can be found in the review section at the end of this book.)

Antonio Conte was the last person Terry saluted and the Italian looked as happy as I'd ever seen him. What an incredible journey... and it wasn't over just yet. "This season can become fantastic if we are able to win the FA Cup," said the Blues boss later in the day. "We must find the right motivation because the level is the same between ourselves and Arsenal, we lost 3-0 in the first game and then won 3-1. Now we have the opportunity to play the third game. We must find the right fire in our soul to work very hard this week and feel this game. It's a great opportunity to win the Double."

We must find the right fire in our soul
We must find the right fire in our soul

A new Conte mantra which reminded me of...

Pay attention and be focused
Pay attention and be focused

When Saturday comes...

22 May

Antonio Conte won the two main prizes (Manager of the Year and Premier League Manager of the Year) at the League Managers' Association's annual awards evening. The associated positive vibe was erased almost immediately as news filtered through about the murderous, barbaric atrocity perpetrated against innocent children, parents and families who had attended an Ariana Grande concert at the Manchester Arena. Initial reports indicated that 22 people died and at least 60 more were maimed. The world came together to show solidarity with Manchester. It was truly sobering to think about the pure evil of this type that existed in our society and how close to home it had become.

23 May

Two days after the supposed 26th minute betting 'coup' had been exposed by a press hungry for John Terry's blood, cfcuk fanzine editor

THE ITALIAN JOB

David Johnstone, a co-author of the *Eddie Mac Eddie Mac* book, accompanied the revered and much loved Mr McCreadie to Chelsea's Cobham training ground where they met several times with Antonio Conte. In his own 'inimitable style', Johnstone told the Italian manager that Chelsea's supporters absolutely loved him and that he was on course to become the club's greatest ever manager.

24 May

Chelsea announced the cancellation of the victory parade scheduled to take place on Sunday. A statement on the club's official website read, "Everyone associated with Chelsea Football Club offers our heartfelt condolences to those affected by Monday's terror attack in Manchester. Our thoughts go out to all the victims, and their families and friends. In light of these tragic events, we feel it is inappropriate to go ahead with the victory parade in London on Sunday."

There was some disagreement on social media about the decision, with arguments being reasoned that the football club was yielding to terrorism. I didn't subscribe to this concept, though I could understand the thinking. One of my best friends has served as a bobby on the streets of inner London for over 20 years and he was constantly saying how the emergency services were already seriously stretched. With the terror threat raised to 'critical' by Her Majesty's government, it was a simple case of common sense not to divert important resources away from their duties.

*****

In the shadow of the tragic consequences of the massacre of innocents on their doorstep back home Manchester United deservedly won the Europa League beating Ajax 2-0 in Stockholm. The victory provided a much-needed fillip for British people irrespective of football allegiances and furthermore ensured the Red Devils would play in next season's Champions League competition... which again was a good thing.

United's qualification also meant that Tottenham Hotspur would now find themselves in Pot Three when the draw for the group stages of Europe's elite club competition was made meaning progress would be that little bit harder as the quality of opposition Spurs would face was likely to be tougher. Shame that.

United winning the trophy reminded me of a comment their current manager José Mourinho had made when returning to be Chelsea boss for a second time in 2013. "I don't want to win the Europa League. It would be a big disappointment for me. I don't want my players to feel the Europa League is our competition." A couple of days before Man U had played Celta Vigo in the semi-final of this season's Europa League, the Portuguese advised, "It's the only competition that Manchester United have never won, and it would be great to close that circle and say we are a club that won every single competition in the football world." We'll leave it there eh José. Never kid a kidder.

27 May

FA Cup Final
Chelsea 1 Arsenal 2
Wembley
Attendance: 89,472
Referee: Anthony Taylor

Chelsea (3-4-3): Thibaut Courtois, Cesar Azpilicueta, David Luiz, Gary Cahill (c), Victor Moses, N'Golo Kante, Nemanja Matic (Cesc Fabregas 61), Marcos Alonso, Pedro (Willian 72), Diego Costa (Michy Batshuayi 88), Eden Hazard.
Scorer: Costa 76
Sent off: Moses 68
Booked: Moses 57, Kante 59

Arsenal (3-4-3): Ospina, Holding, Mertesacker (c), Monreal, Bellerin, Ramsey, Xhaka, Oxlade-Chamberlain (Coquelin 82), Ozil, Sanchez (Elneny 90+3), Welbeck (Giroud 78).
Scorers: Sanchez 4, Ramsey 79
Booked: Ramsey 9, Holding 54, Xhaka 81, Coquelin 83

We must find the right fire in our soul
We must find the right fire in our soul

Pay attention and be focused
Pay attention and be focused

Well that didn't work out the way we all had hoped.

Chelsea's Double dream evaporated on a balmy early summer afternoon at Wembley as a full-strength Blues side inexplicably failed to turn up against an injury and suspension-ravaged Arsenal team who were supposedly there for the taking.

THE ITALIAN JOB

Antonio Conte's mantras went out of the window as early as the fourth minute when N'Golo Kante uncharacteristically allowed Gunners danger man Alexis Sanchez the freedom of Wembley (inadvisable) to score what proved to be a contentious and game-defining goal.

The build-up had seen Thibaut Courtois cleanly catch a corner ball from Mesut Ozil, but the Belgium international's throw-out clearance was poor and allowed Arsenal to retake the initiative easily. Sanchez gained possession and chipped the ball forward but David Luiz cleared with a header which as it dropped down certainly looked to glance across the Chilean's hand. "Hand Ball!" we cried. Not given. Kante had to do better, but didn't. It was horribly un-Chelsea-like. Sanchez flicked the ball forward in the direction of Aaron Ramsay who was clearly offside. "Offside!" we cried. Assistant referee Gary Beswick raised his flag, but Ramsay had had the common sense to stand back leaving Sanchez to sprint forward and knock the ball past Courtois into the bottom right-hand corner.

Momentarily we laughed at the Gooners cheering a non-goal.

Match referee Anthony Taylor ran across to Beswick and no-doubt advised him that he hadn't seen Ramsay touch the ball meaning he wasn't offside...

Goal given! Gooners fans cheered again... we cursed Chelsea's misfortune.

Come on you Blues, Come on you Blues...

But they didn't.

Antonio Conte's team were playing as if they had spent the entire afternoon in Station 31, a curry house come bar adjacent to the stadium that my mate Jeff Warren had organised as a meeting point for many. £18 for a double helping of curry was good value and we'd had plenty of lager to wash it down as we'd chatted about the Double and how many we were going to beat Arsenal by.

complacency a feeling of smug pleasure and / or security which overrides potential danger. (We all got suckered this time didn't we.)

It's fair to say that for the remainder of the first-half Arsenal swarmed all over Chelsea. Gary Cahill cleared a Sanchez effort off the line. Danny Welbeck hit the post. Cahill again cleared off the line this time from

Welbeck.

Somewhere in the midst of the siege Diego Costa did manage to force a superb save out of Arsenal keeper David Ospina, but when half-time came we were left shrugging our shoulders and wondering what was going on? Conte would certainly have words at the lemon-break.

We must find the right fire in our soul
We must find the right fire in our soul

Whatever the Italian said at the interval seemed to work as Chelsea recommenced battle with a different mind-set. *Champions of England, we know what we are...* chanted the Blue half of Wembley. The Blues had their chances, but Ospina was in inspired form nullifying efforts from Kante and Victor Moses.

Moses, booked in the 57th minute for a blundering challenge on Welbeck, found himself the centre of attention 10 minutes later when he decided to take a blatant dive in the Arsenal box in a bid to win Chelsea a penalty. Even from my distant vantage point, it was clear that the Nigeria international had deliberately taken a tumble when going past Alex Oxlade-Chamberlain. Referee Taylor had no alternative other than to show Moses a second yellow card followed by a red one. What a plonker! Moses, not Taylor. What was the 26-year old thinking?

The Blues were down to 10 men and really up against it now. What we needed was a bit of glorious unpredictability... and suddenly, there it was. Willian on as a substitute for Pedro found his natural-born-countryman Diego Costa with a neat ball and the striker calmly drilled the ball past Ospina into the bottom-left corner of the net. Goal! 1-1 Game on!

Pay attention and be focused
Pay attention and be focused

Nope!

Within a couple of minutes, Olivier Giroud, who'd replaced Danny Welbeck moments after Chelsea equalised, chipped a precise ball to Aaron Ramsay who powered a downward header into the Blues net.

Stunned disbelief!

As the time ticked down, Costa brought another fine save out of Ospina but the squandered chance deflated Chelsea who had the woodwork to thank again when Ozil hit the post with Courtois beaten.

With two minutes left Costa was substituted... I wondered if Conte had done it purposefully so that the striker could be applauded as I was firmly convinced this was to be his last game for Chelsea. It was a puzzling move to be honest. Substitute Michy Batshuayi had little time to make an impression.

The game was over, the chance of the Double gone.

At the final whistle, there were no complaints. Galling as it might be, the best side had won. There was an ironic chant of *Arsene Wenger we want you to stay* that was neutered by a *Champione, Champione, Olé, Olé, Olé...* which soon fizzled out.

It was a shame because predictably Chelsea's defeat was a cue for the social media super critics and pseudo analysts to wade in and wallpaper over what had been a brilliant season up to this point by focussing on the cup loss and denigrating the players who hadn't performed on the day.

Post-match Antonio Conte had no excuses. "The first-half we didn't start well, we didn't have the right approach and we suffered in first 25 minutes. We started to play better in the second-half and the red card was decisive." The Blues boss was quick to show his support for miscreant Moses though by adding, "There is disappointment for the final result but it can happen and there was a lot of pressure. Victor Moses has been good and played an important season."

28 May

The story of Antonio Conte's first season as Chelsea manager had to end somewhere and Chelsea's end of season awards dinner at Battersea Evolution seemed like as good a place as any to draw a line in the sand.

Picking up awards on the night were Eden Hazard whose brilliant individual goal against Arsenal in February was voted the season's best by supporters. Hazard also came out on top of the fans poll for player of the year, the third time he has won the award.

N'Golo Kante was voted player of the year by his teammates. He'd already been handed the trophy in the dressing room at Cobham so didn't pick up the gong on the night.

Mason Mount captain of the Double-winning Under-18s side was voted Academy Player of the Year. Mount collected the award from youth team manager Jody Morris who in the relatively modern era of Chelsea remains one of those rare beasts to have blazed a trail from youth team to first team at Stamford Bridge.

Fond farewells and tributes were made to captain, leader, legend John Terry who received a 'Special Recognition' award and first team coach Steve Holland.

*****

Final words… Antonio Conte of course.

Oh and what shimmering words of Conte-esque beauty they were… posted by the man himself to his Facebook page the day after Chelsea won the title at West Brom.

"We started the season mired in difficulty, but it ended in a single word: VICTORY! A heartfelt thanks to my players, to my staff, to all the people working at Chelsea Football Club who have contributed in a silent, but fundamental way. To the Club and our splendid fans who have always sustained us and believed in our team. Thanks to Betta and Vittoria for the sacrifices made the is year, trying to make me always feel at home despite the distance. Now we are ready for the next match, which is always the most important one! Blue is the colour, football is the game!"

TO BE CONTINUED

REVIEW

MANAGER

Antonio Conte
Matches (all competitions): 47
Won 37: Drawn 3: Lost 7:
For 109: Against: 44
Win rate 78%

Under Antonio Conte's inspired management Chelsea rose phoenix-like from the flames of the shocking season that had gone before. The Italian swiftly cleared up the mess left behind after the Mourinho debacle... reprogrammed the hearts and minds of his new players, made a couple of inspired signings, reinvented the way football would be played in the English top-flight... and duly won the Premier League.

There was scarcely time for Blues supporters to catch their collective breaths once Conte had made the switch to 3-4-3 and sent the London club on their way up the table, and the unassuming manner in which he addressed the media throughout the campaign, in good times and bad, was a joy.

It's too early perhaps to talk of Conte as being Chelsea's greatest ever manager, although had he masterminded the Double it might have settled a few early arguments. Should he remain at Stamford Bridge (and the temporary home beyond wherever that may be) for the foreseeable future, success seems certain to follow and his legend and stature will only be enhanced.

It's very rare for one man to be able to completely transform the whole philosophy of a football club and do so without ruffling feathers... but Conte achieved that in his first season with Chelsea.

Veni, Vidi, Vici (I came, I saw, I conquered) proclaimed the slogan on a brilliant Chelsea Supporters Group Conte tribute t-shirt that was worn by plenty of us at the end of the season… @Camberleycfc on Twitter can assist with acquiring one... a nice bit of Latin to recognize a notable achievement.

Manager of the year, man of the year… Antonio Conte, grazie per tutto!

PLAYERS

Cesar Azpilicueta
Appearances 47: Goals 2: Yellow Cards 4:

My personal choice for Player of the Year

Azpilicueta's name was nowhere to be seen on the nomination lists for the external POTY awards handed out this season. Teammate N'Golo Kante, named both PFA and Football Writers Association Player of the Year, raked in the plaudits and while Eden Hazard ran him close for the prizes 'Dave' was overlooked… a scandalous injustice given his contribution to Conte's title-winning cause.

Versatility is the name of Azpilicueta's game, and when Conte made the pivotal call last September to switch to 3-4-3 it was the 27-year old he selected to play on the right-hand-side of his new-look three man central defence. It came as little surprise to Chelsea fans that Azpi has excelled in the role because since arriving at Stamford Bridge from Marseilles in the summer of 2012 for what now looked like an absolute bargain fee of £6.5 million he had played in every position across the Blues backline and done so with aplomb.

Signed as right-back cover for Branislav Ivanovic by then manager Roberto Di Matteo, Azpilicueta found opportunities to play in that position limited by the form of the Serbia international who was still at the top of his game. The return of José Mourinho as Chelsea boss a year later brought with it a switch to left-back and the displacement of club legend Ashley Cole. Mourinho was so impressed with his ability and work-rate that he remarked that if he had 11 Azpilicueta's the Blues would win the Champions League!

That didn't stop the Portuguese from signing specialist left-back Filipe Luis from Atletico Madrid for £15.8 million in July 2014, but it was Azpi who kept his place in the team as Chelsea went on to win the Premier League in the season that followed. Luis spent just a year at Stamford Bridge before returning to Atletico for an undisclosed fee.

As age finally caught up with Ivanovic, it seemed logical that Azpilicueta would finally move across to his natural right-back position, but fate and Conte's tactical wizardry deemed otherwise.

Conte may have uncovered the fact that Azpilicueta's best position is as a mobile centre-back, but in the 4-3 home win over Watford towards the end of the season, the Blues boss deployed the player as a wing-back, and the Spaniard's buccaneering runs forward brought him a goal when he rifled home Chelsea's second to put the Blues 2-1 up. After that game, mirroring somewhat the observation that Mourinho had made three years previously, Conte mused that Azpi was the type of player coaches loved and that if he asked him to play in goal he would be ready.

While the wider football world seemed continually blind to Azpilicueta's attributes, his peer group at Chelsea knew his abilities very well and voted him Players Player of the Year at the end of the 2013/14 campaign. Short-listed but nothing more at this season's ceremony when perhaps he was most deserving, Cesar Azpilicueta has for me become without any shadow of doubt the most underrated player in the Premier League if not world football.

Gary Cahill
Appearances 43: Goals 8: Yellow Cards 5:

Having endured a tough start to the season and been the subject of finger-pointing and social media trolling following issues away at Swansea and Arsenal, Cahill rose above the storm when John Terry lost his place in Conte's starting XI through injury. Taking on Terry's indomitable 'captain, leader, legend' role, Cahill led the Blues with gusto. Defence may be the centre-back's role in life, but big goals came easy too and none were bigger than the epic 87th minute winner away at Stoke in March.

Pedro
Appearances 43: Goals 14: Yellow Cards 8:

Two-time goal of the month winner Pedro was one of a number of players who exceeded expectations under Antonio Conte's management. The Spain international flourished in Conte's 3-4-3 system to such an extent that he deposed Willian, a firm favourite with Chelsea supporters, from the Italian's preferred starting XI. The 29-year olds devastating pace and eye for a spectacular goal have endeared him to Blues fans keen to see him take on Europe's elite defences when Chelsea return to Champions League action.

Eden Hazard
Appearances 43: Goals 17: Yellow Cards 3:

Completely reinvigorated by Antonio Conte, Hazard started the season in scintillating form and got progressively better as Chelsea got in their club record breaking winning groove. The 26-year olds world-class strike against Arsenal at Stamford Bridge in February still has the capacity to mesmerise even now having watched it back at least 100 times on YouTube. The goal was voted by Blues supporters as the best of the season and the fans also voted Hazard as their player of the year.

Hazard's tally of 16 Premier League goals was his best in five full seasons as a Chelsea player and at the time of writing (28 May 2017), the rumour mill was in overdrive suggesting he might be heading to the Bernabeu and Real Madrid. I really hoped the deal wouldn't materialise, irrespective of the likely world record transfer fee. It's not as if Mr Abramovich needed the money now was it?

Diego Costa
Appearances 42: Goals 22: Yellow Cards 11:

Costa surpassed himself in the pantomime villain stakes with a controversial January which saw him fall out with one of Conte's fitness coaches at the same time as his agent was agitating for a move to the Chinese Super League for silly money. It's a shame because in the first-half of the season the Brazil-born Spain international had surprised everyone by staying out of trouble on the pitch and focussing on what he did best... scoring goals.

Understandably, with his head turned by the riches on offer in China, the second-half of Costa's season was less productive and his form erratic. Shortly after scoring for Chelsea in the FA Cup Final, Diego declared that he was still under contract at Stamford Bridge and had no intention of leaving... but if the Blues decided to sell him in the summer he would stay in Europe and only be prepared to go to one club and that everyone knew the club concerned (Atletico Madrid obviously). A bold statement. Player power eh. Let's see how this story plays out then.

Willian
Appearances 41: Goals 12: Yellow Cards 3:

It was a tragic circumstance, the untimely death of his mother Donna Zee, that saw Willian lose his place in the side to Pedro. The incredible new-found form of his teammate made it difficult for Conte to drop the Spaniard, so much so that he didn't. 20 of the Brazil international's appearances consequently came from the substitutes bench and with his old guvnor José Mourinho repeatedly rumoured to be interested in taking him to Old Trafford, Willian's long-term Chelsea future looked uncertain as the season ended.

A brace against Tottenham Hotspur in that blistering one-hour FA Cup semi-final cameo at Wembley was a reminder of the 28-year olds capabilities. If he turned out to be surplus to Conte's exacting requirements, I hoped Chelsea would have the common sense to sell him to a foreign club. Willian in a Man U shirt just wouldn't sit right somehow.

N'Golo Kante
Appearances 41: Goals 2: Yellow Cards 11:

Pound for pound, Kante was easily the best value signing made by any Premier League club in the past year. PFA and FWA Player of the Year awards may have borne testimony to his superlative box-to-box midfield skills, but it was former Chelsea defender and fellow France international Marcel Desailly who brought the most notable of 'Kante facts' to a wider audience. 71% of the earth is covered by water, the remaining 29% is covered by N'Golo Kante tweeted Dessaily on 14 March.

Kante later joked that it was a bit of fun… but the truth was the indefatigable 26-year olds ability to cover every blade of grass on a football pitch over the course of 90 minutes made him a class apart from any other midfielder in the English top-flight… and the return on investment for the £32 million paid to Leicester City for his services was almost immediate.

Could Chelsea have won the Premier League without N'Golo Kante in their ranks? With Conte as manager, the seemingly impossible appears possible… but even the Italian admitted that Kante proved himself to be a decisive differential. "N'Golo is a fantastic guy, fantastic player, great commitment, great behaviour. A great example."

Despite my championing the cause of Cesar Azpilicueta, Blues players underlined their manager's view of Kante by voting him their Player of the Year.

Nemanja Matic
Appearances 40: Goals 2: Yellow Cards 4:

Eden Hazard may have scored Chelsea's best goal of the season against Arsenal, but Matic's thunderous volley that rippled the Tottenham Hotspur net at Wembley in that epic FA Cup semi-final and signalled the start of a fire drill in the Spurs end of the stadium will also live long in the memory.

Matic's season was intriguing as it was clear that his position in midfield supporting N'Golo Kante was the only one that Antonio Conte was never 100% sure of. Kante and Matic, Kante and Fabregas, Matic and Fabregas… or something else. When the Serbia international did play, which was most of the time, certainly in league games, he scarcely disappointed proving himself to be an effective shield for the back three.

Was Matic a true Conte player? Looking ahead, that poor showing in the FA Cup Final against Arsenal wouldn't help his cause. Time and the summer transfer window would ultimately tell if he still had a future at the Bridge.

Victor Moses
Appearances 40: Goals 4: Yellow Cards 4: Double Yellow Cards 1:

Antonio Conte sprang plenty of surprises as he fettled his team into one that would eventually win the Premier League, and the inclusion of Moses who'd had spent the majority of his first four years as a Chelsea player out on loan was probably the biggest of them all.

Since arriving at the Bridge in August 2012, Moses had been neglected by a succession of Chelsea managers and all but forgotten by Blues supporters… but Conte was impressed enough by the Nigeria international in pre-season to assimilate him into his squad and when the Italian went with 3-4-3, it was the former Crystal Palace and Wigan Athletic player he turned to for the vacant right-wing-back role… and the rest… well that was wonderful history. Wonderful… right up until the last game of the season, the FA Cup Final at Wembley, when Moses had a mare! Unfortunate, and costly in the end… but let's leave it there because overall the 26-year old did a fantastic job.

Thibaut Courtois
Appearances 39: Goals 0: Yellow Cards 1:

It's fair to say that Courtois spent a lot of the early part of the campaign standing on my own personal naughty step. If there's one thing that winds me up it's a player who doesn't seem to be that bothered about playing for Chelsea, and the Belgium international appeared to be forever banging on about returning to Spain's La Liga where he'd spent three successful seasons on-loan with Atletico Madrid. As a consequence, there was never any shortage of stories linking him with a move back to the Spanish capital and of course it was Real Madrid not city rivals Atletico who were rumoured to be interested in signing him.

Curiously, once Chelsea started flourishing under Conte the stories stopped and Courtois declared himself happy with life at the Bridge. The keeper of course proved himself to be in a class of his own in the Premier League with some excellent displays that would ultimately bring him the Golden Gloves title for the most clean sheets. Maybe he had the defence in front of him to thank in part for that, but Courtois did have an outstanding season and at 25-years of age he still has time on his side to become a genuine Chelsea great.

David Luiz
Appearances 38: Goals 1: Yellow Cards 7:

The summer transfer window deadline day return of Luiz to Stamford Bridge caught everyone by surprise, me especially. Having been sold to Paris Saint-Germain in June 2013 for an eye-popping £50 million by José Mourinho, the flamboyant Brazillian defender who'd won three consecutive domestic trebles with the Lique 1 club was back and interestingly he'd taken a pay-cut to pull on a Chelsea shirt again.

Luiz is one of those players whose persona lends itself perfectly to him being referred to as 'Proper Chels', and once established as the ball-playing enabler in the middle of Antonio Conte's centre-back trio he was in his element.

A wiser head now on football visionary shoulders, Luiz still managed to treat us to a samba-style piece of irrational genius when stealing countryman Willian's thunder and blasting home a free-kick against Liverpool at Anfield. If there was a prize given out for cheekiest goal of the season, Luiz's only goal of a stellar campaign would have won by a country mile.

Cesc Fabregas
Appearances 37: Goals 7: Yellow Cards 9:

A season of mixed fortunes for Chelsea's assist king who found himself on the periphery of Antonio Conte's first-team thinking for much of the campaign with 19 of his 37 appearances coming from the bench.

11 top-flight assists coming at a rate of one every 112 minutes made Fabregas the Premier League's goal creator in chief and a return of seven goals in all competitions proof that his famous magic hat still had its mystical powers.

Despite being 30 years of age now, there would be no shortage of clubs willing to take Cesc on should he feel the need to move to get week-in-week-out first team football, but with the Champions League now back on the fixture list at Stamford Bridge, many supporters were hoping they would still be singing *Fabregas is magic…* next season.

Marcos Alonso
Appearances 35: Goals 6: Yellow Cards 3:

Marcos who? God's honest truth that was my first reaction when I heard the news that Chelsea had signed the then 25-year old Spanish left back from Fiorentina in a £24 million deadline day deal. The Blues recent habit of squandering money on left backs (step forward Baba Rahman and Filipe Luis) suggested Alonso's arrival might be another folly. Just goes to show how wrong you can be.

Alonso proved himself to be nothing short of a revelation when eventually deployed at left-wing-back in Conte's 3-4-3 system. Defensive nous coupled with buccaneering runs down the left flank and an athletic ability to always be in the right place at the right time brought assists and goals and virtually untouchable status in Chelsea's Premier League starting XI. That £24 million spent looked like a bargain come Christmas.

Michy Batshuayi
Appearances 28: Goals 9: Yellow Cards 0:

I couldn't help feeling sorry for Michy who'd joined Chelsea full of hope and expectation last summer. At £33 million, the Belgium international was expected to play a fuller role for the Blues than he ended up doing. The fact that 21 of his 27 appearances for the London club came from the subs bench told its own story… but the 23-year olds enthusiasm never waivered, and a nine-goal haul was proof that the striker could do what he was signed for… find the back of the net. Clearly Antonio Conte was unconvinced about Batshuayi's suitability for the style of football he advocates and so as the season ended what the future held for the player at Stamford Bridge remained uncertain.

Branislav Ivanovic
Appearances 16: Goals 1: Yellow Cards 2:

Brana's nine-year career as a Chelsea player which embraced 261 appearances and brought 21 goals ended during the January transfer window when the then 32-year old left the Blues for Zenit Saint Petersburg. The Serbia international didn't make the cut when Conte switched to 3-4-3 and a move to Russia presented an opportunity for regualr first team football.

An outstanding career at Stamford Bridge was rounded off nicely with a farewell goal in the 4-0 FA Cup hammering of Brentford in January. The Muppet Show themed chant *Ivanovic, do, do do, do, do* never sounded sweeter and I'm sure it will be reprised from time to time when the mood takes the Chelsea massive.

Nathaniel Chalobah
Appearances 15: Goals 0: Yellow Cards 3:

Having been with the Chelsea academy since the age of 10, versatile midfielder Nathaniel Chalobah was one of those players who seemed destined for the loan treadmill (apprenticeships served at Watford, Nottingham Forest, Middlesbrough, Burnley, Reading, Napoli!!) and then a move away from the Bridge. However, in a similar fashion to Victor Moses, Chalobah impressed Antonio Conte in pre-season sufficiently to warrant a place in the Italian's first team squad and the then 21-year old continued to impress when given the chance to do so. Now 22, under Conte, Chalobah looks set to continue his progress as a Chelsea player... which can only be a good thing surely.

John Terry
Appearances 14: Goals 1: Yellow Cards 1: Red Cards 1:

The Premier League may be a melting pot of football stars from around the globe these days with Stamford Bridge one of its most cosmopolitan venues, but for years the beating heart of Chelsea Football Club had remained quintessentially English. Captain, leader, legend John Terry. In a day-and-age when our national game seemed to be losing all sense of tradition and identity, Terry, although every inch a modern footballer, had a *Roy of the Rovers* comic-book-hero quality to his persona whimsically redolent of a wonderfully homespun bygone era.

Roy Race had already been playing for Melchester Rovers for 15 years when I first came across him as an eight-year old kid reading *Tiger – The Sport and Adventure Picture Weekly*. Youthful Roy had made his debut for Rovers in 1954 alongside best friend Blackie Gray, and in a glittering career that followed he won nine league titles, eight FA Cups, three League Cups, three European Cups, four European Cup Winners Cups and one UEFA Cup... he was also capped 42 times by England. In 1975, Race became Melchester's player-manager... a position he retained until the mid '90s... by which time I'd long since given up reading his adventures.

The mid '90s also saw John Terry, a promising 14-year old schoolboy central midfielder who'd been on West Ham United's books for four years, arrive virtually unannounced at Stamford Bridge. Joining Chelsea full-time on leaving school as a 16-year old YTS earning £46 per week, Terry's duties included cleaning the boots of Denis Wise, Eddie Newton and David Lee. On the pitch, he soon impressed, moving into central defence for the Blues youth team and securing his first professional contract a year later. The money improved to £250 per week with a promise that once he'd played 20 games for the first team he would be offered a new contract worth £1000 per week. But as with Roy Race, for JT it wasn't about the money, it was about playing football... about proving you were good enough to make it in the top-flight

Unlike Race, who didn't have to go out on loan to gain experience to convince Melchester Rovers manager Ben Galloway he was worthy of a regular first team place, John Terry, having made an inauspicious debut for Chelsea in October 1998 as a late substitute in a League Cup tie with Aston Villa, found himself swapping a blue shirt for a red one in March 2000 as Blues boss at the time Gianluca Vialli loaned him out to Nottingham Forest.

Terry impressed in a short, unbeaten, six-game loan spell at Forest, but World Cup winning France international duo Marcel Desailly and Frank Leboeuf were Vialli's first choice centre-back pairing. So what would the future hold for the precocious youngster? How different would JTs career have been had current Aston Villa manager Steve Bruce, then with Huddersfield Town, been successful in his bid to sign him? £750,000 was put on the table, a lot of money for a 19-year old, and Chelsea were willing to sell... but Terry didn't want to leave Stamford Bridge.

The importance of Terry's decision, and his stubbornness and determination to prove that he was good enough to play for Chelsea, cannot be underestimated when assessing how the Blues future mapped out

THE ITALIAN JOB

the way it did. Five games into the 2000-2001 season, Vialli was sacked by then Bridge supremo Ken Bates. Among those tipped as potential replacements were the Italian's assistant Graham Rix, Gianfranco Zola, George Graham, Terry Venables, Glenn Hoddle and Ray Wilkins... but out of nowhere came another Italian coach Claudio Ranieri.

Ranieri saw qualities in Terry that his countryman had failed to spot giving him 23 starts in his first campaign as manager... and the rest as they say is history... modern history. The affable Italian was also responsible for signing Frank Lampard who along with Terry was an influential member of the Chelsea side that succeeded in qualifying for the Champions League at the end of the 2002-2003 season, a notable feat viewed as the catalyst for Russian billionaire Roman Abramovich buying the London club.

The comic book analogy rang truer and truer with every passing year. Blues supporters had to pinch themselves to believe what was happening, and no doubt John Terry did as well. For Roy of the Rovers, read John of the Chelsea. Terry has gone on to become the Blues most successful captain, skippering the team to a bountiful haul of silverware that has brought him 15 winners medals. Sparkling in his collection are gongs for the Champions League, Europa League, Premier League x5, FA Cup x5 and League Cup (in various guises) x3. Not quite as many as Roy Race... but then he was fictional character after all.

Fact... fiction... fiction... fact... the lines between the two are often blurred.

Roy Race was almost, but not quite, a one-club man. Having made 245 appearances for Melchester Rovers between 1955 and 1983, Race had his head turned by Walford Rovers, but the dalliance lasted just 21 games before he was back at Mel Park. A further 256 appearances followed before injuries sustained in a helicopter crash in 1993 ended his playing career at the remarkable age of 55.

Having resisted Steve Bruce's attempts to lure him away from Stamford Bridge, John Terry went on to make 717 appearances for Chelsea scoring 67 goals... only Ron Harris (795) and Peter Bonetti (729) played more games for the Blues. At the time of writing, JT had yet to decide whether or not to continue his playing career elsewhere. I chuckled at the thought that at 36-years of age, if he had the Peter Pan-like qualities of Roy of the Rovers, John of the Chelsea would have been kept on by Antonio Conte and easily have surpassed Chopper's appearance record for the Blues, but obviously that wasn't going to happen. I hoped John would retire or at least not carry on playing in this country. It would feel very strange to see him wearing the colours of another English club.

Could John Terry end up managing Chelsea one day? Why not? Roy Race managed his beloved Melchester. The future is unwritten… or is it? There is another spooky little parallel between Roy and John worth highlighting. In 1976, Race married Melchester club secretary Penny Laine and a year later he became a father to twins, Roy and Melinda. Roy junior, nicknamed Rocky, would go on to play for Melchester Rovers under the stewardship of his Dad. Curiously, John Terry and his wife Toni are proud parents of twins, son, Georgie John, and daughter Summer Rose… what price would a bookmaker give you on Terry senior being manager of Chelsea one day and naming Terry junior in a Blues starting XI? Long odds I expect. Just like that bet on the 26th minute substitution in his final game at Stamford Bridge… ha ha ha. Actually, I really fancied some of that. It had a ring to it like those lucky folk in the know who backed tennis maestro Andy Murray when he was a kid at astronomical odds to be a future winner of Wimbledon and the same went for golfing whizz kid Rory McIlroy winning the British Open.

Whatever happens in the years to come, just like Roy of the Rovers, John of the Chelsea's legacy will surely stand the test of time. His valorous achievements as the Blues captain, leader, legend are unlikely to be surpassed… and for those of us who have followed his career and love a bit of sentiment with our football there is something deeply comforting about this eventuality.

Kurt Zouma
Appearances 13: Goals 0: Yellow Cards 0:

Having been out for almost a year through injury, Chelsea supporters welcomed *Zouma, Zouma, Zouma* back to the fold when he returned to first-team action in the Blues 4-1 FA Cup rout of Peterborough United in January.

Things looked promising, but curiously, Conte, having opted to start Zouma for the home league game with Manchester City in April, replaced him at half-time and the centre-back's chances were subsequently limited. At 22-years of age, with a World Cup season looming, the France international may decide he needs to move away from the Bridge to secure the first-team football he will need to ensure he has a chance to be selected to play in the tournament.

Ruben Loftus-Cheek
Appearances 11: Goals 0: Yellow Cards 0:

Failed to live up to the expectations created during the 2015/16 season when it was thought that he would be the first academy graduate to nail down a regular first-team berth since John Terry. Deployed as a striker during pre-season by Conte, RLC failed to make the most of the limited opportunities that came his way. At 21-years of age and seemingly now eclipsed by the likes Nathaniel Chalobah the feeling is that his Chelsea ship has sailed and regular first-team opportunities will have to be sought elsewhere.

Oscar
Appearances: 11: Goals: 0: Yellow Cards 1:

Oscar's five and a half year sojourn at Stamford Bridge ended at just before Christmas when Chelsea confirmed the Brazil international's departure to Chinese Super League side Shanghai SIPG managed by former Blues boss Andre Villas-Boas for a mind-boggling £60 million. Oscar had failed to impress Conte and didn't fit into the Italian's new system. With a dazzling array of creative midfield talent to choose from, the money was too good to turn down.

Asmir Begovic
Appearances 8: Goals 0: Yellow Cards 0:

A capable deputy for Thibaut Courtois, Begovic was the subject of a £10 million bid from Bournemouth in the January transfer window but Conte wisely resisted the temptation to sell the Bosnia international keeper. The 29-year old should be playing regular first team football and it will be a surprise if he is still at the Bridge next season.

Ola Aina
Appearances: 6: Goals: 0: Yellow Cards 0:

Having played all six of Chelsea's pre-season matches, plenty (me included) thought that right-back Aina, then 19 years of age, was in contention for a first team berth when the league campaign started… but it wasn't to be and the youngster found opportunities hard to come by. A loan move looks a distinct possibility for 2017/18.

Nathan Ake
Appearances 5: Goals 0: Yellow Cards 1:

Commenced the season on loan at Bournemouth, a deal meant to last the whole campaign. 12 appearances and three goals later, the Holland Under-21 international was recalled to the Bridge in January by Conte who had been monitoring his progress as we all had. Ake had played a series of blinders for the Cherries and later proved his worth to Chelsea notably in the FA Cup semi-final triumph over Tottenham Hotspur when he deputised for Gary Cahill and played with the type of maturity that suggested he had to have a future with the Blues. It's Conte's call ultimately and it will be interesting to see how Ake's career unfolds.

Kenedy
Appearances: 2: Goals: 0: Yellow Cards 0:

Started the season on loan at Watford but struggled with injuries and returned to the Bridge in December. Kenedy featured in the cup win over Brentford and against the Hornets in the league. At 21-years of age, Conte is likely to monitor the Brazil starlet closely during the summer and assess whether or not to include him in his plans for next season.

STATISTICS 2016/2017

PREMIER LEAGUE – Champions!

38 matches 93 points

Home: Won: 17 Drawn: 0 Lost: 2 For: 55 Against: 17
Away: Won: 13 Drawn: 3 Lost: 3 For: 30 Against: 16
Total: Won: 30 Drawn: 3 Lost: 5 For: 85 Against: 33

FA CUP – Runners Up

6 matches

Home: Won: 3 Drawn: 0 Lost: 0 For: 9 Against: 1
Away: Won: 1 Drawn: 0 Lost: 0 For: 2 Against: 0
Wembley: Won 1: Drawn 0: Lost 1 For 5: Against 4
Total: Won 5: Drawn 0: Lost 1 For 16: Against 5

EFL CUP – 4th Round

3 matches

Home: Won: 1 Drawn: 0 Lost: 0 For: 3 Against: 2
Away: Won: 1 Drawn: 0 Lost: 1 For: 5 Against: 4
Total: Won: 2 Drawn: 0 Lost: 1 For: 8 Against: 6

COMBINED LEAGUE AND CUP RECORD

47 matches

Home: Won: 21 Drawn: 0 Lost: 2 For: 67 Against: 20
Away: Won: 15 Drawn: 3 Lost: 4 For: 37 Against: 20
Wembley: Won: 1 Drawn 0: Lost: 1: For 5: Against 4
Total: Won 37: Drawn 3: Lost 7: For 109: Against 44

ATTENDANCES

Premier League:

Home: Highest: 41,622 v West Brom - Lowest: 41,168 v Southampton
Home Total: 788,645
Home Average: 41,508

Away: Highest: 75,272 v Man United - Lowest: 11,283 v Bournemouth
Away Total: 682,860
Away Average: 35,940

Total: 1,471,505
Total Average: 38,724

FA Cup:

Home: Highest: 41,042 v Brentford - Lowest: 40,801 v Man United
Away: One game only: 30,193 v Wolves

Wembley: Highest 89,472 v Arsenal - Lowest 86,355 v Tottenham Hotspur

Total: 328,866
Total Average: 54,811

EFL Cup:

Home: Highest: 39.276 v Bristol Rovers - Lowest: 39,276 v Bristol Rovers

Away: Highest: 45,957 v West Ham - Lowest: 29,899 v Leicester City
Total: 115,132
Total Average: 38,377

All Competitions (47 games)
Total Attendance: 1,915,503
Total Average Attendance: 40,755

TRANSFERS AND LOANS 2016/2017

TRANSFERS IN

Michy Batshuayi (Marseille) £33.15 million
N'Golo Kante (Leicester City) £30.43 million
David Luiz (Paris Saint-Germain) £29.75 million
Marcos Alonso (Fiorentina) £19.55 million
Eduardo (Dinamo Zagreb) Undisclosed

TRANSFERS / LOANS OUT

Oscar (Shanghai SIPG) £51.00 million
Mohamed Salah (AS Roma) £12.75 million
Papy Djilobodji (Sunderland) £8.08 million
Patrick Bamford (Middlesbrough) £5.87 million
Juan Cuadrado (Juventus) £4.25 million (loan fee)
Stipe Perica (Udinese) £3.83 million
Marko Marin (Olympiacos) £2.55 million
Bertrand Traore (Ajax) £1.70 million (loan fee)
Mario Pasalic (AC Milan) £0.85 million (loan fee)
Loic Remy (Crystal Palace) £0.85 million (loan fee)
Baba Rahman (Schalke 04) £0.425 million (loan fee)
Branislav Ivanovic (Zenit St. Petersburg) free transfer
John Mikel Obi (TJ Teda) free transfer

The following players were on season-long loan deals ending 30 June 2017 unless stated.

Andreas Christensen (Borussia Monchengladbach)
Tammy Abraham (Bristol City)
Isaiah Brown (Huddersfield Town)
Mukhtar Ali (Vitesse Arnhem)
Christian Atsu (Newcastle United)
Victorien Angban (Granada)
Lewis Baker (Vitesse Arnhem)

Nathan Baxter (Solihull Motors) loan ended 14 May
Jamal Blackman (Wycombe Wanderers)
Jeremie Boga (Granada)
Jake Clarke-Salter (Bristol Rovers)
Charlie Colkett (Swindon Town)
Cristian Cuevas (Sint-Truiden)
Fakaty Dabo (Swindon Twon)
Jay Dasilva (Charlton Athletic)
Matej Delac (Mouscron)
Islam Feruz (Swindon Town)
Michael Hector (Eintracht Frankfurt)
Tomas Kalas (Fulham)
Alex Kiwomya (Crewe Alexandra)
Matt Miazga (Vitesse Arnhem)
Nathan (Vitesse Arnhem)
Kenneth Omeruo (Alanyaspor)
Kasey Palmer (Huddersfield Town)
Danilo Pantic (Excelsior)
Lucas Piazon (Fulham)
Jhoao Rodriguez (Cortulua)
Fikayo Tomori (Brighton & Hove Albion)
Marco van Ginkel (PSV Eindhoven)
Wallace (Gremio)

ALSO BY MARK WORRALL

Fiction
Blue Murder: Chelsea Till I Die
This Damnation

Football
Over Land and Sea
One Man Went to Mow
Chelsea Chronicles (five volume series)

Collaborations
Chelsea Here, Chelsea There
Chelsea Football Fanzine the best of cfcuk
Making History Not Reliving It
Eddie Mac, Eddie Mac

Printed in Great Britain
by Amazon